AMERICAN SAGE

AMERICAN SAGE

The Spiritual Teachings of
Ralph Waldo Emerson

BARRY M. ANDREWS

University of Massachusetts Press
Amherst and Boston

Copyright © 2021 by University of Massachusetts Press
All rights reserved
Printed in the United States of America

ISBN 978-1-62534-607-0 (paper); 606-3 (hardcover)

Designed by Sally Nichols
Set in Berkeley
Printed and bound by Books International, Inc.

Cover design by Frank Gutbrod
Cover art by Efim Volkov, *October,* 1883, oil on canvas. WikiArt.com.

Library of Congress Cataloging-in-Publication Data

Names: Andrews, Barry M., author.
Title: American sage : the spiritual teachings of Ralph Waldo Emerson /
Barry M. Andrews.
Description: Amherst : University of Massachusetts Press, [2021] | Includes
bibliographical references and index.
Identifiers: LCCN 2021016960 (print) | LCCN 2021016961 (ebook) | ISBN
9781625346063 (hardcover) | ISBN 9781625346070 (paperback) | ISBN
9781613768822 (ebook) | ISBN 9781613768839 (ebook)
Subjects: LCSH: Emerson, Ralph Waldo, 1803–1882—Religion. | Emerson, Ralph
Waldo, 1803–1882—Knowledge and learning. | Spiritual life in
literature.
Classification: LCC PS1642.R4 A525 2021 (print) | LCC PS1642.R4 (ebook) |
DDC 814/.3—dc23
LC record available at https://lccn.loc.gov/2021016960
LC ebook record available at https://lccn.loc.gov/2021016961

British Library Cataloguing-in-Publication Data
A catalog record for this book is available from the British Library.

To the two most important women in my life:
my mother, Judith, and my wife, Linda.

CONTENTS

PREFACE

Ralph Waldo Emerson was often said to be the Sage of Concord. The title is not off the mark, nor is it simply a timeworn cliché. Classical philosophy depicted the sage as an ideal figure. The notion is based on a type of ethics that emphasizes the cultivation of virtue. Steeped in the classical tradition and the virtue ethics of Harvard and the Unitarian church, the nature of his spirituality was further shaped by religious and intellectual crosscurrents of the nineteenth century—particularly the Romantic revolution, the rise of secularism, and the discovery of Eastern forms of spirituality. As a result, Emerson's spiritual teaching is both timeless and modern, universal and uniquely American.

As a minister, I have gained wisdom and guidance through Emerson's teachings and spiritual practice. As a teacher, I have seen how he enriches the spiritual lives of others when they grasp his meaning. In this book, I have taken Emerson's message seriously and explained as best I can the substance of his writings. Mine is not an academic or critical study, treating its subject at arm's length. Such books are important, but so are books—and there are only a few—that make Emerson's writings intelligible to seekers curious to know what he was all about, written for the most part in everyday language. At the same time, I have sought to ground my efforts in solid scholarship, paying attention to accuracy and historical detail. Emerson is not for everyone. But if readers learn nothing else, it is that each of us must find our own spiritual path. That is all that Emerson ever wanted for his audience.

My own appreciation of Emerson—both the man and his message—began as a high school student. Rudy Gilbert, minster of the Unitarian church in Spokane that I attended, spoke of Emerson in such reverent tones that I began reading "Self-Reliance," "The Over-Soul," and other famous essays. Studying for the ministry at the Unitarian Universalist seminary in Chicago and the University of Chicago, I delved deeper into Emerson's writings and his important role in Unitarian history and theology. While a minister of the Community Church of New York in the 1980s, I attended a class by Dr. Richard Geldard titled Emerson as Spiritual Guide, which offered me a model of how I might introduce Emerson to others who wanted to read and reflect on his spiritual message. Taking a cue from Dr. Geldard, I wrote *Emerson as Spiritual Guide: A Companion to Emerson's Essays for Personal Reflection and Group Discussion*. Along the way I have led adult workshops and taught graduate students about Emerson and others in the Transcendentalist movement.

Over the years I have benefited enormously from the work of scholars specializing in Emerson studies, including David Robinson, Robert D. Richardson Jr., Phyllis Cole, Alan Hodder, Len Gougeon, and many others. Many of my colleagues in the Unitarian Universalist ministry have also contributed to my understanding of Emerson and his place in Unitarian history, especially Jenny Rankin, John Buehrens, William Houff, and Bruce Bode. I am also indebted to Dr. Daniel McKanan at Harvard Divinity School and Gloria Korsman, research librarian at the Andover-Harvard Theological Library.

Books may be attributed to a single author, but they are actually a collaborative effort involving many people. My closest collaborator has always been my wife, Linda. For the publication of my books, I wish to acknowledge Mary Dougherty, Matt Becker, and the staff at the University of Massachusetts Press for their efforts in bringing my latest writings into print. Kimberly French deserves much credit for helping me polish my writing and prepare it for publication.

I especially wish to thank those who have participated in classes, workshops, and study groups I have led in the congregations I have served in Spokane, New York City, San Diego, Long Island, and elsewhere. The opportunity to teach and the comments I have received have deepened my understanding of Emerson and enriched my spiritual life.

AMERICAN SAGE

INTRODUCTION

Ralph Waldo Emerson forever changed American spirituality. Eight years after Emerson's death, the poet Walt Whitman observed, "I know our age is greatly materialistic, but it is greatly spiritual, too. Even what we moderns have come to mean by *spirituality* . . . has so expanded and color'd and vivified the comprehension of the term, that it is quite a different one from the past."[1] The difference Whitman refers to is largely because of Emerson's influence. Before Emerson, the word "spirituality" always referred to a specific religious tradition, such as Catholic spirituality or Christian spirituality. Emerson is the first American writer to separate the word from its sectarian associations. For Emerson, spirituality was the essence of religion, and he sought to rescue it from forms he viewed as decaying: dry preaching, ancient texts, rote rituals.[2]

The nature of his spirituality is hard to pin down. My hope is that it will become clearer in the pages that follow. Today's readers need to understand, first, that Emerson's spirituality was shaped by religious and intellectual crosscurrents of the late eighteenth and early nineteenth centuries, both abroad and in the United States—particularly the Romantic revolt against the Enlightenment, the rise of secularism, and the discovery of Eastern forms of spirituality.

The rise of Romanticism was a watershed event in modern history. According to historian of ideas Isaiah Berlin, "The importance of romanticism is that it is the largest recent movement to transform the lives and thought of the Western world. It seems to me to be the greatest single shift in the consciousness of the West that has occurred, and all the other shifts which have occurred in the course of the nineteenth and twentieth centuries appear to me in comparison less important, and at any rate deeply influenced by it."[3]

Emerson and the Transcendentalists were captivated by Romantic ideas. In many ways, Transcendentalism was a younger generation's revolt

1

against classical Unitarianism, which was rooted in the rationalism of the Scottish Enlightenment, especially the empiricism of John Locke. In 1836 a group of young ministers, including Emerson, gathered to discuss what they considered to be the aridity of Unitarian worship and theology and the weaknesses of Locke's "sensuous philosophy." This was the first meeting of what came to be called the Transcendental Club.

The group hailed the "new views" of religion, culture, and society then coming out of Europe and Britain, advanced by Romantic poets and philosophers, including Samuel Taylor Coleridge, William Wordsworth, and Thomas Carlyle, each of whom Emerson met on his trip to Britain in 1833. Looking back on that era, Frederic Henry Hedge, one of the young radicals, remarked that the work of these writers "created a ferment in the minds of some of the young clergy of that day." There was, he said, "a promise in the air of a new era of intellectual life."[4] Romanticism was a reaction to forces then and still at work today: tyranny, materialism, industrialism, skepticism, and conventionality. It was such a break with the past that Emerson called it "a crack in Nature."[5]

The modern, or Romantic, period emphasized subjectivity, a "Feeling of the Infinite," a consciousness of one Mind common to all, and nature as a source of divine revelation, Emerson said in a series of lectures titled The Present Age in the winter of 1839–40.[6] Those notions were so far removed from Christian orthodoxy that a new language was needed to express them. Emerson's friend, Thomas Carlyle, in his book, *Sartor Resartus*, coined the term *natural supernaturalism*. "The Mythus of the Christian Religion looks not in the eighteenth century as it did in the eighth," Carlyle wrote. And those who wish to salvage it must seek "to embody the divine spirit of that religion in a new Mythus, in a new vehicle and vesture, that our Souls, otherwise too like perishing, may live."[7] For Emerson, who was moving away from historical Christianity, natural supernaturalism meant expressing religious experience in the language of symbolism taken from the natural world.

Emerson and the Romantics also critiqued materialism and commerce. "There is nothing more important in the culture of man than to resist the dangers of Commerce," he said. Trade and the desire for riches have infected every facet of society. They have subordinated the needs of the soul to gross materialism. Education and even religion have been bent to serve instrumental ends. "Commerce, dazzling us with the perpetual discovery of new facts," he observed, "has availed so far to transfer the devotion of men from the soul to that material in which it works."[8]

Another major intellectual trend during this period was the rising tide of secularity. Charles Taylor, in his book *A Secular Age*, tells us that there are three ways of understanding secularity: The first is the removal of religion from the public sphere, that is, the separation of church and state. The second is the decline of religious belief and practice. The third is viewing religious belief as a choice among options, including atheism.[9]

In Massachusetts, where Emerson lived, church and state had been closely entwined for centuries, growing out of New England's Puritan tradition. Citizens had long been taxed to support the parish churches in their community. In the early nineteenth century, some were Congregationalist, and some were Unitarian. As other religious groups became established in the state, including Baptists, Catholics, Quakers, Universalists, and Episcopalians, this arrangement began to break down. Subsequently, taxes in support of local churches were abolished in Massachusetts in 1833, although they remained in place in Concord, for instance, until 1856.

In addition, Unitarian churches were undergoing significant changes in worship and polity, or church governance. Transcendentalist ministers did away with the tradition of pew rentals and ownerships, a source of revenue for the churches. This practice separated the wealthier members of the congregation from those who could not afford to rent or purchase pew-boxes, relegating them to side balconies. One prominent Transcendentalist minister, James Freeman Clarke, implemented what he called the Voluntary Principle, which brought lay members of his congregation into leadership positions. Some ministers also resisted sectarian labels, naming their congregations Free churches instead of Unitarian.

Simultaneously, powerful forces were undermining the nature of religious belief. In a broad sense, the Enlightenment challenged the notion of a supernatural deity actively involved in human events. Reason and science pushed God into the background. Although God created and designed the world, he was in a sense removed from it. A providential Deism—as reflected, for example, in the language of the Declaration of Independence—replaced the medieval conception of God. Puritanism was losing its hold in New England. The notion of sinners in the hands of an angry God gave way to that of a benevolent deity ruling over an ordered universe.

New biblical scholarship also threatened traditional Christian ways of thinking. The University of Göttingen in Germany was the leading center of the "higher criticism" of the Bible. Several Unitarians, later on the faculty of Harvard College, went there to study. Frederic Henry Hedge, one of the original members of the Transcendentalist group, and Emerson's brother William studied there also. The university took a historical approach to the study of the Bible, which led many students to conclude that the Bible was an amalgam of myths, legends, and conflicting accounts of questionable historical value. Disillusioned, William Emerson ceased studying for the ministry. William's letters to his younger brother convinced Waldo, as he preferred to be called, that there was no biblical sanction for serving the Lord's Supper. This became an issue precipitating Waldo's resignation from his pastorate at Boston's Second Church in 1832. The "vast body of religious writings which came down to this generation as an inestimable treasure," Emerson concluded, "have been suddenly found to be unreadable and consigned to remediless neglect."[10]

The Transcendentalist movement is an early instance of Taylor's third form of secularity. Taylor identifies Emerson as proponent of "a third path: the search for a new age of faith, a new positive form of religion." Emerson occupies a space between historical Christianity and a thoroughgoing religious skepticism. In Taylor's view, Emerson "hovered on the borders where theism, pantheism, and non-theism all meet."[11]

The other important influence on Emerson's spiritual growth was the discovery of Eastern religions. Unitarians played an important role in bringing Eastern religions to public attention. Hannah Adams and Joseph Priestly, both Unitarians, were the first in America to write about the religions of India and China. But Rammohun Roy, a Hindu reformer who cofounded the Calcutta Unitarian Society, sparked the most interest. American readers were intrigued by lengthy articles about Roy in the *Christian Register* and the *Christian Examiner*, both Unitarian publications. Emerson's aunt Mary Moody Emerson (1774–1863), who for many years mentored her young nephew, brought them to Waldo's attention in 1822 when he was nineteen years old. Roy also translated numerous Hindu texts, making them accessible to New England readers.

By the 1830s, Asian literature was widely read and discussed in Transcendentalist circles. Emerson, along with Theodore Parker, Margaret Fuller, Henry David Thoreau, Bronson Alcott, James Freeman Clarke, and others, was an eager student of Eastern spirituality. The *Dial* magazine, the organ of the Transcendental Club, carried a regular column featuring "ethnical scriptures" chosen by Emerson and Thoreau from Indian, Chinese, and Persian sources. Elizabeth Palmer Peabody published the first Buddhist text in America in 1844, also in the *Dial*. Several of the Transcendentalists, most notably Lydia Maria Child, James Freeman Clarke, and Samuel Johnson, wrote lengthy studies of Eastern religions, laying the groundwork for academic departments of comparative religions in the years that followed.

Emerson himself was most attracted to the Vedic tradition of India, the Confucian philosophy of China, and the Sufi teaching of Persia. The Bhagavad Gita was his favorite work, and he was delighted to get his own copy of it in 1845. As we will see, his essays are laced with references to Hindu and Confucian literature. Several of his best-known poems are on Indian themes. He, like other Transcendentalists, considered these texts a form of perennial philosophy, just as they did the writings of Greek and Roman philosophers and religious figures of the Middle East. In taking Eastern teachings seriously and incorporating strains of their wisdom into their own spiritual outlook, Emerson and the Transcendentalists demonstrated an unprecedented religious cosmopolitanism.

Romanticism, secularism, and religious cosmopolitanism: these were the three major intellectual and cultural currents that shaped Emerson's spiritual life. There were other important factors, too, including the influence of his Aunt Mary, who played Socrates to her Platonic nephew, and the classical education he received at Harvard College. Over the years, Emerson's spirituality developed from the providential Deism of his youth to a form of deep pantheism later in life.

I will trace this development by examining his writings, including his journals and letters, in more or less chronological order, beginning with the religious crisis that led to his resignation from the ministry in 1832. Charles Taylor suggests that Emerson and Walt Whitman not only shaped the nature of American spirituality of their own day but also continue to offer wisdom and guidance to spiritual seekers today.[12] I hope to reinforce that view.

I have been reading Emerson for many years, seeking to understand him better and learning what he has to teach me in my own spiritual growth. But I also wish to convey his spiritual message to those who are curious to know more about him and his teachings but struggle to decipher his writing. Although I have taught both at the undergraduate and graduate levels of higher education, most of my students have been adult spiritual seekers, active in the churches I have served as a Unitarian minister and religious educator, who themselves are well-educated but impatient with academic writing. In my own writing and teaching I try to convey Emerson's philosophy in a scholarly but accessible way, focusing on the central ideas of his lectures and essays. I have also attempted to clarify certain terms, which sometimes have meanings different from current usage. I encourage students to relate Emerson's message to their own lives. For Emerson, philosophy was a way of life, not a matter of dialectics and sophisticated arguments. Everything he said and wrote had to do with "the conduct of life," the title of one of his best books of essays.

Emerson says every book is different to different readers and that we can hear only what we are prepared to learn. My reading of Emerson may differ from that of others. Although we write in individual and solitary ways, what we have to say is a collaborative effort drawing on the work of many others tilling the same scholarly fields. In acknowledging the contributions of others, I take responsibility for any mistakes I may have made.

Understanding Emerson's ideas has been an important part of my own spiritual growth, and I have always felt that his message can benefit that of others as well. Philosopher John Lysaker, author of *Emerson and Self-Culture*, speaks of "taking Emerson personally," and that is what I seek to do. English poet and critic Matthew Arnold wrote of Emerson that "he is the friend and aider of those who would live in the spirit."[13] For me, Emerson is a spiritual guide, a mentor and midwife in the cultivation of the soul. It is with this in mind that I have written this book.

1

AN AMERICAN SAGE

Even during his lifetime, Emerson was called the Sage of Concord. He was probably amused by this but undoubtedly also found the sobriquet somewhat embarrassing. For it is in the nature of the sage to be humble and to realize that sage-hood is never fully attained. It is a process, not an achievement. Intended as an honorific recognizing his status as a widely known and highly esteemed purveyor of philosophical wisdom, in Emerson's case the label is justified.

Emerson's readers have had a hard time pinning him down. What was he? Poet? Philosopher? Public intellectual? Scholar? Essayist? Mystic? Those who have written about him over the years have typically emphasized one aspect or another in trying to get a handle on him. (His friend Henry James Sr. actually described him as a "man without a handle.")[1] But "sage" is not just one more descriptor to add to the list. Rather, the notion of the sage encompasses all the other aspects of his life and writing.

We think of the sage as a wise and virtuous person. Greek and Roman philosophy depicted the sage as an ideal figure, which means that no living person is ever a fully realized example. The notion serves an aspirational purpose, encouraging us to strive toward achieving the model. It is based on a type of ethics that emphasizes virtue over conduct. Modern ethics has much to do with rules and duties. Virtue ethics, on the other hand, focuses on developing character rather than following rules. Although virtue implies doing good, it also means living well.

For the ancients, the goal in life is to achieve *eudaimonia*, commonly referred to as "happiness" but more accurately defined as "flourishing," according to classical scholar Julia Annas.[2] Eudaimonia is not a state of feeling but a way of living. What is good for us to do is that which is conducive to human flourishing or living virtuously. The sage, in this view, is someone who has cultivated the art of living well. The epitome of the sage varied with the different schools of philosophy. But most agreed that a sage exhibited equanimity of soul, authenticity of character, simplicity in lifestyle, and detachment or indifference in regard to the messy details of everyday life.[3] This is essentially what Emerson means by self-reliance, an inner freedom coming from a sense of personal wholeness or integrity.

The sage was not categorically different from other people. He or she was an example of what everyone might aspire to and a model for individual self-improvement. The different philosophical schools— Stoicism, Epicureanism, and those of Plato and Aristotle—each offered theories of how to accomplish this in a disciplined way, by means of spiritual exercises.

Classical thinkers believed there were essentially two ways the virtuous or self-reliant person could be developed. "One conception of the sage is that of the person living according to an ideal which transcends the everyday," Annas writes, "rising above it and regarding ordinary life, its concerns and troubles, as petty and fleeting." In this view, the sage exhibits tranquility and calmness, untroubled by the cares that concern most people as he or she has risen above them. Epicurus writes that those who follow his path, eschewing "the pleasures of the profligates and those that consist in sensuality," will not "be disturbed waking or asleep" but "shall live like a god among men."[4]

In the second way, the sage is seen as a "person whose ideal virtue is displayed not in rising above the everyday but precisely in staying at that level and dealing with it," Annas continues. "This is arguably the more challenging notion, since instead of contrasting the ideal and the practical it tries to bring them into relation, showing how ideal virtue can be found in actual practical, goal-directed activity."[5] The Stoics are example of this path. Although they are often viewed as indifferent to the world, they were not without emotions or desires. They believed the problems that disturb us are caused by our attachment to things we feel we can't live without. While it is rational that we should prefer some things, like good health, to other things, such as making money, they are "indifferent" so far as happiness is concerned.

The Stoic sage views everyday life from a "higher platform," as Emerson would say, that is, from the perspective of divine Reason. In thinking of ourselves as part of a larger whole, we loosen the grip of everyday concerns. Rather than avoiding life, the Stoic takes an active part in it. "The Stoics are not tempted by the ideal of detachment from practical life in order to study transcendent objects," Annas says. Rather, they "see the life detached from everyday practical concerns, devoted to a transcendent ideal, as selfish and self-indulgent."[6] For the Stoics, virtue meant living life well: mindfully, focusing on that which promotes eudaimonia, or human flourishing.

Emerson was well acquainted with the classic schools of ancient philosophy. He was especially drawn to Stoicism, frequently mentioning it and Stoic philosophers, including Epictetus, Cicero, Seneca, and Marcus Aurelius, in his journal, addresses, and essays. Stoicism is a thread that runs through much of Emerson's writing. Key essays, such as "Experience" and "Fate," exhibit considerable Stoic influence.

There are several reasons for considering Emerson a sage, especially in Annas's second sense of the term. For one thing, he exhibited the persona of a sage. George Santayana, though critical of Emerson's philosophy, beautifully described the impression he made on his audiences:

> Those who knew Emerson, or who stood so near to his time and to his circle that they caught some echo of his personal influence, did not judge him merely as a poet or philosopher, nor identify his efficacy with that of his writings. His friends and neighbors, the congregations he preached to in his younger days, the audiences that afterward listened to his lectures, all agreed in a veneration for his person which had nothing to do with their understanding or acceptance of his opinions. They flocked to him and listened to his word, not so much for the sake of its absolute meaning as for the atmosphere of candor, purity, and serenity that hung about it, as a sort of sacred music. They felt themselves in the presence of a rare and beautiful spirit, who was in communion with a higher world. More than the truth his teaching might express, they valued the sense it gave them of a truth that was inexpressible.[7]

I love this description, but I disagree with Santayana's implication that the impression Emerson made on people was incidental to his philosophy. For one to be considered a sage, it was essential that the persona match the philosophy. In fact, his persona was a reflection of his philosophy.

Many others have similarly described Emerson as a person serene and aloof from everyday concerns. Emerson's reputation as the Sage of

Concord peaked in the years immediately following his death in 1882. The focus on Emerson's exemplary personal character overshadowed the ideas contained in his writing. "The genteel critics diverted attention from Emerson's writings while enshrining him as a cultural icon, leaving the impression that he was someone who demanded reverence but not necessarily careful reading," according to American studies scholar Charles E. Mitchell.[8]

Emerson was not the remote figure depicted in these early accounts. Although he did view daily affairs from a higher platform, he was a devoted friend, family member, and citizen of Concord. He provided financial support to the Alcott family, enabling them to purchase a home in Concord; took in and looked after his mother and brothers; and in Concord served on the School Committee, taught in the Sunday school, and joined the Fire Company and the Social Circle.[9] Although he considered much of American society selfish and superficial, he sought to elevate it, not abandon it.

The importance of the persona is that the sage is depicted, as Annas says, "in terms of doing the actions which ordinary people do, but from wisdom, thus transforming the way in which those actions are performed. The sage is the person who does what we do, but succeeds where we fail. He does it all *well*, in a manner that cannot be criticized in any respect."[10] Emerson had his critics, but his audiences and those who knew him best saw him as a person who exhibited the art of living life well.

My argument for considering Emerson a sage does not rest on his persona alone. There are additional reasons. The sage was an exemplar of what is called "virtue ethics." The ancient Greeks believed that virtuous living entailed the cultivation of character. Morality was not a matter of right and wrong or of following commandments issued by a deity. It was assumed that the moral person would pursue the good, or behavior that is "according to nature." Thus human laws were a reflection of the laws of nature. The Greeks also believed that morality was developmental. Every person had the capacity to be a virtuous person, but some were more virtuous than others because they had cultivated morality.

Emerson was born into a Unitarian family. His father, who died when Waldo was still a boy, had been a prominent minister in Boston. The Unitarians at the time were still in the process of breaking away from the Calvinist churches of the Standing Order in Massachusetts. Although they became known as Unitarians for believing that God was one "person," not three, the primary disputes centered on the issues of original sin and election to salvation. Historian David Robinson, in his book *The Unitarians and the Universalists*, explains that the Calvinist viewpoint "undermined human moral exertion. The idea of the taint of Adam, communicated to all people regardless of their action or character, seemed to deny the possibility of the moral life; the idea of God's preordained selection of a few to salvation, regardless of their character or action, seemed to undercut the motivation for it. The liberals countered therefore with a moral system that affirmed human capability, as evidenced in the moral sense." In *Apostle of Culture: Emerson as Preacher and Lecturer*, Robinson notes, "Because human nature, according to the Unitarians, was not essentially corrupt, salvation came to be seen as the developing and unfolding of a potential inner virtue, rather than a wrenching inner change from corruption to righteousness."[11]

Another factor accounting for the Unitarians' break with New England Congregationalism had to do with the impact of the Great Awakening, which stressed the importance of enthusiasm in the process of conversion. Liberal Christians were rationalists and therefore suspicious of religious fervor as an evidence of faith. Charles Chauncy (1705–87) opposed the revivals of the Great Awakening because enthusiasm undermined the authority of reason. As Robinson points out, Chauncy "described 'real religion' as 'a sober, calm, reasonable thing' that ought to be judged not by the excesses of the emotions but by its moral results in the lives of [the faithful]." Chauncy judged religion by its moral results. "This stress on moralism, as it evolved into an ethic of character building and self-cultivation," Robinson notes, "also became a touchstone of the liberal movement in theology."[12]

The Unitarians' emphasis on the moral sense, human potential, and self-development was a form of virtue ethics. The most persuasive exponent of this point of view was William Ellery Channing (1780–1842), whose Federal Street Church in Boston is where Emerson and his family attended after his father died. "We believe that all virtue has its foundation in the moral nature of man, that is, in conscience, or his sense of duty, and in the power of forming his temper and life according to conscience," Channing asserted in his sermon "Unitarian Christianity."[13] Later, as Emerson prepared for the ministry himself, he considered Channing his mentor.

Though raised in genteel poverty, his mother saw to it that Waldo and three of his brothers were educated at Harvard.[14] By the time Emerson studied there, Harvard had become a Unitarian institution of higher learning, with a predominance of Unitarian scholars on its faculty. The curriculum was grounded in a moral philosophy promoted by intellectuals of the Scottish Enlightenment, primarily Thomas Reid (1710–96) and Dugald Stewart (1753–1828), who held that human beings were endowed with an innate moral sensibility. This meant all people had a capacity for discerning right from wrong intuitively, without divine mandates. "The difference between good and evil, or right and wrong," historian Daniel Walker Howe points out, "is regarded as part of 'the nature of things' and self-evident." Even though people were born with this capability, they did not necessarily exercise it. The moral sense needed to be developed. "Nineteenth-century Unitarians no longer thought of the good life primarily in terms of obedience to God," Howe says; "for them the good life meant achieving a delight in virtue."[15]

Another potent influence on Harvard moral philosophy was Neoplatonic philosophy, which added a spiritual dimension to the theory. Scottish moral philosophy was essentially rational, based on what was called "common sense." Neoplatonism elevated reason beyond its analytic power of discernment (what would come to be called "understanding") to that of Reason, with a capital R, or, in other words, the soul or mind of the universe itself. This type of Reason has to do with eternal truths and first principles. The ancient Greeks called it *nous*, the highest or divine intellect, "the eye of the Mind." For Unitarians it involved not only the formation of moral character but also, more importantly, the cultivation of our higher or spiritual nature—in Channing's words, "likeness to God."

As a student, Emerson absorbed the *rational intuitionism* taught by the Harvard faculty. But he questioned one important aspect. Morality might be intuitive, but what did these intuitions rest on? What evidence do we have that they are true? To answer this question, the Unitarians turned to the philosophy of John Locke, who argued that moral intuitions are grounded in empirical reality, assured by the veracity of divine revelation.

Since the Middle Ages, theologians have made a distinction between *natural religion* and *revealed religion*. Natural religion encompasses all that can be known about God and the world by means of the unaided human reason. But, according to this view, such knowledge is incomplete; it needs to be supplemented by revealed religion, given to us through divine revelation or scripture, namely, the Christian Bible, a position called *supernatural rationalism*.[16] Locke pointed to the miracles of Christ as evidence of the truth of the Gospels and, by extension, the authority of moral intuitions. Emerson challenged Locke's philosophy on this point, arguing there is no reason to believe the so-called witnesses in the contradictory accounts presented in the Gospels. He eventually dispensed with the need for revealed religion altogether, grounding moral law in human consciousness and the book of nature rather than the Christian Bible and the teachings of the church.

The theory and practice of ancient virtue ethics differed among the various schools of Greek philosophy, and ancient virtue ethics is not the same as the moral philosophy that was taught at Harvard College. Yet there are important similarities. For one, both Greek virtue ethics and Harvard moral philosophy focused on developing character rather than following rules. For another, they held that the moral sense was innately human, even if in the case of nineteenth-century Unitarians specific duties and obligations were enjoined by divine revelation. Moreover, the two viewpoints are essentially aspirational, focused on living a virtuous life, rather than avoiding the consequences of failure to follow rules and commandments.[17] Both were more concerned with *how* we ought to live than what we ought to *do*. They are teleological in the sense that they viewed eudaimonia, or human flourishing, to be the goal of a life well lived and democratic in the sense that every person has the capacity to pursue the good life. They viewed philosophy not as discursive arguments or theoretical proofs but rather as a way of life and looked for human examples of good character and virtuous living.

The more that Emerson distanced himself from his Unitarian upbringing and Harvard education, the more pronounced his affinity with the theories and practices of ancient virtue ethics became. Although he never ceased to believe that the moral sense was grounded in the human soul, he did alter his understanding of it. Historian David Robinson observes that Emerson "moved from an early position in which he felt the moral sense to be a simple discriminator of right and wrong actions, not unlike what we might call the conscience, to a more dynamic conception of it as that power by which man was inspired to the good by an ideal of perfection . . . which transcended the world ordinarily available to his senses."[18]

This perfectionist impulse is a distinctive feature of what Christopher Gowans calls "self-cultivation philosophies," which include ancient virtue ethics and Harvard moral theory. Here's how Gowans describes these philosophies: "Self-cultivation philosophies propound a program of development for improving the lives of human beings. On the basis of an account of human nature and the place of human beings in the world, they maintain that our lives can and should be substantially transformed from what is judged to be the problematic, untutored condition of human beings into what is put forward as an ideal state of being. As such, self-cultivation philosophies are preeminently practical in their orientation: their primary purpose is to change our lives in fundamental ways."[19]

These philosophies share two general characteristics. First, they promote a cultivation of the self that is radically different from ordinary conceptions of the self. Second, such philosophies have a practical orientation in teaching their followers how to live a good life. Gowans identifies a fourfold pattern typical of these philosophies. They begin with a baseline understanding of human nature. Second, they conclude that the existential condition of human beings is problematic. Third, they posit an ideal state of being—often the opposite of our present unsatisfactory condition—that we should aspire to attain. Finally, they prescribe a spiritual regimen designed to achieve a transformation of the self.

This pattern appears in the writings of the Stoic and Epicurean philosophers of ancient Greece and Rome. In antiquity, to be a philosopher meant living a philosophical life rather than engaging in abstract, theoretical discourse. The philosophical life was achieved by means of spiritual exercises. "In all philosophical schools, the goal pursued in these exercises is self-realization and improvement," writes Pierre Hadot, one of the foremost authorities on these philosophies. "All schools agree that man, before his philosophical conversion, is in a state of unhappy disquiet. Consumed by worries, torn by passions, he does not live a genuine life, nor is he truly himself. All schools also agree that man can be delivered from this state."[20] Philosophy is an art of living that alleviates suffering by teaching a radically new way of life.

Ancient virtue ethics and Harvard moral theory are both *aspirational*, meaning they invite us to aim for a better way of living. Our lives might be better—that is, we might be happier, more creative, and more productive—if we would develop our innate capacities. In the case of

Harvard moral theory, this was expressed in terms of cultivating the soul, in short, self-culture.

William Ellery Channing explained this notion in his address titled "Self-Culture" to a Boston working-class audience in 1838. "Self-culture," he said, is "the care which every man owes to himself, to the unfolding and perfecting of his nature." Little is to be gained in life "unless we are roused to act upon ourselves, unless we engage in the work of self-improvement." We can do this by virtue of "two powers of the human soul which make self-culture possible, the self-searching and the self-forming power." We are able to enter into and examine ourselves, to learn "what our nature is and what it was made for." Moreover, "we have a still nobler power, that of acting on, determining and forming ourselves." We are capable "not only of tracing our powers, but of guiding and impelling them; not only of watching our passions, but of controlling them; not only of seeing our faculties grow, but of applying to them means and influences to aid their growth." This power over ourselves "transcends in importance all our power over outward nature. There is more divinity in it, than in the force which impels the outward universe; and yet how little we comprehend it! How it slumbers in most men unsuspected, unused! This makes self-culture possible, and binds it on us as a solemn duty."[21]

The emphasis on self-culture coincided with (or was perhaps prompted by) what Emerson called "the age of the first person singular," which was a growing focus on the individual person apart from his or her ties to family, church, and state. "The individual self [during the eighteenth century] did not yet enjoy the unambiguous moral legitimacy that it has today," Howe observes. But in the nineteenth century this began to change. Though many were severely restricted by class, gender, and the practice of slavery, Americans became progressively freer to engage in what Thomas Jefferson had called "the pursuit of happiness." The nineteenth century allowed greater opportunities for self-definition and cultural pursuits. "In sum," Howe remarks, "the expansion of the market economy widened the scope for personal autonomy on a scale previously unparalleled: choice of goods and services to consume, choice of occupations to follow, choice of lifestyles and identities."[22]

Prior to the rise of state colleges and public schools in the nineteenth century, Americans were largely self-educated. Those who could afford them had tutors and went to private colleges. To meet the needs of working people seeking self-improvement, a number of institutes, associations, and lyceums sprang up in New England during the 1820s and 1830s. These included the Society for the Diffusion of Useful Knowledge, the Mechanics' Apprentices' Library Association, the Lyceum, and many other such societies. They provided an array of lectures, workshops, and classes for young men and women.[23] Channing delivered his iconic lecture on self-culture to one such group in Boston. All organizations promoted the notion of self-culture as a means of advancement. Self-culture was, in the words of historian Mark G. Vásquez, "the defining characteristic of the age." And it was the Unitarians who elevated it into a spiritual practice: "The Unitarians were the first to make self-culture an end in itself. In Unitarian thought self-culture included the unabashed quest for secular learning, which Unitarians associated with the inculcation of a disinterested spiritual elevation akin to religious belief. Self-culture became a life-long enterprise for Unitarians and indeed continued into the afterlife; they imagined heaven as a place devoted to self-culture."[24]

Much of this learning was practical, intended to equip persons for a better position in the workforce or in society more generally. Continuing in the twentieth century and today, this trend fed a burgeoning market for self-help literature, from *How to Win Friends and Influence People* to the latest "hacks" for time management. But for Channing and the Unitarians, self-culture served not only instrumental purposes but also moral, religious, and intellectual purposes, to some degree acting as a sort of check on the utilitarian uses of knowledge. "The exaltation of talent, as it is called, above virtue and religion, is the curse of the age," Channing observed. "Education is now chiefly a stimulus to learning, and thus men acquire power without the principles which alone make it good. Talent is worshipped; but, if divorced from rectitude, it will prove more of a demon than a god."[25]

For Emerson and the Transcendentalists, self-culture served another, even greater purpose: as a form of spiritual practice (which will be explored at greater length in a later chapter). As such, it was promoted by Emerson in his lecture series on human culture, Bronson Alcott in his "Doctrine and Discipline of Human Culture," and James Freeman Clarke in his best-selling book *Self-Culture*.[26] Frederic Henry Hedge, one of the original members of the Transcendentalist Club, described just how seriously they pursued self-culture as a spiritual practice in "The Art of Life, the Scholar's Calling," published in the *Dial* magazine:

> The work of life, so far as the individual is concerned, . . . is self-culture—the perfect unfolding of our individual nature. To this end above all others the art, of which I speak, directs our attention and points our endeavor. There is no man, it is presumed, to whom this object is wholly indifferent—who would not willingly possess this too, along with other prizes, provided the attainment of it were compatible with personal ease and worldly good. But the business of self-culture admits of no compromise. Either it must be a distinct aim, or wholly abandoned. . . .
>
> Of self-culture, as of all other things worth seeking, the price is a single devotion to that object—a devotion which shall exclude all aims and ends that do not directly or indirectly tend to promote it. In this service let no man flatter himself with the hope of light work and ready wages. . . . The only motive to exchange in this work is its own inherent worth, and the sure satisfaction which accompanies the consciousness of progress, in the true direction towards the stature of a perfect man. . . . No emoluments must seduce him from the rigor of his devotion. No engagements beyond the merest necessities of life must interfere with his pursuit. A meagre economy must be his income.[27]

Each of the Greek and Roman models of self-cultivation included elements of theory and practice. Theory encompassed metaphysics (the nature of reality) and epistemology (how we know what we know). The ancient philosophers were not content with abstract theorizing, however. For them, philosophy was all about the art of living. "The philosophical act is not situated merely on the cognitive level, but on that of the self and of being," Pierre Hadot explains. "It is a process which causes us to *be* more fully and makes us better. It is a conversion which turns our entire life upside down, changing the life of the person who goes through it. It raises the individual from an inauthentic condition of life, darkened by unconsciousness and harassed by worry, to an authentic state of life, in which he attains self-consciousness, and exact vision of the world, inner peace, and freedom."[28] For this reason each school prescribed a series of spiritual exercises intended to achieve this result.

Emerson founded no school of philosophy and took pride in the fact that he had not one disciple after "writing and speaking what were once called novelties for twenty-five or thirty years."[29] Mythologist Joseph Campbell tells this story of the Quest of the Holy Grail, epitomizing the process of individuation and self-reliance: The knights of King Arthur's court were gathered at the Round Table when a vision of the Holy Grail appeared to them. The knights were in awe. When the vision disappeared, Sir Gawain proposed that the knights should go in search of it. "That is the way a life is," Campbell writes. "Someone at some time in your life reveals to you a potential fulfillment journey. But then you have to undertake it." Since the knights thought it would be a disgrace to go as a group, each entered the forest of the adventure separately, where there was no way or path. "What we seek is the fulfillment of what was never on land or sea, namely of our own highest potentials," Campbell says. If we go to someone else, either saint or sage, thinking they can tell us the way, then we are not on our own path. Individuation "means bringing into fulfillment *your* talents, *your* destiny, *your* potentiality which is different from everyone else's."[30]

Why had Emerson not wanted to attract followers? "Not that what I said was not true," he wrote, "not that it has not found intelligent receivers but because it did not go from any wish in me to bring men to me, but to themselves. I delight in driving them from me. . . . This is my boast that I have no school and no follower. I should account it a measure of the impurity of insight, if it did not create independence."[31] Observing the journey by which Emerson came to his own theory and practice of self-culture has made it possible for others to discover their unique talents, destiny, and potential—both in his own lifetime and continuing through today. This is what I hope to show in the following chapters.

2

THE HERO'S JOURNEY

Scholars and literary historians have long puzzled over accounting for Emerson's genius. "Few American thinkers have influenced posterity in such varied and pervasive ways: its literature, its religion, its philosophy, its social thought," Lawrence Buell wrote in his bicentennial tribute to Emerson in 2003.[1] How did he come to be so influential? What was his secret?

An early historian of the Transcendentalist movement, Octavius Brooks Frothingham (1822–95), described it this way: "That secret lies in the writer's pure and perfect idealism, in his absolute and perpetual faith in thoughts, his supreme confidence in the spiritual laws. He lives in the region of serene ideas; lives there all the day and all the year; not visiting the mount of vision occasionally, but setting up his tabernacle there, and passing the night among the stars that he may be up and dressed for the eternal sunrise."[2] While this may have been a popular view, Emerson did not become a sage by being aloof from the world's affairs. He considered it essential to view life and society from the perspective of "the mount of vision" but said his visits there were few and far between. Although he may have wished to philosophize from the solitary comfort of his study, he earned his living as a celebrated public speaker. His faith in moral laws drew him into social reform and antislavery activism. By 1850, he had developed an international reputation as America's foremost public intellectual.

19

HOUR OF DECISION

Emerson's future prominence was hardly predictable given his early performance. He was an average student, graduating in the middle of his Harvard class. His brothers Edward and Charles showed greater promise. At loose ends following his graduation, he assisted at Edward's school in nearby Roxbury, south of Boston. "My years are passing away," he confided to his journal. "Infirmities are already stealing on me that may be the deadly enemies that are to dissolve me to dirt and little is yet done to establish my consideration among my contemporaries and less to get a memory when I am gone."[3] Though just nineteen years of age, he suffered from rheumatism in his hip, symptoms of tuberculosis, and problems with his eyesight.

Tired of teaching, he decided to enter the ministry, following in the footsteps of his father, William, who had been minister to Boston's prestigious First Church before his untimely death in 1811. In fact, there were six generations of ministers in the family. Yet he had doubts about his fitness for the profession. In his journal Emerson assessed his strengths and weaknesses. "In Divinity I hope to thrive," he wrote. While he inherited from his father "a passionate love for the strains of eloquence," he admitted that he was ill at ease around others. "What is called a warm heart, I have not."[4]

Despite his uncertainty, he enrolled in Harvard Divinity School. His studies were interrupted by his numerous health issues. In search of relief, he traveled to the South, going as far as St. Augustine, Florida, and returned six months later. In October 1826 he was licensed to preach, even though he had not completed his ministerial education. He said afterward that if the authorities had examined him, they would not have approved him.[5]

For several years he preached at various churches that invited him when they needed someone in the pulpit, called "supply preaching." At one of these churches, in Concord, New Hampshire, he met his first wife, Ellen Louisa Tucker, then sixteen, who was a beautiful and vivacious young woman with a gift for poetry. They were engaged the following year and wed in September 1829.

After several years of supply preaching, he accepted the call to become junior pastor of Boston's Second Church in January of 1829. From the beginning of their marriage, his young wife suffered from consumption, or pulmonary tuberculosis. In spite of efforts to loosen its grip, she died at only nineteen years of age. They had been married for just a little over a year. He was devastated by her death. Every day he walked several miles to visit her tomb. Once, he even went so far as to open her coffin for a look inside. He was desperate to hold on to his young wife's memory, which was fading all too quickly. The specter of illness and death hung over him during these months. His brothers Edward and Charles, with whom he was very close, also showed symptoms of tuberculosis. Another brother, Bulkeley, was committed to a mental hospital. Waldo himself was often laid low by debilitating attacks of diarrhea, in addition to his other health problems.

Following the illness of the senior minister at Second Church, Emerson was invited to take his place. He enjoyed preaching and was good at it. His sermons "were characterized by great simplicity and an unconventional style, which brought him into closer *rapport* with his hearers than was commonly achieved by the pulpit in those days," according to his friend and fellow Transcendentalist Frederic Henry Hedge. While the more orthodox Christians in his flock were shocked by what they heard, "those who listened with unprejudiced and appreciative minds, especially the young, were charmed by his preaching as by no other."[6] His greatest shortcoming was in his pastoral role. He was shy and introverted. Making parish calls was difficult for him. But he worked at those duties, performing numerous weddings and baptisms, meeting with church committees, and undertaking civic responsibilities, including a turn as chaplain of the Massachusetts State Senate. According to church reports, the congregation was pleased with his efforts.

At a deeper level, however, Emerson was undergoing a profound transformation in his spiritual life. His views on religion and ministry were changing to such an extent that he began to feel it impossible for him to continue on his present course. He was raised and educated a liberal Christian, as first-generation Unitarians called themselves. In 1819, his mentor, William Ellery Channing, had given an address on Unitarian Christianity that defined the Unitarian position. Unitarians, Channing said, were committed to the Bible as the source of religious truth, but it "is a book written for men, in the language of men, and that its meaning is to be sought in the same manner as other books."[7] Readers of the Bible should not take it literally, apart from its historical context. To be sure, the Bible contained divine revelation, but it also included material that was not inspired at all. Taking a historical approach to biblical study would allow readers to distinguish between revealed truth and literary fiction.

In 1823 William Emerson, Waldo's older brother, acted on Channing's advice and left to study for the ministry at the University of Göttingen in Germany, arguably the most advanced institution of higher learning anywhere.[8] In particular, he hoped to attend the lectures of Johann Gottfried Eichhorn, the foremost biblical scholar in the world and a pioneer in the "higher criticism" of the Bible, focusing on the Bible's composition and history. Though William admired Eichhorn, he was troubled by the skepticism the professor's "higher criticism" seemed to engender among scholars. He soon became disillusioned himself, questioning his call to the ministry and regretting his decision to study in Germany. On a visit to Weimar, he sought Johann Wolfgang von Goethe's advice. To his great disappointment, the renowned author advised him to "preach to the people what they wanted; his personal belief was no business of theirs; he could be a good preacher and no one need ever know what he himself had for his own private views."[9] On his return to America, William decided to study for the law instead.

William's return coincided with Waldo's enrollment in Harvard Divinity School. In an 1830 letter to his uncle, Ezra Ripley (1751–1841), who served as the minister at First Parish in Concord for sixty-three years, William explained that he did not doubt the genuineness of Jesus's teachings but he did question the forms those teachings had taken in Christian worship. In particular, he did not feel the "external ceremonies of the communion table are at this day binding and important."[10] Undoubtedly, his brother's experience in Germany made an impression on Waldo. William's views on religious forms, especially the Lord's Supper, played a huge role in Waldo's decision to resign from Second Church.

The nature of the Unitarian ministry itself was also changing. Increasingly, congregations expected more from their ministers than eloquence and scholarship—they wanted a personal relationship, a friend and spiritual guide, not just a leader or preacher. While he excelled in eloquence and scholarship, Emerson came across as aloof and socially awkward to his parishioners.

Orthodox Christians viewed the liberal Christians as infidels, atheists, and disturbers of the peace. The Unitarians had separated themselves from the Calvinist churches early in the nineteenth century. They held that God was one, not three, and they rejected the Puritan doctrines of predestination and human depravity. At that time the Unitarians sought to avoid stirring further controversy about doctrine, focusing instead on ethics. Until Channing came out as an avowed Unitarian in 1819, liberal Christians had been reluctant to use that label. Even after they founded the American Unitarian Association in 1825, ministers were careful to avoid controversy in their relations with the orthodox and within their own congregations.

Both issues—the changing role of the minister and the conservatism of first-generation Unitarians—added to Emerson's growing discomfort with the ministry. Perhaps influenced by hearing Goethe's advice to his brother, Waldo became increasingly determined to say what was in him to say and not tailor his words to avoid controversy. At first this was scarcely an issue, as he was very much a Channing Unitarian theologically, and he dutifully observed the forms of Unitarian worship. But in March 1831 he posed this query to his journal: "Why unsettle or disturb a faith which presents to so many minds a helpful medium by which they approach the idea of God?" His answer was that the popular view of religion is "pernicious" because it puts a medium or a screen between the individual and God.[11] Ministers and religious institutions were obstacles in the way of directly perceiving religious truth.

He was especially uncomfortable with sectarian labels. "I suppose it is not wise, not being natural, to belong to any religious party," he wrote a few months later. "In the Bible you are not directed to be a Unitarian, or a Calvinist or an Episcopalian. Now if a man is wise, he will not only not profess himself to be a Unitarian, but he will say to himself, I am not a member of that or of any party. . . . Religion is the relation of the soul to God, and therefore the progress of Sectarianism marks the decline of religion." Such thoughts continued to trouble him the rest of the year. He felt pinched by the constraints of his clerical position, as he noted in a journal entry dated January 10, 1832: "It is the best part of the man, I sometimes think, that revolts most against his being the minister. His good revolts from official goodness. . . . The difficulty is that we do not make a world of our own but fall into institutions already made and have to accommodate ourselves to them to be useful at all. And this accommodation is, I say, a loss of so much integrity and, of course, of so much power."[12]

By June, Emerson's doubts and misgivings had come to a head. "I have sometimes thought that in order to be a good minister it was necessary to leave the ministry," he wrote in his journal on June 2. "The profession is antiquated. In an altered age, we worship in the dead forms of our forefathers. Were not a Socratic paganism better than an effete, superannuated Christianity?"[13] The tipping point came in a disagreement with his church over the issue of the Lord's Supper. Following his studies in Germany, William Emerson had concluded that there was no biblical mandate for the ordinance of Communion. Waldo agreed with his brother's assessment and, in a letter to the standing committee of his church a few days later, asked to be relieved of the responsibility of administering the rite. On June 21 the committee denied his request but hoped that he would stay on as the congregation's minister.

The church was undergoing repairs at the time, so Emerson took the next four weeks off to decide what to do next. He went into the White Mountains with his brother Charles and Aunt Mary. The trip proved to be both a catharsis and a turning point. "Here among the mountains the pinions of thought should be strong and one should see the errors of men from a calmer height of love and wisdom." From this lofty perspective certain things became clearer to him. For one, he concluded that religion is not about doctrines or rituals at all. "It is a life," he said. "It is not something else *to be got*, to be *added*, but is a new life of those faculties you have." For another, he was determined to be "the vehicle of that divine principle that lurks within and of which life has afforded only glimpses enough to assure me of its being. We know little of its laws—but we have observed that a north wind clear cold with its scattered fleet of drifting clouds braced the body and seemed to reflect a similar abyss of spiritual heaven between clouds in our minds." Once having had such an "experience we strive to avail ourselves of it and propitiate the divine inmate to speak to us again out of clouds and darkness."[14] To summon the soul and communicate its wisdom to others would be his life task.

This was "the hour of decision" about his future at Second Church. It was "a bad sign," he said, "to be too conscientious, and to stick at gnats. The most desperate scoundrels have been the over-refiners. Without accommodation society is impracticable. But this ordinance is esteemed the most sacred of religious institutions, and I cannot go habitually to an institution which they esteem holiest with indifference and dislike." He did not wish to force the issue with his congregation and decided to resign. The illness that had plagued him on and off for months caused him to delay announcing his decision until September. In a sermon based on a verse from Paul's Letter to the Romans—"The kingdom of God is not meat and drink; but righteousness and peace and joy in the holy ghost"—Emerson explained his position and his reasons for leaving his pulpit.[15]

This was not the end of his ministry. He continued to preach, as needed, in other churches and for a time served the Unitarian congregation in East Lexington. But it was a turning point in his career and in his evolving spiritual development. It was also the beginning of a revolution—in the conception of a religious life and a reliance on the God within rather than the teachings of the Christian church. The seeds of this revolution had been planted by his Aunt Mary, herself a religious rebel, who instilled in her young nephew independence of mind, love of learning, endless curiosity, and the value of "enthusiasm"—the immediate apprehension of divine spirit. All these qualities helped form Emerson's idea of self-culture and his influence as America's preeminent spiritual seeker.[16]

Joseph Campbell has written eloquently about the hero's journey. It begins with a feeling that the life we are living is not authentic. "There comes a point," he says, "a threshold crossing, where everything that you've been taught is of no use to you whatsoever." In Emerson's case, the ministry was stifling his creativity, his intellectual independence, and his spiritual growth. "The visionary or hero's journey begins when one feels there is something missing and drops out," Campbell continues. "It is what I refer to . . . as the 'call to adventure,' the feeling that we need to go away, that societal rules don't fit." One leaves the world of social achievement in search of "the inner power and harmony that is missing."[17] The hero's quest is not only in search of his own healing and wholeness but also in pursuit of a saving knowledge, a "boon" with which to enlighten humankind upon his return. Campbell's paradigm of the hero's journey well describes Emerson. His resignation from the parish ministry was a crossing of the threshold for him, a break with a way of life that he considered inauthentic. Seeking both inspiration and relief from his suffering, he was lured abroad for the next stage of his sage-hood.

A "NEW MYTHUS"

It was with a mixture of exhaustion and expectation that he sailed for Europe on Christmas Day 1832. A fitting coda to this period of his life is a poem he wrote in October as his service to Second Church was coming to a close:

> I will not live out of me
> I will not see with others' eyes
> My good is good, my evil ill
> I would be free—I cannot be
> While I take things as others please to rate them
> I dare attempt to lay out my own road.
> . . . .
> Henceforth, please God, forever I forego
> The yoke of men's opinions. I will be
> Lighthearted as a bird and live with God.[18]

Although he felt liberated, it was hard for those around him to see his decision as anything but a sign of failure. "Leaving the Second Church in Boston was a repudiation of the world of his father," writes Robert D. Richardson Jr. in *Emerson: The Mind on Fire.* "He was also giving up institutional affiliation and support, a guaranteed social position, and a generous and assured salary."[19] After a rough voyage, Emerson arrived in Malta at the beginning of February. From there he went on to Sicily, then to Naples, Rome, Florence, Venice, Milan, and other cities and towns along the way. After three months in Italy he stopped briefly in Switzerland, spent a month in Paris, and arrived in London near the end of July.

In Britain there were three people he wanted to see: Samuel Taylor Coleridge, William Wordsworth, and Thomas Carlyle, writers central to the Romantic movement. Coleridge lived in London. Emerson paid him a visit first, unannounced, on August 5. Finding him still in bed, he returned later in the day. By that time Coleridge (1772–1834) was sixty years old and in ill health. Although he had been a Unitarian in his younger years, he was now firmly in the Anglican fold. Coleridge did all the talking and at one point went on a tirade about "the folly and ignorance of Unitarianism." When Emerson interjected that he himself was a Unitarian, Coleridge said, yes, he "supposed so and continued as before." Altogether, it was a disappointing visit, "rather a spectacle than a conversation, of no use beyond the satisfaction of my curiosity," he wrote in his book, *English Traits*.[20]

Emerson next traveled to Scotland and on August 26 set out from Dumfries in a carriage to visit historian Thomas Carlyle (1795–1881) and his wife, Jane, on their farm sixteen miles into the countryside. Emerson had been reading Carlyle's essays for several years and sensed in him an intellectual soul mate. He wrote in his journal: "A white day in my years. I found the youth I had sought in Scotland and good and wise and pleasant he seems to me." They went for a long walk over the hills "and talked of the immortality of the soul."[21]

Two days later, on August 28, Emerson called on William Wordsworth (1770–1850) at his home at Rydal Mount in the English Lake District. Like Coleridge, Wordsworth was getting on in years. The poet offered to recite some of his latest compositions. When it was time for his young visitor to leave, Wordsworth insisted on walking with him part of the way back to his lodgings. "To judge from a single conversation," Emerson noted uncharitably, "he made the impression of a narrow and very English mind; of one who paid for his rare elevation by narrow tameness and conformity."[22]

Perhaps there was no way Coleridge and Wordsworth could have lived up to their literary reputations. They had grown older and more conservative. Despite his negative impressions on meeting them face to face, Emerson was wise enough to realize that the two of them, along with Carlyle, were his greatest sources of inspiration. In these three writers he found answers to some of the questions that had been nagging at him.

Emerson had begun reading Coleridge in earnest three years earlier. He was more interested in Coleridge's prose than his poetry, which was better known. As Emerson gushed in a letter to his Aunt Mary, Coleridge was an example of "the restless human soul bursting the narrow boundaries of antique speculation and mad to know the secrets of that unknown world, on whose brink it is sure it is standing."[23]

He was especially drawn to *Aids to Reflection* and *The Friend*. In both works, Coleridge drew an important distinction—derived from his reading of German philosopher Immanuel Kant—between what he called the Reason and the Understanding. "Reason," he stated in *Aids to Reflection*, "is the power of universal and necessary convictions, the source and substance of truths above sense, and having their evidence in themselves. . . . On the other hand, the judgments of the Understanding are binding only in relation to the objects of our senses, which we reflect under the forms of the Understanding."[24] Today we associate the word "reason" with rationality and logical thought. But for Coleridge, Reason, with a capital *R*, meant intuition or vision. In contrast to Reason was Understanding, which meant empirical knowledge, as provided by data from the senses. (He sometimes uses the word "reason" in lowercase to refer to discursive reason, as opposed to its uppercase intuitive Reason.)

Emerson elaborated on this distinction in a letter to his brother Edward in 1834: "Philosophy affirms that the outward world is only phenomenal and the whole concern of dinners, of tailors, of gigs of balls whereof men make such account is a quite relative and temporary one—an intricate dream—the exhalation of the present state of the Soul—wherein the Understanding works incessantly as if it were real, but the eternal Reason, when now and then he is allowed to speak, declares it is an accident, a smoke nowise related to his permanent attributes. . . . Reason is the highest faculty of the soul—what we mean often by the soul itself; it never *reasons*, never proves, it simply perceives; it is vision. The Understanding toils all the time, compares, contrives, adds, argues, near sighted but strong-sighted, dwelling in the present, the expedient, the customary." What he is saying here is, first, the Understanding shows us the *actual* world, whereas Reason gives us a vision of the *real* world behind the smokescreen of appearances. Second, when he says "near sighted but strong-sighted," what he means is that in everyday life the Understanding, though limited and secondary to Reason, nevertheless predominates. As he puts it in his own colorful language, "Understanding, that wrinkled calculator, the steward of our house to whom is committed the support of our animal life, contradicts evermore these affirmations of Reason, and points at Customs and Interests and persuades one man that the declarations of Reason are false and another that they are at least impracticable."[25]

This distinction is important to Emerson—as it was to Coleridge, Carlyle, and the American Transcendentalists—because it helps answer one of his most troublesome questions. Emerson was deeply religious while at the same time skeptical of Christian scriptures and church doctrines. If faith does not rest on scriptures and doctrines, what, then, does it rest on for its authority? The answer, at least in part, is that faith is a revelation of the Reason. It is experienced intuitively. Scriptures and doctrines, on the other hand, belong to the category of the Understanding. Because the Understanding is "strong-sighted," it promotes scriptures and doctrines and denies the revelations of Reason. But the attempt to validate religious truth on an empirical basis is bound to fail and will inevitably lead to atheism.

For Coleridge, as for Emerson, these two modes of cognition are not opposed to each other but are complementary. Both are necessary functions of human consciousness. In everyday life, however, they are out of balance. The predominance of the Understanding, with its emphasis on matter and utility, has resulted in a sense of alienation from the world. We feel divorced from nature. In Coleridge's view, the Understanding and the Reason represent two poles of a bipolar unity. Nature and spirit are interrelated. Their relationship is consummated, intuitively, in a vision of a marriage of the two. Even so, there continues to be a push and pull between them, two alternating modes of consciousness. Their relationship is dynamic, not static.

Coleridge also influenced Emerson's opinion of Wordsworth. Prior to 1833, Emerson had been dismissive of Wordsworth's poetry. But after reading that Coleridge ranked Wordsworth with Milton, Emerson took another, closer look at Wordsworth's poetry. There he found another part of the answer to his quandary. The Unitarians made a distinction between natural and revealed religion. Natural religion was based on all we can know about God, morality, and immortality from observing the natural world. Revealed religion, on the other hand, was based on what God had directly communicated to the writers of the Gospels. For the liberal Christians, revealed religion completed natural religion, supplementing it with knowledge of God's special revelation concerning man's salvation. In rereading Wordsworth's poetry, Emerson concluded that nature is a revelation of God sufficient unto itself. In nature, Wordsworth wrote,

> I have felt
> A presence that disturbs me with the joy
> Of elevated thoughts; a sense sublime
> Of something far more deeply interfused,
> Whose dwelling is the light of setting suns,
> And the round ocean, and the living air,
> And the blue sky, and in the mind of man,
> A motion and a spirit, that impels
> All thinking things, all objects of all thought,
> And rolls through all things.[26]

In his essay "Thoughts on Modern Literature," published in the *Dial* magazine in 1840, Emerson acknowledged Wordsworth's influence. His poetry, he said, "awakened in every lover of nature the right feeling. We saw the stars shine, we felt the awe of mountains, we heard the rustle of wind in the grass, and we knew again the ineffable secret of solitude. It was a great joy. It was nearer to nature than anything we had before."[27] His poetry was characterized, Emerson noted, by "subjectiveness" and "the Feeling of the Infinite," as shown in these lines from *The Prelude*:

> Of Genius, Power,
> Creation and Divinity itself
> I have been speaking, for my theme has been
> What passed *within* me. Not of outward things.
> . . . .
> Points we have all of us within our souls,
> Where all stand single.
> . . . .
> For there's not a man
> That lives who hath not had his godlike hours,
> And knows not what majestic sway we have,
> As natural beings in the strength of Nature.[28]

He also found in Wordsworth an expression of certain experiences that haunted him all his life. These were "godlike hours," moments of transcendence in which the eye of Reason opens and reveals the world as it truly is. Sadly, such moments never last long, and we find ourselves back in the everyday world. We struggle to retain and express the wisdom gained from these profound yet evanescent experiences. Wordsworth described them in his famous "Ode" as:

Those shadowy recollections,
Which, be they what they may,
Are yet the fountain light of all our day,
Are yet a master light of all our seeing.[29]

Emerson quoted these lines numerous times in his essays, lectures, and journal entries. He also felt that Wordsworth captured the pathos associated with the fading of such moments in these lines from *The Excursion*:

to converse with heaven—
This is not easy:—to relinquish all
We have, or hope, of happiness and joy,
And stand in freedom loosened from this world,
I deem not arduous; but needs confess
That 'tis a thing impossible to frame
Conceptions equal to the soul's desires;
And the most difficult of tasks to keep
Heights which the soul is competent to gain.[30]

Regaining these heights and framing "conceptions equal to the soul's desires" became the central task of Emerson's life and work.

Around 1827 Emerson had begun reading essays of Thomas Carlyle that appeared anonymously in the *Edinburgh Review*. Three in particular were of special interest: "State of German Literature," "Signs of the Times," and "Characteristics." In the first, Carlyle makes the same distinction Coleridge did between Reason and Understanding. He, too, was an interpreter of Kant's transcendental philosophy. He focused especially on the consequences of materialistic utilitarianism for the future of faith. In this essay he wrote, "Should Understanding attempt to prove the existence of God, it ends, if thorough-going and consistent with itself, in Atheism . . . should it speculate on Virtue, it ends in *Utility*."[31] Emerson, too, feared that empiricism led to religious skepticism. This was the basis of his objection to the philosophy of John Locke, who had argued that knowledge comes to us, empirically, by way of the senses. Locke's argument became a central issue in the "miracles" controversy resulting from Emerson's Divinity School Address in 1838, which I discuss in chapter 4.

In "Signs of the Times," Carlyle declares that we are living in the Mechanical Age. "It is the Age of Machinery, in every outward and inward sense of that word; the age which, with its whole undivided might, forwards, teaches and practices the great art of adapting means to ends."

The virus of mechanism has infected all aspects of society, including education, religion, art, and philosophy. He singles out the philosophy of John Locke as "an indication of the spirit of these times. His whole doctrine is mechanical, in its aim and origin, in its methods and results." In opposition to this mechanistic view, Carlyle says, there is a dynamic spirit that accounts for "the primary, unmodified forces and energies of man, the mysterious springs of Love, and Fear, and Wonder, of Enthusiasm, Poetry, Religion, all of which have a truly vital and *infinite* character," and thus promises the redemption of society.[32]

Carlyle's essay "Characteristics" anticipates Emerson's argument in his celebrated "American Scholar" address in 1837. In this essay Carlyle once again focuses on the effects on society of mechanism and a mercantile economy. "Society was what we can call *whole*," he wrote. "The individual man was in himself a whole, or complete union; and could combine with his fellows as the living member of a greater whole. For all men, through their life, were animated by one great idea; thus all efforts pointed one way, everywhere there was *wholeness*." He likens the present, fallen condition of society to a disease brought about by mechanism, which has gotten the upper hand. "Man has subdued this planet, his habitation and inheritance; yet reaps no profit from the victory." He prophesizes, "The genius of mechanism . . . will not always sit like a choking incubus on our soul, when by a new magic word the old spell is broken, become our slave, and as familiar spirit do all our bidding."[33]

Despite his pessimism about the current state of society, Carlyle nevertheless heralded, in a letter written to Goethe, "a period of new Spirituality and Belief, in the midst of old Doubt and Denial; as it were, a new revelation of Nature, and the Freedom and Infinitude of Man, wherein Reverence is again rendered compatible with Knowledge, and Art and Religion are one."[34] Nowhere is this more manifest in Carlyle's writing than in that strange classic *Sartor Resartus*, or the Tailor Retailored. The narrator, Professor Diogenes Teufelsdröckh, declaims "that the Mythus of the Christian Religion looks not in the eighteenth century as it did in the eighth. . . . Wilt thou help us to embody the divine Spirit of that Religion in a new Mythus, in a new vehicle and vesture, that our Souls, otherwise too like perishing, may live?"[35] This new mythus is expressed in terms of what Carlyle calls "natural supernaturalism." Nature, not biblical scripture, is the revelation of God: "We speak of the Volume of Nature: and truly a Volume it is,—whose Author and Writer is God. To read it! Dost thou, does man, so much as well know the Alphabet thereof? With its Words, Sentences, and grand descriptive Pages, poetical and philosophical, spread out through the Solar Systems, and Thousands of Years, we shall not try thee. It is a Volume written in celestial hieroglyphs, in the true Sacred-writing; of which even true Prophets are happy that they can read here a line and there a line."[36]

For Emerson, natural supernaturalism meant expressing the revelations of nature in familiar religious imagery and symbolism. An example is the imagery of the divine marriage. In the New Testament Book of the Apocalypse, the coming of the new heaven and the new earth at the end of time will be heralded by the marriage between Christ and the heavenly city, a "new Jerusalem, prepared as a bride adorned for her husband." Wordsworth used this imagery in the "Prospectus" of *The Excursion*:

> Paradise, and groves
> Elysian, Fortunate Fields—like those of old
> Sought in the Atlantic Main, why should they be
> A history only of departed things,
> Or a mere fiction of what never was?
> For the discerning intellect of Man,
> When wedded to this goodly universe
> In love and holy passion, shall find these
> A simple produce of the common day.[37]

In his first book, *Nature*, Emerson also invokes the imagery of the divine marriage as a way of imaginatively overcoming the separation between man and nature, which will be discussed in chapter 4.

Emerson was not enamored of Carlyle's writing style, but he agreed with Carlyle's message. A new mythus *was* called for, and it needed to be written in the language of nature, not the Bible. On his return from Europe, Emerson set himself to develop and articulate this new mythus, drawing on the ideas of Coleridge and Wordsworth, as well as Carlyle. For him now, God was immanent in nature, not apart from it, and no longer viewed as a supernatural being but as a vital force. In the transition from the pulpit to the podium, Emerson went from being a liberal Christian to an avowed pantheist. This new mythus was the "boon," the saving knowledge, that Emerson returned with from his hero's journey.

3

BECOMING A SAGE

The foundation stones of Ralph Waldo Emerson's education were the classic writings of ancient Greece and Rome. When he was nine years old, he was enrolled in the Boston Public Latin School, where he was drilled in Latin and Greek and studied the classical authors such as Virgil and Homer. At the age of fourteen, in 1817, he entered Harvard College, where his education in the classics continued. Then and for years afterward, he studied the writings of the ancient schools of philosophy, including those of Epicurus, Epictetus, Plato, Aristotle, Pythagoras, and Plotinus.

Each of these schools included elements of theory and practice. Theory encompassed metaphysics and epistemology. As we have seen, Emerson did not establish a school of philosophy and took pride in the fact that he had not attracted any disciples. Nevertheless, he did develop a theory and practice for cultivating the soul. The theory was what he called the "First Philosophy." The practice was "self-culture." Even if he did not attract disciples, at least he left a pattern for others to follow.

FIRST PHILOSOPHY

Just as on his outbound voyage to Europe, Emerson's emotions on the return were a mixture of excitement and anxiety. His reading and his travels had filled his mind with ideas, but in deciding to leave the ministry he fretted about his future course without a professional position. At sea in September he wrote in his journal, "I like my book about nature and wish I knew where and how I ought to live."[1] It took another two years to finish his book about nature. Most pressing was finding a way to support himself. On arriving in Boston in early October 1833, he continued to preach at churches in and around the city. But soon an even better opportunity presented itself.

The lyceum movement, offering public lectures to adult audiences, was gaining momentum in the late 1820s and early 1830s. Local lyceums were thriving in towns throughout New England and beyond. Emerson's strengths—eloquence and a love of books—were ideally suited to this new platform. The lyceum gave him the freedom to speak to a wider audience and to choose his own topics. He began lecturing soon after his return, first in Boston and then in other towns nearby. More money could be made by selling subscriptions to a series of lecture series than to individual talks. Between November 1833 and November 1835, he developed lecture series on science, biography, and English literature.

He was also reading voraciously, delving more deeply into Coleridge, Wordsworth, and Carlyle, and tackling a wide range of thinkers across the ages. His reading lists from 1831 to 1834 include works by Socrates, Plato, Aristotle, Zoroaster, Plutarch, Plotinus, Cicero, Seneca, Montaigne, Shakespeare, Milton, Swedenborg, Thomas Hobbes, David Hume, Jean-Jacques Rousseau, Friedrich Schiller, Friedrich Shelling, Madame de Staël, Goethe, Victor Cousin, Edward Gibbon, and many others.[2]

His manner of reading was somewhat peculiar. He seldom read books from cover to cover, and he didn't try to master their subject matter. Rather, he read for the "lusters," the ideas that caught his attention and resonated with his own experience. In his journal he copied Coleridge's four types of readers: the Hour-glass, "all in and all out"; the Sponge, "giving it all out a little dirtier than it took in"; the Jelly-bag, "keeping nothing but the refuse"; and the Golconda, "sieves picking up the diamonds only."[3] Emerson was definitely a reader of the Golconda type—named after the diamond-rich region in India—looking only for the most valuable gems. Even as he took in all these many influences, he was determined to think for himself. On October 6, 1834, he wrote, "Insist on yourself. Never imitate," foreshadowing his famous essay "Self-Reliance."[4]

Drawing on his reading, Emerson began to develop what he called the First Philosophy. Something was nagging at him, an itch he couldn't quite scratch. It prompted him to think more deeply about his life and the human condition. "We are always getting ready to live but never living," he observed.

> We have many years of technical education; then, many years of earn-
> ing a livelihood, and we get sick, and take journeys for our health, and
> compass land and sea for improvement by travelling, but the work of
> self-improvement—always under our nose,—nearer than the nearest, is
> seldom engaged in. A few hours in the longest life.
>   Set out to study a particular truth. Read upon it. Walk to think
> upon it. Talk of it. Write about it. The thing itself will not much
> manifest itself, at least not much in accommodation to your studying
> arrangements. The gleams you do get, out they will flash, as likely at
> dinner, or in the roar of Faneuil Hall, as in your painfullest abstraction.
>   Very little life in a lifetime.[5]

This quandary is at the heart of Emerson's writing. We humans are troubled by a sense that there is more to life than our daily routine. From
time to time and in unexpected places we catch glimpses of a richer,
more radiant life. We ponder ways of maximizing these moments, but
they elude our efforts. The harder we try, the more evasive they seem
to be. Yet Emerson was convinced that "the work of self-improvement,"
properly understood and diligently undertaken, would make us more
receptive to the promptings of the spirit.

In 1834 and 1835, Emerson filled his journal with musings on this
dilemma. During this time he also faced the challenge of supporting himself and launching his career as a lecturer and writer. He spent much time
at the Boston Athenaeum, a private library founded by his father, studying
for his lectures. He prepared sermons for his supply preaching. He moved
from one temporary home to another. Once his dead wife's estate was
finally settled, the legacy he inherited freed him for a while from needing
a salary as a minister or teacher. It also allowed him to pursue answers to
questions that had been troubling him well before he left for Europe.

A central dilemma was his disillusionment with historical Christianity.
He questioned the legitimacy of the Bible and church teachings. He no
longer believed in a supernatural God. If faith no longer rests on belief in
these, what does it rest on? If, as he had written to his brother Edward,
"the outward world is only phenomenal . . . relative and temporary,"
then what, if anything, can we rely on? If, as Carlyle argued, we need a
new religious mythus, retailored to the spiritual needs of today, what is
that mythus? These questions, as he noted in his journal, had to do with

the problem initially posed by Plato, namely, "for all that exists conditionally . . . to find a ground that is unconditional and absolute."[6]

In July 1835 Emerson set down in his journal the rudiments of his First Philosophy, or the original laws of the mind. "It is the Science of what *is*, in distinction from what *appears*." He explored more deeply Coleridge's ideas on Reason and Understanding. These original laws of the mind, which are the revelation of Reason, are more easily obeyed than expressed. To the Understanding, our habitual way of perceiving, they seem glimpses of a world in which we do not yet live. We are conscious, he says, of having a twofold nature that puts us at odds with ourselves: the Reason and the Understanding. "Reason is the superior principle," Emerson asserts. "Its attributes are Eternity and Intuition. We belong to it, not it to us." This mode of consciousness exists in all persons, though for many it lies dormant. "The authority of Reason cannot be separated from its vision."[7] They are one and the same.

The Understanding, on the other hand, is empirical. "It divides, compares, reasons, invents. It lives from the Reason yet disobeys it. It commands the material world, yet often for the pleasure of the sense." It incarnates the ideas of Reason, though imperfectly. "Heaven," for instance, "is the projection of the Ideas of Reason on the plane of the Understanding." In so doing, it commits what Alfred North Whitehead calls the fallacy of misplaced concreteness, that is, taking symbolism too literally.[8] At the same time, it dismisses the revelations of Reason, such as those uttered by Jesus in his Sermon on the Mount, as nonsense. The Understanding tends to contradict the Reason.

The challenge of the spiritual life is to awaken the mind. In the materialistic worldview of empirical philosophy, the Understanding has the upper hand, to the neglect and disadvantage of the Reason. In living for "the pleasure of the sense," we pursue a superficial existence, living one-dimensional lives in which appearances count for everything. "We walk about in a sleep," Emerson observes. "A few moments in the year or in our lifetime we truly live; we are at the top of our being; we are pervaded, yea, dissolved by the Mind: but we fall back again presently."[9] The practical-minded, those in whom the Understanding predominates, are not awake. The question is, how to arouse the Mind from the lethargy of inaction, the superficiality of our habitual existence. This will be the topic of the next chapter.

Much of what follows in my examination of Emerson's spiritual philosophy depends on the validity of the distinction between the Understanding and the Reason. Is this just a quaint notion Emerson seized
on in his reading of Coleridge? And who is to say Coleridge is right to
make such a claim? Critics such as David Van Leer have pointed out
that Coleridge derived his views on this distinction from a misreading
of Immanuel Kant's *Critique of Pure Reason*. But important here is not
whether Coleridge understood Kant correctly but the use Emerson
made of Coleridge's distinction.[10] Kant, as filtered through Coleridge,
gave Emerson a vocabulary and a framework for mediating between
idealism and empiricism, a dichotomy that goes back to the differing
philosophies of Plato and Aristotle.[11]

Emerson concluded that of the two modes of consciousness, one of
them, the Understanding, predominates, to the neglect of the other.
His conclusion would seem to be supported by research into the bilateral structure of the human brain. Iain McGilchrist, a psychiatrist who
has studied neuroimaging, writes in *The Master and His Emissary: The
Divided Brain and the Making of the Western World*: "My thesis is that for
us as human beings there are two fundamentally opposed realities, two
different modes of experience; that each is of utmost importance in
bringing about the recognisably human world; and that their difference
is rooted in the bihemispheric structure of the brain. It follows that the
hemispheres need to co-operate, but I believe they are in fact involved in
a sort of power struggle, and that this explains many aspects of contemporary Western culture."[12]

Studies show that the left hemisphere processes sensory data, using
language to describe, define, categorize, and communicate information
about everything. It develops understanding by means of deductive
reasoning and organizing facts in a linear and methodical way. It puts
everything into an orderly sequence, thereby creating the concept of
time. The left hemisphere is also the locus of the ego and our sense of
self. With its "brain chatter," it continually reminds us of the details of
our life. Without this ability we would forget who we are and thus lose
our identity.[13]

The left hemisphere, because of its ability to create and understand
language, predominates over the right. So dominant is the left side of
our brain that we might not have understood the importance of the right

side had it not been for a treatment for epileptic seizures that surgically separated the two hemispheres. As a result, researchers discovered that the two hemispheres function independently, each with unique characteristics.

In contrast with the analytic operations of the left brain, the right brain is holistic. It is rich with sensations, thoughts, and emotions and registers distinct, memorable impressions. In the absence of logical constraints imposed by the left side of the brain, the right side is spontaneous, carefree, and imaginative, expressing itself in artistic and creative ways. The right brain has no sense of time, only of what is happening in the present moment. It perceives us as one with the universe and as equal members of the human family. Intuitively, we see that everything is interconnected and that we are part of a cosmic whole. In right brain cognition we lose the awareness of being an individual, isolated self and gain a sense of kinship, compassion, and empathy for others. These two modes of consciousness coexist, McGilchrist notes, "but they have fundamentally different sets of values, and therefore priorities, which means that over the long term they are likely to come into conflict."[14]

While both hemispheres play crucial roles in human experience, the relationship between them is asymmetrical. The left hemisphere, which has to do with language and logic, has taken precedence over the important function of the right. "An increasingly mechanistic, fragmented, decontextualised world, marked by unwarranted optimism mixed with paranoia and a feeling of emptiness, has come about, reflecting," McGilchrist believes, "the unopposed action of a dysfunctional left hemisphere."[15] Carlyle, Emerson, and the American Transcendentalists reached the same conclusion. They argued that the excessive emphasis on rationalism, empiricism, and materialism—not only in science but also in business and patterns of consumption—has been detrimental to human flourishing.

Note that McGilchrist asserts the two modes of consciousness have not only a difference in perception but also a difference of *values*. The left hemisphere—for Emerson, the seat of the Understanding—is shortsighted and self-centered, whereas the right hemisphere—Emerson's locus of the Reason—is visionary and altruistic. McGilchrist maintains there needs to be a balance between them, rather than the left hemisphere predominating over the right. However, Emerson argues that

"Reason is the superior principle." And the Understanding is subordinate to the Reason. That brought Emerson back to the question, How is Reason to be accorded its proper place?

While Emerson's metaphysics is abstract, it has very practical consequences. In today's world ethics struggles to keep up with technological change. Data mining, artificial intelligence, and military weaponry are a few examples in which privacy and human life are threatened. Avid consumerism depletes natural resources and produces greenhouse gases and pollution. Unrestrained capitalism has caused an unjust gap between wealth and poverty. Emerson's metaphysics has spiritual consequences also. As he writes in "Lecture on the Times," we are tormented by unbelief, uncertainty as to what we ought to do, distrust of the value of what we do, and "distrust that the Necessity (which we all at last believe in) is fair and beneficent."[16] In his view, the only remedy for our dis-ease is to achieve a balance between Reason and Understanding, and the way to do that is by means of self-culture.

SELF-CULTURE

Self-culture was a familiar term in nineteenth-century America. Although its origin is uncertain, most people used it interchangeably with "self-education." But Emerson used "self-culture" to address the spiritual dilemma he faced. At the end of his outline of the First Philosophy, he observed: "We stand on the edge of all that is great yet are restrained in inactivity and unacquaintance with our powers. . . . We are in the precincts, never admitted. There is much preparation—great ado of machinery, plans of life, travelling, studies, profession, solitude, often with little fruit. But suddenly in any place, in the street, in the chamber, will the heaven open, and the regions of wisdom be uncovered, as if to show how thin the veil, how null the circumstances. As quickly, a Lethean stream washes through us and bereaves us of ourselves." How can we retrieve this knowledge that we only occasionally catch sight of? "What a benefit if a rule could be given whereby the mind, dreaming amidst the gross fogs of matter, could at any moment east itself and find the Sun."[17] He knew these revelations could not be summoned at will. They came unannounced. But perhaps such a rule *could* be found.

This was the goal he set for himself in two series of lectures in the winters of 1836 and 1837, under the rubric of "Intellectual and Moral Culture." He laid the metaphysical framework in the first series of lectures, called "The Philosophy of History." There is one Universal Mind, he declared, of which each individual person is an incarnation. All the properties of this Mind consist in every incarnation of it. We are "a bundle of relations," he says, our lives "intertwined with the whole chain of organic and inorganic being."[18] While there is variety, each aspect of it is part of a larger whole, an all-encompassing Unity. There is no dualism of God and man or of man and nature.

We belong to this Mind, not it to us. It is what constitutes us as human beings. The notion of individualism runs counter to this view. "The individual always craves a private benefit," Emerson says, which puts our outward interests at odds with our inner well-being. Virtue consists in surrendering our individual will to the Universal Mind. Right is what is in accord with nature; wrong is what is in opposition to it. Although awareness of this nature often lies dormant, from time to time we sense its presence. We see that "as there is no screen or ceiling between our heads and the infinite heavens, so there is no bar or wall in the Soul, where man the effect ceases, and God the cause begins."[19] Although Emerson continues to use the word "God," he does not mean God as a supernatural being. God is immanent, not transcendent. In other words, God exists within the world and everything in it, not outside or above it.

In the daily course of our lives, Emerson says, we are seldom mindful of this Reality. It has three features. The first is universality. There is a "unity of the human soul in all the individuals." Second, it is efficacious. Being in harmony with it is beneficial to our existence. Third is its power to elevate us. "It is an influx of the Divine Mind into our mind. It is an ebb of the individual rivulet before the flowing surges of the Sea of Life."[20] It stirs a sense of awe in us. He finds that this understanding of reality is reflected in the scriptures of China and India, as well as in the teachings of Jesus, the philosophy of Plato and Plotinus, and the visions of the Christian mystics.

"Everywhere," Emerson asserts, "the history of religion betrays a tendency to enthusiasm," a mixture of awe and delight in the presence of the Universal Soul. The Understanding seeks to incorporate these revelations in religious doctrines and formulas, but these are imperfect representations. "You might as easily preserve light or electricity in barrels."

Like manna from heaven, it cannot be kept, but "tomorrow must be gathered anew." The more alienated we are from the vision itself, the more we succumb to idolatry. As a result, the "established churches have become old and ossified under the accumulation of creeds and usages."[21] Skepticism creeps in. Emerson knew that faith could not be sustained on empirical grounds but only on the basis of intuition.

With this framework in mind, Emerson got to the question that most intrigued him in his second lecture series, Human Culture: Even if spiritual visions couldn't be summoned at will, was there a way to make the individual more receptive or to promote conditions favorable to their recurrence? He took up this topic in the winter of 1837–38.

"His own Culture," Emerson announced, "the unfolding of his nature, is the chief end of man. A divine impulse at the core of his being, impels him to this." Self-culture, he said, "does not consist in polishing and varnishing" one's personality but in "educating the eye" to distinguish between what is Real and what is Actual in our experience. What is Real is the Ideal (a revelation of the Reason), which "is the presence of universal mind to the particular." What is Actual (the world of the Understanding) is the conditional and transitory nature of everyday life. "The Ideal is the shining side of man," he insisted. "We say that all which is great and venerable in character is measured by the degree in which this instinct predominates." But we have become subservient to the Actual, "which is as if the head should serve the feet." The much-needed "great Reform," he said, is to do justice to the Ideal by restoring it to its rightful sovereignty.[22]

How is this possible? What are the means of self-culture? Emerson answers that it is possible by virtue of "the related nature of man." We have a symbiotic relationship with the natural world. This world, of which we are a part, educates us by its symbolism. "The light that shines on [our] shoes came from the sun, and the entire laws of nature and the soul unite their energies in every moment and every place." There is nothing that does not speak to us. "Our culture comes not alone from the grand and beautiful but also from the trivial and sordid." In addition, we have agency, the ability to "look at all things in a new point of view from the popular one"—in other words, from the point of view of the Reason rather than the Understanding.[23]

In teaching his listeners to "educate the eye," to distinguish between

Real and Actual, Emerson introduces the term *the Culture of the Intellect*, which means something different from what we might assume. His earliest influence was Neoplatonism, a school of Hellenistic philosophy. Its most prominent figure was Plotinus, for whom Intellect was the intuitive faculty of perceiving the Divine Mind. It is not a form of mental activity but a passive reception of spiritual truth.[24] The cultivation of the soul requires a systematic surrender to the Intellect to allow in those fleeting moments of vision. "True growth is spontaneous in every step. The mind that grows could not predict the times, the means, the mode of that spontaneity. God comes in by a private door into every individual: thoughts enter by passages which the individual never left open."[25]

It may seem paradoxical to suggest that the soul could be cultivated intentionally. Emerson explains that "you cannot with your best deliberation and heed, command your intention upon any speculative or practical question with such success as shall follow the spontaneous glance you give to the matter as you rise from your bed or walk abroad in the morning. Always our thinking is an observing. Into us flows the stream evermore of thought from we know not whence. We do not determine what we will think; we only open our senses, clear away as we can all obstruction from the facts, and let God think through us." We seek spiritual truth. We think hard, and roam about looking for it. "Then in a moment and without observation the truth we sought appears. A certain wandering light comes to us and is the distinction, the principle we wanted. But the oracle comes because we had previously laid siege to the shrine."[26]

How can we do that—lay "siege to the shrine"? First, self-reliance is required. We are offered a choice between Truth and Repose. We can have one or the other, but not both. Repose is the comfort of believing we have already found or know the answers we need. Those who seek it will adopt "the first creed, the first philosophy, the first political party" they meet—most likely, that of their parents. Truth is an ongoing search, always questioning. Those who seek the truth will avoid the easy path, abstain from dogmatism, and embrace "the inconvenience of suspense and imperfect opinion."[27] Think for yourself, he admonishes us. Do not surrender independence of mind to the thoughts of others.

Second, Emerson stresses the importance of solitude and contemplation: "The simple habit of sitting alone occasionally to explore what facts of the moment lie in the memory may have the effect in some more favored hour to open to the student the kingdom of spiritual nature. He may become aware that there around him roll new at this moment and inexhaustible the waters of Life; that the world he has lived in so heedless, so gross, is illumined with meaning, that every fact is magical; every atom alive, and he is heir of it all."[28]

Third, he recommends keeping a journal. "Pay so much honor to the visits of Truth to your mind as to record those thoughts that have shown therein." This is not for the purpose of recalling pleasant remembrances of the past "but for the habit of rendering account to yourself of yourself in some more rigorous manner and at more certain intervals than mere conversation or casual reverie of solitude require."[29]

Next on his list of means is the importance of nature. "We need Nature, and cities give the human senses not room enough. The habit of feeding the senses daily and nightly with the open air and firmament, presently becomes so strong that we feel the want of it like water for washing." We divorce ourselves from nature, depriving ourselves of the sense of wonder it evokes and the ability to detect "the miraculous in the common." In its presence we discover that "Nature is an Eternal Now."[30]

Conversation is yet another spiritual practice Emerson recommends. Society, he says, is as necessary as solitude. "We see that our being is shared by thousands who live in us and we live in them." It is based on friendship and intercourse. Conversation is the best means of creating society and cultivating friendship. "In able conversation we have glimpses of the universe, perceptions of immense power native to the soul, far-darting lights and shadows of a mountain landscape, such as we cannot at all attain unto in our solitary studies."[31]

These methods can teach us to be and to live in the present moment. "There is very little life in a lifetime," Emerson observes. "So much of our time is preparation, so much is routine, and so much is retrospect that the real pith of each man's genius seems to contract itself in a very few hours." To the extent that we can focus on the needs of the soul rather than the desires of the self, we "will weave no longer a spotted patchwork web" but "live with a divine unity."[32]

In later lectures and essays, Emerson expanded his list of spiritual practices to include reading, walking, simple living, and several others. His Transcendentalist friends adopted a similar regimen. Whether practiced methodically or informally, these disciplines were nonetheless spiritual exercises meant "to bring about a transformation of the individual, a transformation of the self," as historian of philosophy Pierre Hadot suggests.[33]

What are we to make of the notion of self-culture today? Is this merely a relic of what George Santayana called "the genteel tradition" of polite, refined, and culturally conservative literature popular in the later decades of the nineteenth century, as antiquated now as Victorian houses in old neighborhoods?[34] Although the phrasing may have changed over the years, I believe the cultivation of the soul is still a pressing need. Spiritual self-help books fill numerous shelves in our local bookstores. Emerson sought to address many of the same issues we wrestle with. Like us, he was trying to integrate his ideals with everyday living. Like us, he questioned the prevailing values of society. Like us, he struggled to achieve a loftier perspective from which to resolve the problems of life.

His success is largely due to his tenacity in pursuing his own self-culture. Life in his world was really no easier than ours; if anything, it was more difficult. The pressures to find a career and make a living were just as great. It was a struggle to get an education, to marry and raise a family. Opportunities—especially for women—were limited. The mid-nineteenth century experienced the longest workweek of any period for which we have records. Political problems seemed intractable, especially the evil of slavery. The cultivation of the soul was not a luxury for the leisured elite but a necessity for anyone trying to achieve a sense of wholeness and peace of mind in a turbulent world.

"Self-culture is part and parcel with how a human life unfolds," philosopher John T. Lysaker writes in *Emerson and Self-Culture*. "The question is thus not whether to pursue self-culture, but how best to do so."[35] Today some follow a Buddhist path. Some engage in disciplines such as yoga and insight meditation. Others have developed their own spiritual regimen. Judging from my own experience as a minister and teacher, many people have adopted what Emerson recommended as spiritual practices: reading, conversing, walking in nature, living simply, acting from principle, and seeking wisdom from other religious and philosophical traditions. In his life and writing, Emerson offered us a model for what self-culture looks like and how to achieve it.

4

AWAKENING THE GIANT

Even as Emerson struggled to make a name for himself as a lecturer he continued to preach almost every Sunday, filling pulpits not only in and around Boston but also some in Maine, New Hampshire, and New York. Several churches asked him to become a settled minister. While preaching in Plymouth, Massachusetts, in March 1834, he met Lydia Jackson, the cultured daughter of a prominent family. Soon afterward, she had a premonition they would marry. Following a courtship conducted largely by letter, they were wed a year and a half later. (He insisted she change her name to Lidian because he knew people back home would pronounce Lydia as Lydiar, which sounded harsh to his ear.) With the money he received from his first wife's estate, he purchased a large house in Concord. There they took in family members and received a steady stream of visitors.

An avid spiritual seeker, Emerson often addressed religious topics in his lectures, though many of them also dealt with secular subjects. He felt compelled to give expression to what he termed the First Philosophy, his vision of the spiritual life. In May 1836, he wrote the following in his journal: "The generic soul in each individual is a giant overcome with sleep which locks up almost all his senses, and only leaves him a little superficial animation. Once in an age at hearing some deeper voice, he lifts his iron lids, and his eyes straight pierce through all appearances, and his tongue tells what shall be in the latest times: then he is obeyed like a God, but quickly the lids fall, and sleep returns."[1] He not only was determined to awaken the giant in himself—to pay attention to those fleeting moments of spiritual insight—but also wanted to awaken it in others.

Emerson's reputation was slow to develop. He was known primarily in the Boston area as a somewhat unorthodox Unitarian minister with a modest following among his peers, according to historian Mary Kupiec Cayton. Ironically, he became better known after *Nature* was published—anonymously—in 1836. His reputation grew "because his message shifted from being heard in religious and literary terms to being heard as discourse pertaining to something else," Cayton says. That something else was neither secular nor religious exactly, "since both he and his audiences perceived something spiritual in his utterances."[2] He was beginning to awaken the sleeping giant.

Several of the writings he produced between 1836 and 1842 were foundational to his philosophy, and he later gathered them into a collection published as *Nature, Essays and Lectures* in 1849. In these he addressed topics he continued to revisit in his later writing and public speaking. Especially important are three manifestos written in successive years: *Nature* (1836), "The American Scholar" (1837), and "The Divinity School Address" (1838).

NATURE

On his trip to Paris in July 1833, Emerson visited the Cabinet of Natural History in the Jardin des Plantes. Viewing the many displays of animals, fish, insects, birds, and snakes, he felt a strong sense of identity with the natural world. He perceived "an occult relation between the very scorpions and man. I felt the centipede in me—the cayman, carp, eagle, and fox. I am moved by strange sympathies, I say continually, 'I will be a naturalist.'"[3] This may have been the stimulus to begin writing his first book, *Nature*.

Nature is rightly considered an important manifesto of the Transcendentalist movement. To understand its impact, one needs to view it against the background of Unitarian theology at the time, in particular the distinction that was made between "natural religion" and "revealed religion," as explained in chapter 1. The liberal Christians held that revealed religion completed natural religion. That is what was known as *supernatural rationalism*.

Emerson's book fundamentally departed from this view. It is his first sustained effort to articulate a new religious mythus. Revelation no longer comes to us from Christian scriptures and the teachings of the church, he says, but directly from nature. Using biblical language to describe the sacredness of nature, Emerson's book illustrates what Carlyle called *natural supernaturalism*.

Emerson announces his break from the past in the opening paragraph of the book. "Our age is retrospective," he says. "The foregoing generations beheld God face to face; we through their eyes. Why should not we also enjoy an original relation to the universe? Why should we not have a poetry and philosophy of insight and not of tradition, and a revelation to us, and not the history of theirs?"[4]

He distinguishes between traditional views of nature and nature perceived afresh, in an unfiltered way. Properly seen—that is, when our "inward and outward senses are . . . truly adjusted to each other"—the manifold objects of nature awaken in us a sense of reverence and delight. He describes an ecstatic experience while crossing the Boston Common at twilight, under an overcast sky: "Standing on the bare ground,—my head bathed by the blithe air, and uplifted into infinite space,—all mean egotism vanishes. I become a transparent eye-ball. I am nothing. I see all. The currents of the Universal Being circulate through me; I am part or particle of God." At such moments we sense "an occult relation" between us and the natural world. "In the woods," he says, "we return to faith and reason."[5]

Emerson introduces a hierarchy of four ways that nature ministers to us. At its first and most basic level, that of *commodity*, nature provides resources for human needs, from food and produce to the raw materials for trade and commerce. Second, "a nobler want" served by nature is that of *beauty*. Natural objects "give us a delight *in and for themselves*." They have a therapeutic value in restoring our spirits through "their eternal calm."[6] There is beauty, too, in virtuous action and, higher yet, in the production of art.

Third, nature provides us with *language*. "Words," he says, "are signs of natural facts." For instance, "*right* means *straight*; *wrong* means *twisted*." Moreover, every aspect of nature has symbolic meaning. "Who looks upon a river in a meditative hour," Emerson asks, "and is not reminded of the flux of all things?" If nature is symbolic it is because there is a "radical correspondence between visible things and human thoughts." Thus, by contemplating nature, human beings can read the mind of God. "A life in harmony with Nature," Emerson insists, "will purge the eyes to understand her text. By degrees we may come to know the primitive sense of the permanent objects of nature, so that the world shall be to us an open book, and every form significant of its hidden life and final cause."[7]

Fourth, and higher still, is *discipline*. Nature educates both the Understanding and the Reason. Dealing with sensible objects—weighing, measuring, comparing, and so on—exercises the Understanding. Nature educates the Reason by demonstrating that natural laws are also moral laws. "The moral law lies at the centre of nature and radiates to the circumference," Emerson says. "It is the pith and marrow of every substance, every relation, and every process. All things with which we deal, preach to us." Because we are infinitely related, part of the unity of nature, nature's laws apply to us as well. "A leaf, a drop, a crystal, a moment of time," he writes, "is related to the whole, and partakes of the perfection of the whole. Each particle is a microcosm, and faithfully renders the likeness of the world."[8]

Up to this point Emerson has been discussing the ministry of nature primarily in its material manifestation. He asks, where does matter come from? He doesn't dispute what his senses tell him, but neither does he believe the material world he senses is ultimate reality; it is more like "a great shadow pointing always to the sun behind us." He stops short of concluding that "the world is a divine dream" because to do so would mean that we have no consanguinity with it. As it stands, however, we are estranged from nature and alienated from God. This condition will not be addressed by means of the Understanding but only "by untaught sallies of the spirit, by a continual self-recovery, and by entire humility."[9]

The cause of our alienation is a denial of our kinship with nature. We relate to it based on the Understanding alone, mastering it "by a penny-wisdom." Here and there we have "gleams of a better light." But the problem lies with us in our lack of perception. "The ruin or blank that we see when we look at nature, is in our own eye," Emerson tells us. "The axis of vision is not coincident with the axis of things, and so they appear not transparent but opaque. The reason why the world lacks unity, and lies broken and in heaps, is because man is disunited with himself."[10] The marriage of matter and spirit is not celebrated. However, he believed that with new eyes we may come to see not a dualism but a unity. Emerson was convinced that resolving this dichotomy would bring about a revolution in all areas of life.

Emerson makes several important claims in *Nature*. The first of these is that nature is a unity. Every aspect of it "betrays its source in universal Spirit." Human beings know intuitively, in moments of insight, that they are part of the universal Spirit and that there exists "an occult relation" between themselves and the natural world. Because of this intimate relationship and common origin, nature can be for us both an ethical teacher and a spiritual guide. From the revelations of nature "we learn that the highest" is present to the human soul and pervades all of creation. As plants are nurtured by the universal Spirit, so human beings are likewise "nourished by unfailing fountains" and draw "inexhaustible power" from the same source.[11] The ultimate function of nature, then, is to feed the spirit that is in us and liberate its capacities.

Emerson returned to the subject of nature several times in later lectures and essays. But his focus changed. In *Nature* Emerson showed the various ways nature ministers to us, why we have become alienated from nature, and how we can overcome this estrangement. In later works he seized on Coleridge's distinction between *natura naturata* and *natura naturans*, or "nature natured" and "nature naturing," respectively.[12]

In *Nature*, Emerson deals with natura naturata, the outward manifestation of nature, or how it appears to us. But "The Method of Nature," an address given at Waterford College in Maine in 1841, and his essay "Nature" (1844) found in *Essays: Second Series* focus on natura naturans, the inner impulse of nature that creates its outward forms. The book *Nature* displays a structured, hierarchical model of nature, influenced by Emerson's reading of Neoplatonist philosophers; by contrast, "The Method of Nature" and "Nature" draw heavily on Coleridge's distinction between the two forms of nature and show the fluidity and restlessness of the natura naturans.

In the essay "Nature," Emerson urges us to pay "homage to the Efficient Nature, *natura naturans*, the quick cause, before which all forms flee as the driven snows . . . and in undescribable variety." The direction of this impulse is forever onward. It inhabits every atom, creature, and human being. If we resist, we will be overcome. But if we go with the flow, we will find that "we are escorted on every hand through life by spiritual agents, and a beneficent purpose lies in wait for us."[13]

In his lecture at Waterford College, Emerson sounds the same refrain. "The method of nature, who could ever analyze it?" he asks. "That rushing stream will not stop to be observed. We can never surprise nature in a corner; never find the end of a thread; never tell where to set the first stone." He describes nature as a "cataract," a "perpetual inchoation," a "torrent," and "a mysterious principle of life . . . which not only inhabits the organ, but makes the organ." It is spontaneous and unpredictable. It does not work toward any private ends "but to numberless and endless benefit." There is "no rebel leaf or limb, but the whole is oppressed by one superincumbent tendency, obeys that redundancy or excess of life which in conscious beings we call *ecstasy*." As with nature, so too with human beings. There is no cease from striving, no rest for the weary. We are spoken to from behind. If we listen and obey, we will be borne along and lead "a heavenly life." Our "health and greatness consist in . . . being the channel through which heaven flows to earth, in short, in the fullness in which an ecstatical state takes place" in us.[14]

Ecstasy is one of Emerson's favorite words, and he uses it repeatedly in his writings. In "Nature" and "The Method of Nature," he equates it with natura naturans. Philosopher Robert S. Corrington describes Emerson's philosophy as a form of *ecstatic naturalism*. It displays a "deep pantheism," Corrington writes, in that "nature is all that there is and the divine is a natural complex within the one nature."[15] Debates have arisen over whether Emerson is a pantheist or a panentheist. Is God wholly within the nature (the pantheist view), or is God somehow greater than nature and at the same time present in it (the panenthiest view)? By this time Emerson had ceased to believe in the personhood of God. For him God is *immanent* in nature. As he says in "Nature" and "The Method of Nature," God is identified with natura naturans, the animating impulse of nature itself. There is nowhere for God to exist apart from it.

Ecstasy also has another meaning for Emerson. It comes from the Greek word *ekstasis*, which means "to stand outside of." It is how we are enabled to hear the voice that is spoken to us from behind or within, as in the case of his "transparent eyeball" experience in *Nature*. "Every man should be open to ecstasy or a divine illumination, and his daily walk elevated by intercourse with the spiritual world."[16] Emerson truly believed that we should be receptive to such experiences at all times, with our daily lives guided by the wisdom gained. This theme recurs in Emerson's writing.

"THE AMERICAN SCHOLAR"

The annual Phi Beta Kappa address was not only the high point of Harvard's graduation festivities but also a major event in the city of Boston.[17] The college had no hall big enough to accommodate all the dignitaries, civic leaders, students, faculty, and other invited guests, so it was held across the street in the First Parish Meetinghouse of Cambridge. The meetinghouse was full on the evening of August 31, 1837, with up to 350 people attending.

It's hard to know how many came specifically to hear Emerson speak. At age thirty-four, he did not have the stature of speakers chosen in previous years. Phi Beta Kappa was the oldest and most prestigious academic honor society in the United States, and Emerson was not the selection committee's first choice to speak. In fact, he received the invitation barely two months before the event. He was not sure he was up to the task. This would be, in effect, his coming-out speech as a public intellectual. What could he say to this discerning and critical audience, many of whom were much more distinguished than he? Contrary to the self-reliant image he came to portray, he felt hesitant and insecure.

By this time Emerson had been publicly speaking as a minister and lecturer for several years. He did not lack experience or self-confidence in front of an audience. But he had not yet found his voice. That is the challenge every writer or speaker faces at the beginning of his or her career. In this address, Emerson found what was in him to say, and he said it. That is, in fact, the central message of his address—a critique of American writers' reliance on the literature of Britain and Europe. His lecture found its mark and had a profound impact, both on his listeners and on Emerson personally. He had found both his voice and his calling. Sometimes people fall into a certain line of work, but their heart isn't in it. They persist because they don't see an alternative. Maybe they are good at it, maybe not. Many of us take a long time to find our true calling. In my experience as a teacher and minister, people often reach their thirties before they discover what they were called to do. This was definitely true in Emerson's case.

In his remarks, Emerson laments that knowledge has been parceled out into so many different disciplines. It "has been so minutely subdivided and peddled out, that it is spilled into drops, and cannot be gathered."[18] Unfortunately, his plea for the humanities is less heeded today than it was then. Colleges and universities continue to drop courses in philosophy, literature, and the arts in favor of more technical and potentially more financially rewarding subjects.

In contrast, Emerson calls for a holistic form of learning and outlines its three components: "The first in time, and the first in importance" is nature. From nature we learn that there is no beginning or end to the web of existence. All things are connected, and each one is a microcosm of the whole. We may classify facts, but we must view them in relation to the whole of which they are a part. In a holistic form of education, the young scholar will discover that both he and nature "proceed from one root; one is leaf and one is flower; relation, stirring in every vein. And what is that Root? Is not that the soul of [one's] soul?" To those who believe education should serve instrumental ends, Emerson's emphasis on the importance of nature must seem superfluous. But Emerson maintains that the experience of nature is essential to the cultivation of the self. "So much of nature as he is ignorant of, so much of his mind he does not yet possess. And, in fine, the ancient precept, 'Know thyself,' and the modern precept, 'Study nature,' become at last one maxim."[19]

The second component of a holistic education is "the mind of the Past." By this Emerson primarily means the knowledge gained from reading. Books are valuable for the information and insights that went into writing them or, as he put it, for "transmuting life into truth." But no book is perfect; each one is only a partial account of the truth. And every age must write its own books. Unfortunately, we attach too much importance to certain books. They become canonical expressions of accepted dogmas. "Meek young men grow up in libraries," Emerson says, "believing it their duty to accept the views which Cicero, which Locke, which Bacon have given, forgetful that Cicero, Locke and Bacon were only young men in libraries when they wrote those books. Hence, instead of Man Thinking, we have the bookworm."[20]

Even though Emerson was a voracious reader himself, he argued that book reading must be balanced with other kinds of learning: "Books are for the scholar's idle times. When he can read God directly, the hour is too precious to be wasted in other men's transcripts of their readings. But when the intervals of darkness come, as come they must,—when the soul seeth not, when the sun is hid, and the stars withdraw their shining,—we repair to the lamps which were kindled by their ray to guide our steps to the East again, where the dawn is. We hear that we may speak."[21]

The third component of a holistic view of education is action. The scholar is not a recluse. "Action is with the scholar subordinate," he says, "but it is essential. . . . Only so much do I know, as I have lived." Action is our everyday being-in-the-world. It furnishes experiences that reside long afterward in the unconscious until they resurface to become thoughts of the mind. He calls the back-and-forth relationship between thought and action "undulation": "That great principle of Undulation in nature, that shows itself in the inspiring and expiring of the breath; in desire and satiety; in the ebb and flow of the sea, in day and night, in heat and cold, and as yet more deeply ingrained in every atom and every fluid, is known to us under the name of Polarity,—these 'fits of easy transmission and reflection,' as Newton called them, are the law of nature because they are the law of the spirit."[22]

One of Emerson's key spiritual insights, then, is that life is a series of polarities: between solitude and society, the individual and the community, nature and culture, feeling and intellect, and so on. Such polarities are a natural part of life. He is sometimes accused of privileging one of these poles at the expense of the other, such as solitude over society. But on close reading, we can see Emerson recognizes that each of these are not in opposition but are, in fact, complementary. He does not try to resolve the tension between them, only to acknowledge that they have a yin-and-yang relationship. When we have had our fill of society, we seek solitude, and vice versa.

Emerson speaks of the scholar's duties, in addition to getting an education. "The office of the scholar," he says, "is to cheer, to raise, and to guide men by showing them facts amid appearances."[23] So much of life is lived on a superficial level. Many people act as though wealth is the measure of their worth. They would rather be entertained than enlightened. They are inclined to accept their privileges as an entitlement. The scholar's responsibility is to dispel the notion that the way things are is the way they should or were meant to be. It is to see through pretension and to call out hypocrisy, bigotry, racism, and injustice. It is his or her duty to uplift people, to show them a vision of a more perfect world, and to bring joy to their lives.

Another duty of the scholar is to celebrate the common and the every-day. "I ask not for the great, the remote, the romantic," he says.

> I embrace the common, I explore and sit at the feet of the familiar, the low. Give me insight into to-day, and you may have the antique and future worlds. What would we really know the meaning of? The meal in the firkin; the milk in the pan; the ballad in the street; the news of the boat; the glance of the eye; the form and gait of the body;— show me the ultimate reason of these matters;—show me the sublime presence of the highest spiritual cause lurking, as always it does lurk, in these suburbs and extremities of nature; let me see every trifle bris-tling with the polarity that ranges it instantly on an eternal law; and the shop, the plough, and the leger [sic], referred to the like cause by which light undulates and poets sing; and the world lies no longer a dull miscellany and lumber room, but has form and order; there is no trifle; there is no puzzle; but one design unites and animates the farthest pinnacle and lowest trench.[24]

Emerson hoped to encourage a vernacular literature distinct from the formality of English prose and poetry. But I take this passage to be a deeply spiritual message also. Like William Blake, who saw "a world in a grain of sand," Emerson believed that even the smallest, most common details of everyday life are parts of a larger whole, shot through and ani-mated by the same "cause by which light undulates and poets sing." This is another example of Emerson's ecstatic naturalism, in which the facts of the natural world suggest spiritual truths.

The third duty of the scholar is to validate the individual. Because everything proceeds from the same source, all of nature is interrelated, including humans. Each individual person is evidence of one Mind, common to all. "In yourself is the law of all nature," Emerson says in his address. "In yourself slumbers the whole of Reason." Thus, in a paradox-ical way, by expressing our individuality we speak universally. "We have listened too long to the courtly muses of Europe." We should begin to think and speak independently, each of us believing we are "inspired by the Divine Soul which also inspires" everyone else.[25]

"The American Scholar" is Emerson's most celebrated address and has become the gold standard of intellectual scholarship in America. Oliver Wendell Holmes hailed it as "our intellectual Declaration of Indepen-dence."[26] But it was not so much about cultural nationalism as it was about education and how it has become undermined by fragmentation and utilitarian concerns. Today's scholars are advised to stick to their chosen field of study, to the exclusion of other branches of learning. Each department has its own terminology and manner of speaking, making communication across disciplines sometimes difficult. Worse is forcing students to make a cold calculation on the return on investment they get from their education in monetary terms only. Science, technology, engineering, math, and computer science are certainly important subjects in today's world. But when universities drop courses in philosophy, literature, or the arts—and society doesn't value them as part of a holistic education—we all lose in ways we cannot easily calculate.

Emerson's is a voice from the past, speaking to us in an idiom somewhat foreign to the modern ear, warning us we need to consider the impact of our technological accomplishments, including artificial intelligence, in relation to the soul. He was concerned our achievements were outpacing our moral capacity for dealing with their potential for harm. Still, Emerson's message is a hopeful one. It is the office of the scholar to both criticize and inspire. To scholars of his day and ours, he encourages self-reflection and original thinking, summarized in the motto, "A thought too bold—a dream too wild."[27]

"THE DIVINITY SCHOOL ADDRESS"

The chapel on the third floor of Divinity Hall at Harvard Divinity School is a small room, seating no more than fifty or sixty people. On its oak-paneled walls are plaques commemorating former students, most of them Unitarians. One of these reads, simply, "On July 15, 1838, Ralph Waldo Emerson read his Divinity School Address. Acquaint thyself at first hand with deity." This room, so quiet and golden in the late afternoon sun, marks ground zero of a religious revolution in America.[28] Here Emerson delivered his famous address to the graduating class of Harvard Divinity School, the American equivalent of Luther's ninety-five theses nailed to the door of the Wittenberg church.

On that cool July evening when Emerson rose to speak, he was breaking from a religious tradition that stretched back to the founding of this country. He did so not with bombast and fanfare but with a quiet self-confidence in the truth of his words. The way had been prepared a generation earlier when the Unitarians had insisted on the right of private judgment. Unitarians had left a door open, and Emerson went out through it. Faith does not rest on sacred scriptures, church teachings, and religious rituals, he said. "It is an intuition," he insisted. "It cannot be received at second hand."[29] In place of the Calvinist notions of predestination and innate depravity, he embraced an ecstatic naturalism.

The chapel was full to overflowing. Some had to sit in the hallway. In addition to graduating seniors, there were professors of the school, family members, and some of Emerson's friends. The graduating students had invited him, and they got what they expected—an expression of the *new views* in theology announced by a small group of young ministers and intellectuals who came to be known as Transcendentalists. Elizabeth Palmer Peabody, who attended that evening, called Emerson's address "the apocalypse of our Transcendental era."[30]

For the divinity school faculty, it was a different story. Andrews Norton, Dexter Professor of Sacred Literature, branded Emerson's remarks "the latest form of infidelity," and the faculty never again permitted the students to choose their own commencement speaker. Norton's name has long been forgotten, whereas Emerson's "Divinity School Address" is required reading today for those preparing for the Unitarian Universalist ministry.

Although Emerson had been feeling dissatisfaction with the ministry well before he had resigned as minister from Second Church six years earlier, he continued to preach nearly every Sunday. He had declined several churches that offered him a pastorate, but he did agree to preach regularly for one, in East Lexington, Massachusetts. A few months before his Divinity School address, he asked to be relieved of that responsibility as well.

His thoughts about the church, the ministry, and the concept of God had changed dramatically from the time he entered Harvard Divinity School as a student and when he gave his famous speech there thirteen years later. In his early sermons, Emerson comes across as a conventional Unitarian in the mold of William Ellery Channing, his childhood minister and mentor. He affirmed the teachings of scripture, the efficacy of prayer, life after death, and the supernatural existence of God. He still used these tenets of Unitarian faith metaphorically as part of his theological vocabulary, but his own beliefs had changed. "Emerson continued to move away from supernaturalism toward a natural religion, a pattern that defined his entire intellectual career and created one of his chief cultural legacies," according to literary scholar David Robinson. "He gradually came to articulate a newer version of a natural and secular faith."[31]

Emerson began his "Divinity School Address" not by quoting scripture or citing church teaching, as might have been expected, but by appealing to nature: "In this refulgent summer, it has been a luxury to draw the breath of life. The grass grows, the buds burst, the meadow is spotted with fire and gold in the tint of flowers." He envisioned a communion with nature. "The corn and the wine have been dealt to all creatures." It is nature that "awakens in the mind a sentiment which we call the religious sentiment, and which makes our highest happiness." By drawing on natural imagery, he is hinting at a deep pantheism, in which nature, not scripture or church teaching, is "the foundation of society and . . . all forms of worship."[32]

Emerson went on to point out the defects of historical Christianity and Unitarian preaching. He questioned reliance on the so-called miracles of Jesus as proof of his divine nature. Instead, Emerson noted, all of life is miraculous. "The word Miracle, as pronounced by Christian churches, gives a false impression; it is Monster," he declared. "It is not one with the blowing clover and the falling rain." Historical Christianity exaggerated the uniqueness of Jesus. All persons have access to the divine, Emerson suggested, just as Jesus did. "The soul knows no persons," he said. "It invites every man to expand to the full circle of the universe."[33] In fixating on the personhood of Jesus, Christianity sealed revelation as a onetime, long-ago event. Emerson believed that revelation is continuous and available to all.

He critiqued Unitarian preaching as too formal and arid, living at second hand on ancient revelation. "It comes out of the memory, and not out of the soul," he asserted. The "famine of our churches" is due to the failure of ministers to make man "sensible that he is an Infinite soul; that the earth and heavens are passing into his mind; that he is drinking forever the soul of God." He implored the ministers-to-be to reject the old models. "Yourself a newborn bard of the Holy Ghost, cast behind you all conformity, and acquaint men at first hand with Deity."[34]

In *Nature*, Emerson asked the question, "Why should not we also enjoy an original relation to the universe?" In this address, he asked,

Why shouldn't we also have an original relation to the divine? In both instances, we don't need mediators, much less gatekeepers. We can experience the universe and the divine for ourselves, directly.

Emerson delivered an argument for ecstatic naturalism, its first expression in America.[35] For him, God is the impersonal ground of Being, immanent in the world and "everywhere active, in each ray of the star, in each wavelet of the pool." The world is the product of one Mind, and because our mind is a manifestation of this one Mind, we can perceive spiritual laws that instruct us to live a life in harmony with nature. "All things proceed out of the same spirit, and all things conspire with it." No wonder he stirred such controversy. His remarks were, indeed, "the latest form of infidelity." Even so, he was not saying anyone should abandon religion or the church; he only urged preachers to breathe new life into the existing forms. The remedy for a decaying church, he said, is an emphasis on the soul: "first soul, and second soul, and evermore, soul."[36]

For the six graduates of Harvard Divinity School that year, Emerson's address was indeed a revelation. But for their Unitarian elders, it rubbed raw. They felt their preaching and theology was under attack. "Unitarianism had its origins in the Boston reaction against the emotional upheaval of the Great Awakening of the 1740s, and a hallmark of the denomination had been its uncompromising rejection of the excess of the revivals," Robinson says. In ministers' eagerness to avoid emotional excess, their preaching had become uninspiring. Emerson sought to enliven Unitarian preaching by appealing to a Romantic aesthetic, using nature as a spiritual source. "The ultimate fruition of this development of an aesthetic religion was Transcendentalism," Robinson concludes.[37]

The most controversial element of Emerson's address was his denial of the personality of God. He had not mentioned God specifically. Instead, he focused on Jesus, whom he viewed as an exemplary figure, a man who "was true to what is in you and me." In elevating the personhood of Jesus to divine status, the church had declared revelation sealed once and for all, which Emerson argued was an example of mistaking the stream for its source. "There is no doctrine of the Reason," he said, "that will bear to be taught by the Understanding." Historical Christianity, he said, "has dwelt, it dwells, with noxious exaggeration about the *person* of Jesus. The soul knows no persons. It invites every man to expand to the full circle of the universe." In declaring, "the soul knows no persons," he was denying the personhood of God as well.[38]

This point of view, so at variance with the common understanding of God and religious faith, required a new language, Emerson recognized. In subsequent essays he uses fresh words and phrases for what was previously meant by God: "the flying Perfect" and "that around which the hands of man cannot reach" (both in the essay "Circles") and "vast-flowing vigor" (taken from Mencius, in the essay "Experience"). But the word most frequently used is *soul*. The doctrine of the soul is spiritual, but not religious in a sectarian sense of the term. "A religious history which is only religious does not satisfy the whole mind of man," Emerson asserts. "True history will be religious, but it will not be a religious history."[39]

Emerson's commitment to speaking the truth as he saw it led him to conclude he must leave the ministry. Keeping with his vow, he did not temper his words before the audience in the Divinity School chapel on that memorable July evening. Whether this was courageous or impudent was for them to judge. His address opened the way toward a post-Christian Unitarian theology and, even broader, toward a nonsectarian form of spirituality available to all religious seekers. Harvard did not invite him back until 1869, when he was presented with a degree, appointed to the Harvard Board of Overseers, and asked to give a series of university lectures.

5

DOUBLE CONSCIOUSNESS

In November 1840, Emerson and some of his friends, including Bronson Alcott and Theodore Parker, attended the Convention of Friends of Universal Reform held at the Chardon Street Chapel in Boston. The meetings and speeches went on for three days. The convention had drawn reformers "of every shade of opinion, from the straitest orthodoxy to the wildest heresy, and many persons whose church was a church of one member only," Emerson wrote in his account for the *Dial* magazine. They came from all parts of New England. The presentations—akin to today's TED talks—were given and received with great zeal and enthusiasm. Emerson described the gathering vividly: "If the assembly was disorderly, it was picturesque. Madmen, madwomen, men with beards, Dunkards, Muggletonians, Come-outers, Groaners, Agrarians, Seventh-day-Baptists, Quakers, Abolitionists, Calvinists, Unitarians, and Philosophers—all came successively to the top, and seized their moment, if not their hour, wherein to chide, or pray, or preach, or protest."[1] Everyone, it appeared, had a plan for remaking society. Some of Emerson's friends had already begun to do so.

Six years earlier, Bronson Alcott had opened his School for Human Culture, better known as the Temple School, introducing significant reforms in the education of the young. He abandoned rote learning, common at the time, in favor of a Socratic approach, drawing answers out of a child rather than putting information in. Elizabeth Palmer Peabody and Margaret Fuller assisted in the school, and both went on to champion educational reforms of their own. Peabody started the first kindergarten in America, ran a bookstore in Boston, and published books and magazines. Soon after Fuller's stint at the school, she offered a series of "conversations" for women—who were excluded from higher education—on topics such as history, mythology, and literature as a means of self-culture and consciousness-raising. Years later, in 1879, Alcott established the Concord School of Philosophy offering summer courses for adults, drawing faculty and hundreds of students from across the country.

In 1841, George and Sophia Ripley established a cooperative utopian community called the Brook Farm Association for Industry and Education, in West Roxbury, just outside Boston. Its purpose was "to insure a more natural union between intellectual and manual labor than now exists; to combine the thinker and the worker, as far as possible, in the same individual."[2] The community continued until 1847, when it suffered a devastating fire and could no longer sustain itself financially.

Virtually all the Transcendentalists opposed slavery, some more ardently than others. Theodore Parker and Thomas Wentworth Higginson were members of the Boston Vigilance Committee, organized for the protection of enslaved persons who had escaped. Henry David Thoreau refused to pay his taxes to protest slavery and U.S. aggression in Mexico and spent a memorable night in jail in 1846 for doing so. He wrote about the experience in "Civil Disobedience," published, incidentally, by Elizabeth Peabody. He went on to deliver additional influential addresses on civil disobedience and slavery, including "Slavery in Massachusetts" and "A Plea for Captain John Brown."

Margaret Fuller wrote the first feminist manifesto in America, *Woman in the Nineteenth Century*, in 1845. As a reporter for Horace Greeley's *New-York Tribune*, she investigated hospitals, asylums, and slums. She led conversations with incarcerated women at New York's Sing-Sing Prison and went on to become the nation's first female war correspondent, sending dispatches to the *Tribune* on the fight for Italian independence, at the same time directing a hospital for wounded soldiers.

By contrast, many viewed Emerson—both during his lifetime and long after—as an abstract thinker, aloof from the affairs of the world and everyday problems. But as he grew in stature as a public intellectual and as pressures for social change—especially the abolition of slavery—escalated, he became more outspoken and directly involved in reform efforts, along with his friends. Even in lectures delivered fairly early in his postministerial career, between 1841 and 1845, Emerson was thinking deeply about the connection between his philosophical idealism and the necessity of social action.

MAN THE REFORMER

Emerson first addressed the issue of social reform in a speech entitled "Man the Reformer" at the Mechanics' Apprentices' Library Association in 1841. "The community in which we live will hardly bear to be told that every man should be open to ecstasy or a divine illumination," he began, rather remarkably, "and his daily walk elevated by intercourse with the spiritual world."[3] What an unusual way to begin a lecture on social change! But he strongly felt that all reform efforts should begin with—and be guided by—spiritual enlightenment and moral principles.

What he has in mind are not individual, piecemeal reforms but the reformation of society as a whole: "Christianity, the laws, commerce, schools, the farm, the laboratory; and not a kingdom, town, statute, rite, calling, man, or woman, but is threatened by the new spirit." Everywhere he looks he finds abuses calling out for reform. Social mobility is hindered by privilege. Commerce is driven by greed and riven with theft and fraud. Consumption is tainted by slavery and exploitation. Our economic system is essentially unjust, inequitable, and self-serving, based not on giving but on taking advantage. We are all complicit. "One plucks, one distributes, one eats." We all partake but none of us feels responsible. "Inextricable seems to be the twinings and tendrils of this evil, and we all involve ourselves in it the deeper by forming connexions, by wives and children, by benefits and debts."[4]

What shall we do? Shall we renounce the luxuries and conveniences of society and go back to the land? Shall we grow our own food and make our own goods? Emerson thinks that knowing how to do these things would be good for our self-culture and sense of independence. We ought to be able to do the work to meet our needs and live more simply. Consider our modes of living. We spend our incomes for trifles— jewelry and fancy clothes, for example—but not for our spiritual growth. It is better to go without life's luxuries than to have them at too great a cost. "Can anything be so elegant as to have few wants and to serve them one's self, so as to have somewhat left to give, instead of being always prompt to grab?" We should ask ourselves, Emerson says, "whether we have earned our bread to-day by the hearty contribution of our energies to the common benefit? and we must not cease to *tend* to the correction of these flagrant wrongs, by laying one stone aright every day."[5]

We must, he says, "revise the whole of our social structure, the state, the school, religion, marriage, trade, science, and explore their foundations in our nature." What are we born for but to be reformers, remakers of what we have made, in the conviction that there is an inherent and infinite worthiness in humankind? Americans, Emerson says, have many virtues, but they lack faith and hope. We are told that we can never construct a heavenly society. "But the believer not only beholds his heaven to be possible, but already to begin to exist," not by people or materials of the state, but by people transformed and "raised above themselves by the power of principles."[6]

Emerson sets a high bar for reform—the complete transformation of society. And he was impatient with reformers who were focused on single issues rather than systemic ills. "It is better to work on institutions by the sun than the wind," he said in his lecture.[7] Persuasion is more effective than coercion. Reformers were impatient with *him*, too. He seemed standoffish. When George Ripley invited him to join Brook Farm, a community organized according to the very principles Emerson expounded in this lecture on reform, Emerson declined.

Even today, critics rarely characterize Emerson as a reformer. One criticism is that Emerson believed social reform begins with individual initiative, not collective action. As we have seen in this lecture on reform, he challenges audience members to consider how they may be complicit in the injustices of society and the efforts each must make to effect social change. In a similar manner, white people today are called to examine the ways in which they have created and benefit from systems of white privilege. No reform is effective without a change of heart.

"Social reformation that comes as a result of the forceful imposition of change upon individuals or institutions from without is not true reformation because it deals with symptoms and not causes, sins and not sinners," historian Len Gougeon writes about Emerson's early views of reform.[8] Indeed, Emerson's Unitarian background and training emphasized the use of "moral suasion" as a tool for social change. He never ceased to believe that social change is incomplete without personal reform.

However, as the issue of slavery increasingly threatened to tear the country apart, Emerson began to realize that although moral self-examination was necessary, it was not in itself sufficient to end the practice of slavery. In his 1855 "Lecture on Slavery," he concluded that "whilst I insist on the doctrine of independence and the inspiration of the individual, I do not cripple but exalt the social action. . . . A wise man delights in the powers of many people. . . . We shall need to call them all out."[9] Emerson's views on slavery are discussed in greater detail in chapter 9.

Another criticism of Emerson's doctrine of reform is that he never really had one. For the past one hundred years, we have been led to believe that he had no political teaching other than his apolitical individualism.[10] Beginning in the decades after the Civil War, Emerson became depoliticized. His early biographers smoothed over Emerson's sharp edges and avoided mention of his reform efforts. They said he offered spiritual uplift but was politically disengaged. More recently, some critics have taken even more extreme views, accusing Emerson of promoting an atomistic individualism that is not only ineffective as a political praxis but also harmful to social cohesion. Communitarian social philosophers, such as Robert Bellah, have concluded that Emerson promotes "ontological individualism," a solipsism of the self, precluding a concern for others.[11]

Since the 1990s, many scholars have challenged this portrayal of Emerson's apolitical individualism. Alan Levine and Daniel Malachuk, in their introduction to *A Political Companion to Ralph Waldo Emerson*, write: "Throughout his public career, Emerson tirelessly advocated for his philosophy of self-reliance, which meant that he also tirelessly advocated for a democracy that would inspire not conformity but reflective, ethical, and engaged citizenship: that is, self-reliance as Emerson defined it. Emerson believed that no message was more important than self-reliance for a nation still in the midst of inventing the world's first representative democracy."[12] Self-reliance is not detrimental to democracy but is, in fact, necessary for it. The myth of Emerson's apolitical individualism is based on not only a misreading of his lectures and essays but also an ignorance of his important role in reform efforts. A Unitarian minister in the early decades of the twentieth century is said to have remarked that if you want to preach socialism, you had better wear a tailcoat tuxedo.[13] Emerson's formality can sometimes conceal the radical nature of his views, but it actually made him an even more effective agent of social change. His deepening involvement as a voice for antislavery "was, in some respects, more influential because he was not thought to be a political player," David Robinson writes.[14]

The spiritual Emerson cannot be separated from the political Emerson. The one does not preclude the other. In fact, Emerson's vision of self-culture and human development demanded political action and social reform. Action from principle became one of the stated means of self-culture. "Political reform thus came to be understood by Emerson as one of the means of self-culture," Robinson writes, "a validation of the whole revolution of thinking that marked the modern age: the elevation of the individual, though the discovery that his 'chief end' is 'the unfolding of his nature.'"[15]

THE TIMES

Also in 1841, Emerson delivered three lectures on "the times" at the Masonic Temple in Boston: an introductory lecture describing the divisions he saw in society that hindered reform, followed by "The Conservative" and "The Transcendentalist." In the first lecture he observes that "the party of the Past and the party of the Future, divide society to-day as of old." Most people accept the past as a given, as a possession, and resist change, perhaps for fear of losing what they have. "It is the dissenter," Emerson says, "who is quitting this ancient domain to embark on seas of adventure, who engages our interest." He names those who accept the past and resist change "the stationary classes," and he calls the dissenters "the movement party," which he divides into two types of people: "the actors, and the students."[16] While he sides with the dissenters, he finds fault with some of their methods.

The "actors" are the reformers and philanthropists. Although the causes they advance are praiseworthy—antislavery, temperance, education reform—most reformers are not, Emerson says. In their zeal they magnify the importance of their one cause, "until it excludes the others from sight." They fail to see that the many reforms society needs are "in reality all parts of one movement." Reformers are perfectionists, comparing our actual behavior with an ideal that seems far out of reach.

Their arguments leave us feeling apologetic and unworthy, that life as it is currently lived is sordid, not poetic—or, as Emerson puts it, "our modes of living are not agreeable to our imagination."[17]

He finds most reformers tribal, trading on fear and anger. Conviction is the soul of reform, he allows, but not the bickering and acrimony that seem always to come with it. "Those, who are urging with most ardor what are called the greatest benefits of mankind, are narrow, self-pleasing, conceited men, and affect us as the insane do." A harsh judgment, indeed! It is enough to drive one to inaction. Emerson argues for an entirely different approach: "Whilst therefore I desire to express the respect and joy I feel before this sublime connexion of reforms, now in their infancy around us, I urge the more earnestly the paramount duties of self-reliance."[18] In other words, think for yourself. Do not blindly adopt the views of others. "Benefactors hope to raise man by improving his circumstances," he writes, but that strategy is backward. Reform must start at the other end. It is by elevating individuals, by means of their own self-culture, that their circumstances will be improved.

Next Emerson addresses the "students," those on the sidelines of activism. They have fallen into despair, he observes. "Our forefathers walked in the world and went to their graves, tormented with the fear of Sin, and the Terror of the Day of Judgment. These terrors have lost their force, and our torment is Unbelief, the Uncertainty as to what we ought to do; the distrust of the value of what we do, and the distrust that the Necessity (which we all at last believe in) is fair and beneficent." People have become passive onlookers, stricken with ennui. As with the "actors," their melancholy stems from their perception that nothing measures up to the height of their aspirations, that is, "the contrast of the dwarfish Actual with the exorbitant Idea."[19]

"The Time is the child of Eternity," Emerson says, but we have become the prisoners of the times we live in. We do not know where we are bound. We do not wish to be deceived. But the answer to our fate lies within ourselves. "Where but in that Thought through which we communicate with absolute nature, and are made aware that, whilst we shed the dust of which we are built, grain by grain, till it is all gone, the law which clothes us with humanity remains new?" Underneath the appearances that distract us and cloud our judgment lies a reality grounded in the moral sentiment. This is the basis of justice and human flourishing.

"For that reality let us stand: that let us serve, and for that speak. Only so far as that shines through them, are these times or any times worth consideration."[20]

THE CONSERVATIVE

In his second address Emerson gives credit to the conservative position. Conservatism defends the present state of affairs against the possibility of a better one—or the risk of losing what we have. In "the counteraction of the centripetal and centrifugal forces," Emerson says, innovation is the impetus, conservatism the pause in between. He argues they are two halves of a whole and a true society must combine both. This is like the interplay of fate and freedom. Fate accepts the past and present; freedom imagines a better world. Fate is a check on freedom's insatiable demands. "Those who quarrel with the arrangements of society," forsaking the good that exists for something better, fail to recognize the "necessity of using the Actual order of things, in order to disuse it; to live by it, whilst you wish to take away its life." Sooner or later, the rebel becomes a conservative, building and then defending a new order of things. "Among the lovers of the new I observe that there is a jealousy of the newest, and that the seceder from the seceder is as damnable as the pope himself."[21]

The conservative says, "We have worked hard to create the world as it is. It has nourished you, has it not? Is it really so bad?" The reformer concedes that improvements exist and that it would be comfortable to take sides with the establishment. But in its conservatism, society has become stagnant. It has developed a sickness that has infected everything, including the trade system and the ballot box. Religion, he says, has become "a lozenge for the sick." Instead of promoting a reliance on the soul, religion preaches "reliance on rotten institutions."[22]

From this stagnant soil springs the hope of a better world. "And this hope flowered on what tree?" Emerson asks. "It was not imported from the stock of some celestial plant, but grew here on the wild crab of conservatism." It is remarkable that a corrupt system has produced a better result. "It predicts that amidst a planet peopled with conservatives, one Reformer may yet be born."[23]

It is remarkable that anyone today would claim that Emerson is a defender of the status quo, and yet this is the picture that his friends in "the genteel tradition" of American letters tried to portray. In a biography published in 1884, two years after Emerson's death, Oliver Wendell Holmes notoriously relegated Emerson's radicalism to the background of his life story. He denied, for example, that Emerson had ever identified himself as an abolitionist or even sympathized with that cause. William James Potter, who founded the Free Religious Association in 1867 along with Emerson and others, considered Holmes's biography "fatally defective." In Potter's view, Emerson was not merely a "serene, scholarly philosopher" but also "one of the leading heroic reformers of this nineteenth century."[24] Other reformers and antislavery activists, such as Theodore Parker, William Lloyd Garrison, and Wendell Phillips, may have been more outspoken. But Emerson's strength was in the power of his words, not the loudness of his voice.

THE TRANSCENDENTALIST

The simplest explanation of Transcendentalism is that, in the view of its followers, human beings have access to knowledge, intuitively, that transcends information given them by the senses. The Transcendentalists took their name from the transcendental philosophy of the German philosopher Immanuel Kant (1724–1804), whose ideas were popularized and promoted by Coleridge, Carlyle, and other intellectuals of the Romantic movement. Their writings caught the attention of a group of young New England intellectuals and ministers who began meeting in 1836 to discuss new ideas about religion and society coming from Europe and Britain. Somewhere along the way they adopted the name Transcendental Club.[25]

The group, numbering about forty people altogether, included women as well as men, most of whom were second-generation Unitarians. They met over a period of four years, ending in 1840, after which they disseminated ideas through publication of the *Dial* magazine from 1840 to 1844. Margaret Fuller served as editor for the first two years, Emerson for the last two. No doubt the public was curious to know more about this group and their ideas. Emerson addressed the topic in the third lecture of his series, The Times. Yet those attending his lecture "The Transcendentalist" must have been puzzled and somewhat disappointed if they came expecting a clear definition of Transcendentalism.

The *new views* entertained by the Transcendentalists were not unique, Emerson said, "but the very oldest of thoughts cast into the mould of these new times." They were a form of philosophical idealism, "as it appears in 1842."[26]

Philosophy divides into two schools of thought, *materialism* and *idealism*. Materialism refers to experience and data perceived by the senses, and idealism, to consciousness and intuition. Both ways of thinking are natural, but Emerson considers idealism of greater importance. The idealist acknowledges the concreteness of things suggested by the senses, but consciousness is what determines their meaning and significance. He gives the example of "the sturdy capitalist" who believes his bank rests on solid granite, when it is actually attached to a globe floating in space, "spinning away, dragging bank and banker with it at a rate of thousands of miles an hour," heading toward "an unimaginable pit of emptiness." Ask the materialist why he has faith in his figures "and he will perceive that his mental fabric is built up on just as strange and quaking foundations as his proud edifice of stone."[27]

Another way of putting this is to say the idealist sees all experience as essentially subjective. The mind determines reality, not the other way around. The idealist views the world from the perspective of the self, "necessitating him to regard all things as having a subjective or relative existence, relative to that aforesaid Unknown Center of him." Individual consciousness is a "mould into which the world is poured like melted wax. The mould is invisible, but the world betrays the shape of the mould." As an idealist, the Transcendentalist "believes in miracle, in the perpetual openness of the human mind to new influx of light and power; he believes in inspiration and ecstasy."[28] He or she is not troubled by accusations of antinomianism, that is, the flouting of convention.

Emerson says there can be no Transcendental *party*, nor is there such a thing as a pure Transcendentalist. There have been "harbingers and forerunners; but of a purely spiritual life, history has yet afforded no example." He describes Transcendentalism as a "Saturnalia or excess of Faith," a faith proper to us, except that our obedience is hindered by self-consciousness. Those to whom it has appealed seem to have withdrawn themselves from society and have adopted "a certain solitary and critical way of living," he says. They hold themselves apart, prefer to ramble in the countryside, and "perish of ennui." They are despondent and melancholy. They find fault with others. They make unreasonable demands. They are immature. "But their solitary and fastidious manners not only withdraw them from the conversation, but from the labors of the world; they are not good citizens, not good members of society."[29]

At this point the audience might have been a bit incredulous. Here is Mr. Transcendentalist himself talking about young people moping about, shunning society, and calling other people hypocrites and phonies. They sound like hippies of the 1960s, with whom there is indeed a similarity. Emerson's portrayal seems like a parody of Transcendentalism: a description more likely to come from its critics than the central figure of the movement. And isn't there a contradiction in how he presents himself, the Transcendentalist par excellence—intellectual, thoughtful, and moral—and this negative depiction of the younger seekers who are part of the movement? The answer is, he often exaggerates for effect. He is pointing out a shortcoming in the idealist position. These young people are seeking a perfection they will never find. Idealism, by definition, posits a perfection that cannot be achieved.

When asked why they feel so alienated, he imagines one of these Transcendentalist youth responding in the following way: "There is a wide difference between my faith and other faith; and mine is a certain brief experience which surprised me in the highway or in the market, in some place, at some time,—whether in the body or out of the body,— God knoweth,—and made me aware that I had played the fool with fools all this time, but that law existed for me and for all; that to me belonged trust, a child's trust and obedience, and the worship of ideas, and I should never be fool more."[30] This is an ecstatic experience similar to the one Emerson had when crossing the Boston Common, and like all such experiences, it does not last for long. Soon enough we return to the world we left, back to our old routines and habits, but with the feeling that our life is superficial by comparison with the one shown to us in the vision. We ask ourselves, he says, "When shall I die, and be relieved of the responsibility of seeing an Universe which I do not use? I wish to exchange this flash-of-lightening faith for continuous daylight, this fever-glow for a benign climate."[31]

This is the dilemma at the heart of Emerson's First Philosophy. The *actualities* of daily life "stand in wild contrast" to the *realities* of the ideal world. If we view our lives in comparison to "these moments of illumination," we seem to play "a mean, shiftless, and subaltern part in the world." He refers to this dilemma as "double consciousness." The Understanding and the Reason give us two views of life: "one prevails now, all buzz and din; and the other prevails then, all infinitude and paradise." How can they be reconciled? Our faith consists of "a thought of serenity and independence, an abode in the deep blue sky." Although these ecstasies cannot be sustained, "we retain the belief that this petty web we weave will at last be overshot and reticulated with veins of the blue, and that the moments will characterize the days."[32]

Emerson acknowledges that some will object to this point of view. The Transcendentalists realize they are open to criticism and ridicule. They may seem naive, but for those willing to follow their lead, they show the way to greater enlargements of the soul. "Their heart is the ark in which the fire is concealed, which shall burn in a broader and universal flame," he says. "Let them obey the Genius then most when his impulse is wildest; then most when he seems to lead to unimaginable desarts [sic] of thought and life; for the path which the hero travels alone is the highway of health and benefit to mankind."[33]

This is the hero's journey, described by Joseph Campbell in *The Power of Myth*. "The usual hero adventure begins with someone from whom something has been taken, or who feels there's something lacking in the normal experiences available or permitted to members of his society," Campbell says. "This person then takes off on a series of adventures beyond the ordinary, either to recover what has been lost or to discover some life-giving elixir. It's usually a cycle, a going and a returning." There are two types of hero: the physical hero who performs a courageous act, and the spiritual hero who experiences something beyond the ordinary range of human spiritual life and returns with a message. The young Transcendentalist is clearly a hero of the spiritual kind. In either case, Campbell says, the quest is essentially the same: "You leave the world that you're in and go into a depth or into a distance or up to a height. There you come to what was missing in your consciousness in the world you formerly inhabited. Then comes the problem either of staying with that, and letting the world drop off, or returning with that boon and trying to hold on to it as you move back into your social world again. That's not an easy thing to do."[34]

This pattern describes Emerson as a Transcendentalist hero. He was dissatisfied with his religious inheritance and at odds with a society dominated by materialism and commercialism. An ecstatic experience revealed to him the possibility of a world transformed by a vision of "infinitude and paradise," in which intrinsic values take precedence over instrumental ones. Society needs persons "speaking for thoughts and principles not marketable or perishable." Soon enough mechanical inventions and so-called improvements will be superseded. But the thoughts of these spiritual forerunners and harbingers "shall abide in beauty and strength, to reorganize themselves in nature, to invest themselves anew in other, perhaps higher endowed and happier mixed clay than ours, in fuller union with the surrounding system."[35] This is the message he brings back from his own spiritual quest.

Transcendentalism is a form of philosophical idealism, Emerson claims. But it isn't always clear what he means by this. He is not a rigorous philosopher to begin with. He uses the word "idealism" in several different ways, interchangeably. Sometimes he uses it in a Platonic sense, drawing on Plato's theory of the forms. This theory holds that there is an essence of things of which there are only imitations in the actual world. It posits a perfection that can never be achieved, which speaks to the perfectionism of the young Transcendentalists who consider themselves failures and everyone else hypocrites and phonies. None, including themselves, can ever match up to such impossible expectations.

In another sense, idealism does not deny the existence of the empirical world of the Understanding, but it considers it superficial or merely phenomenal from the point of view of the eye of Reason. This is the difference between the *actual* and the *real*. We may live in the actual world of getting and spending, but we know that there is more to life than keeping up with the Joneses. As Emerson learned more about Indian philosophies, he adopted the Vedic notion of *maya*, or "illusion," to show that much of what we take for granted is, in reality, superficial and insubstantial.

In yet another sense, Emerson equates idealism with subjectivity, as in this lecture. He does not deny the existence of the physical world but insists that how we see it depends on our own subjectivity. Two people may see the same thing in different ways. The way they view this datum constitutes its reality. In this manner, it is the subject, that is, the individual person, who creates the world. All things have "a subjective or relative existence, relative to that aforesaid Unknown Center of him," he says. This is also why he claims there can be no cohesive Transcendental party, since each person views the world from a different perspective.

These understandings of idealism are common in our own experience. But Emerson's subjective idealism goes even deeper. He challenges the assumption that the world we know is essentially material, even if we view it subjectively or in relative terms. As a student, Emerson was drawn to the philosophical idealism of Irish philosopher George Berkeley (1685–1753), who denied the existence of material substance and believed that objects exist only in the minds of those who perceive them. Emerson goes even further. Berkeley believed the universe was the creation of God's mind. In this sense, he was an *objective* idealist. Emerson, a *subjective* idealist, rejected the concept of a personal God and believed instead that the universe is the creation of the human mind.[36]

By this time Emerson was convinced that God was within and had no existence independent of human consciousness. When he writes in *Nature* that "the Supreme Being, does not build up nature around us but puts it forth through us, as the life of the tree puts forth new branches and leaves through the pores of the old," he is identifying the Supreme Being with the human mind.[37] This view has raised two issues for his critics. One is the arrogance, if not blasphemy, of identifying himself with God. In his journal for 1837 he wrote, "In certain moments I have known that I existed directly from God, and am, as it were, his organ. And in my ultimate consciousness Am He."[38] What he means by God here is "soul" and that the soul becomes consciousness in us, its organ. Though it manifests itself in each individual, it is not individualistic, but universal. It is not the same as the ego.

The other objection critics of this position have raised has to do with the mind-body problem in philosophy. Mind and matter: Which has priority over the other? Philosophers continue to debate this problem. It has simply been assumed that consciousness is an epiphenomenon, or by-product, of the brain. What else could it be? Our materialistic bias posits that at some point in the evolutionary process, matter produced mind. A jolt of energy must have quickened the mind to consciousness. But scientists have been unable to prove this theory. The assumption that we live in a material world is so accepted that even considering the opposite hypothesis—that matter is the product of consciousness—is difficult.

David Chalmers, a philosophy of mind professor at New York University, outlines the trajectory involved in moving from materialism to idealism: "First, one is impressed by the successes of science, endorsing materialism about everything and so about the mind. Second, one is moved by the problem of consciousness to see a gap between physics and consciousness, thereby endorsing dualism, where both matter and consciousness are fundamental. Third, one is moved by the inscrutability of matter to realize that science reveals at most the structure of matter and not its underlying nature, and to speculate that this nature may involve consciousness, thereby endorsing panpsychism [the view that mind itself is a feature of reality]. Fourth, one comes to think that there is little reason to believe in anything beyond consciousness and that the physical world is wholly constituted by consciousness, thereby endorsing idealism."[39] Chalmers examines the varieties of idealism, including objective and subjective idealism. He also describes what he calls *cosmic* idealism, "the thesis that all concrete facts are grounded in facts about the mental states of a single cosmic entity, such as the universe as a whole or perhaps a god."[40] Cosmic idealism has affinities with many nineteenth-century German and British idealists and also with certain schools of Hindu idealism, especially that of Advaita Vedanta. This form of idealism appealed to Emerson as well, so long as it is understood in a nontheistic way. One could argue that we see in *Nature* a version of *objective* idealism; in "The Transcendentalist," a form of *subjective* idealism; and, as we shall see, in "The Over-Soul," an example of *cosmic* idealism.

Has the case for idealism been proven? No. "No position on the mind-body problem is plausible," Chalmers observes. "Idealism is not significantly less plausible than its main competitors. So even though idealism is implausible, there is a non-negligible probability that it is true."[41] But for Emerson, its truth was self-evident. He never surrendered his idealistic philosophy, although in time he moved away from a strict form of idealism toward a more pragmatic understanding of the term.

The notion of double consciousness is central to Emerson's spiritual philosophy. We are alienated from nature because we are disunited in ourselves, he writes in *Nature*. "The axis of vision [the Reason] is not coincident with the axis of things [the Understanding]," Emerson writes.[42]

The marriage of matter and spirit is not celebrated. With new eyes we may come to see not a dualism but a unity. However, there can be no final resolution to this dilemma because we are forever "undulating" or alternating between these two poles of the intellect. Even if unity is always just beyond our reach, we can, through the practice of self-culture, cultivate the Reason and establish its priority over the Understanding.

Recall what Emerson said at the beginning of his lecture "Man the Reformer": "the community in which we live will hardly bear to be told that every man should be open to ecstasy or a divine illumination, and his daily walk elevated by intercourse with the spiritual world." All reform proceeds from a comparison of the existing state of affairs with an ideal envisioned in moments of ecstasy. Reform does not end there, but this is where it must begin.

6

SPIRITUAL PRINCIPLES

Emerson was nearly overwhelmed with the demands on his time as his reputation grew. In addition to his annual winter lecture series, which were important sources of income, he was acting as a literary agent for his friend, Thomas Carlyle, arranging for the publication and promotion of his books in America. With the launch of the *Dial* magazine in 1840, he was providing copy to plump its pages and often filling in for Margaret Fuller as editor. By 1841 he and Lidian had three young children: his namesake, Waldo, born in 1836; Ellen, named for his first wife, born in 1839; and Edith, born in 1841. He also had the care of his younger brother Bulkeley, who was intellectually disabled. His home in Concord was filled with a growing family, servants, and a steady stream of guests.

For several years he had wanted to write another book and was itching to get at it. But between the lectures and other commitments he found little time to work on it. In a letter to Carlyle, he wrote, "Here I sit and read and write with very little system, and as far as regards composition, with the most fragmentary result: paragraphs incomprehensible, each sentence an infinitely repellent particle."[1] He tried to establish a routine, rising at 6:00 a.m., helping himself to a couple of cups of coffee and a piece of pie, and spending the next six hours undisturbed, thinking, reading, and writing. Slowly, his first book of essays took shape.

He drew heavily on his journal and lectures. He had been keeping a journal for many years, making entries almost daily of his thoughts and comments on his reading. He indexed these so that he might use them in lectures and later in published essays. The pattern of writing for his first two books of essays was from journal to lecture to essay, with considerable editing along the way. *Essays: First Series* was finally published in 1841, to mixed reviews. English writer and cultural critic Harriet Martineau called it "a vision of health . . . like a breeze,—like a handful of wild flowers." In a letter to Emerson she wrote, "My prophecy would be that this book will live 1000 years."[2] On the other hand, his Aunt Mary—herself a New Light Puritan theist—called it a book of atheism, a charge other reviewers made as well. Regardless of what anyone said or how much controversy his essays stirred up, Emerson was determined to speak his mind.

The result was a volume of twelve essays, the most brilliant and insightful of his writing career. David Robinson calls it "a guidebook for the culture of the soul." The essays explore a fundamental dilemma of the spiritual life, in which will and acceptance represent contrasting poles and alternate between these two approaches to spiritual growth. In Emerson's model of self-culture, notes Robinson, "a dichotomy existed between willed effort and passive will-lessness. Is the 'unfolding' of the soul the product of strenuous moral effort, or is it better conceived as a coming to oneself in a quietist acceptance?"[3] Emerson suggests that the undulation between intentionality and receptiveness allows the "unfolding" of the soul. It is a bipolar unity in which both elements are necessary.

"SELF-RELIANCE"

Emerson's "Self-Reliance" is both the best known of his essays and the most controversial. In his "Divinity School Address" in 1838, he had said that "it is not instruction, but provocation, that I can receive from another soul." This essay is indeed provocative. "Trust thyself," he insisted, "every heart vibrates to that iron string."[4] The doctrine of self-reliance was central to everything he taught throughout his career. But it is often confused with individualism. That's not what Emerson meant, nor did he mean total independence or self-sufficiency. The worst mistake of all would be to identify it with narcissism, which some of his detractors continue to do.[5]

A closer reading of the essay should dispel such misconceptions. The "self" Emerson is writing about is not the individual, isolated ego but the soul, which is uniquely incarnated in each person and, at the same time, commonly shared by all. "There is one mind common to all individual men," he wrote in "History," the first essay of the book. "Every man is an inlet to the same and to all of the same." Self-reliance is not reliance on the self in *isolation* but on the self in *relation* to that larger self which "makes us receivers of its truth and organs of its activity."[6] He was well aware of the dangers of antinomianism, or flouting convention by mistaking the self for the soul.

At the outset of "Self-Reliance" Emerson makes a bold assertion: "To believe your own thought, to believe that what is true for you in your private heart is true for all men,—that is genius." Is he saying every crackpot with a loony idea is right? Of course not. On the other hand, all serious writers must believe there is truth to what they say, otherwise why bother to tell us what they think? They must say what is in them to say, even when the "whole cry of voices is on the other side."[7] Emerson believes that all great art and literature are inspired—they are works of genius.

Today we use the word "genius" to mean exceptional intelligence, as when we say Einstein is a genius. But for Emerson and others in the Transcendentalist circle, genius meant something else. Their use of the term came from Greek philosophy. For Plato, the Stoics, and others, genius was a daimon, or "guiding spirit." The Stoic philosopher Epictetus described it this way: "[Zeus] has assigned to each man a director, his own good genius, and committed him to that guardianship—a director sleepless and not to be deceived. To what better and more careful guardian could he have committed to each one of us? So that when you have shut your doors, and darkened your room, remember never to say that you are alone; for you are not alone, but God is within, and your genius is within."[8] Emerson uses the term in this sense himself and sometimes characterizes it as a certain tendency or bias in the individual. Genius, then, is a matter of surrendering to this bias or tendency.

"Imitation is suicide," Emerson insists. For better or worse, we must take ourselves as we are, for nothing comes of pretending otherwise. We do not speak or act with power as long as we conform to the opinions of others. Apple founder Steve Jobs, in his famous Stanford Commencement Address in 2005, perfectly expresses Emerson's point of view: "Your time is limited, so don't waste it living someone else's life. Don't be trapped by dogma—which is living with the results of other people's thinking. Don't let the noise of others' opinions drown out your own inner voice. And most important, have the courage to follow your heart and intuition. They somehow already know what you truly want to become. Everything else is secondary."[9] We are too much inclined to doubt ourselves. We are insecure and uncertain. We hesitate because we fear criticism or ridicule. We too readily defer to the authority of others, especially those who tell us what is right and proper. The pressures to conform are overwhelming. Society conspires against uniqueness and originality. "Whoso would be a man must be a non-conformist," Emerson declares. "Nothing is at last sacred but the integrity of your own mind." To those who say self-reliance is too subjective to be the basis of authority, he replies, "No law can be sacred to me but that of my own nature."[10] We have only ourselves to go by, our own sense of right and wrong.

Emerson is unusually harsh in his criticism of philanthropy. His dismissive tone toward the poor and the enslaved suggests that the self-reliant individual is lacking in compassion. The best that can be said for his argument here is that he believes there is no goodness by proxy or out of a sense of duty. We must be motivated by our own conscience, not by the expectations of others. But his uncompromising stance in favor of independence makes Emerson appear aloof and indifferent. It contributes to the view that he espouses an uncompromising individualism.

Emerson may be trying too hard to make his case. Ignore inconsistency, he says. Scorn appearances. "If I am the devil's child, I will live then from the devil." He may be putting on a brave front to mask his own sense of insecurity. Emerson was stung by criticism of the Divinity School address more than he let on, historian Kenneth Sacks points out in *Understanding Emerson: "The American Scholar" and His Struggle for Self-Reliance*. This may explain the defensive tone of his essay "Self-Reliance," written in the wake of the controversy he had stirred on that occasion.[11]

Some critics have argued that self-reliance promotes a radical form of individualism that is detrimental to communities and institutions. But Emerson is trying to find a healthy balance between the needs of the individual and the needs of society. His thumb may be on the individual's side of the scale, but only because he believes our integrity is threatened by social pressures to conform. "The essay is not a blueprint for selfishness or withdrawal: it is not anticommunity," Emerson biographer Robert D. Richardson Jr. writes. "It recommends self-reliance as a starting point—indeed *the* starting point—not as a goal. When a better society evolves, it will not, in Emerson's view, come about through a suppression of the process of individuation, but through a voluntary association of fulfilled individuals."[12]

"I know of no country in which there is so little independence of mind and real freedom of discussion as in America," noted French writer Alexis de Tocqueville (1805–59) after his visit in 1831. "In America the majority raises formidable barriers around the liberty of opinion; within these barriers an author may write what he pleases, but woe to him if he goes beyond them."[13] Emerson was determined to break through those barriers of rigid conformity.

Emerson believed we need community and society. The self he extols in the essay is not the isolated, self-important ego but rather the soul, commonly shared by everything that exists as a manifestation of the oversoul. We are not isolated from one another. We are, in fact, infinitely related. Our individuality sets us apart, but it does not separate us from the larger whole. "For the sense of being which in calm hours rises, we know not how, in the soul, is not diverse from things," Emerson writes, "but one with them, and proceeds obviously from the same source from whence their life and being also proceed. We first share the life by which things exist, and afterwards see them as appearances in nature, and forget that we have shared their cause."[14]

What Emerson means by self-reliance is not independence and autonomy but self-trust and authenticity. "Who is the Trustee?" he asks. "What is the aboriginal Self on which a universal reliance may be grounded?" He believes that this aboriginal self is "the fountain of action and thought."[15] In elevated moments we intuitively perceive the reality behind the show of appearances. But in everyday life the reality of the aboriginal self is obscured by convention, dull routine, and pressures to measure up to other people's expectations. Contemporary spiritual writer Thomas Moore expresses a similar point of view in *Original Self: Living with Paradox and Originality*: "Far below the many thick layers of indoctrination about who we are and who we should be lies an original self, a person who came into this world full of possibility and destined for joyful unveiling and manifestation. . . . Chronically trying to be someone other than this original self, persuaded that we are not adequate and should fit some norm of health or correctness, we may find a cool distance gradually separating us from that deep and eternal person, that God-given personality, and we may forget both who we were and who we might be."[16]

Many people, at some point in their lives, sense that they are not following their own path but one that someone else chose for them. They may occasionally catch a glimpse of their original self and struggle to become who they were meant to be. Emerson himself is an example of this. He was descended from a long line of ministers and expected to follow in his father's footsteps. Suffering a crisis of faith brought about by the death of his first wife and doubts about Christian teachings, he realized he was not cut out to be a minister. After his soul-searching trip to Europe and Britain, he discovered his true calling as a lecturer. Trading his pulpit for a podium, he found a larger audience for his own message.

For Emerson, our original self is identical with the aboriginal self, as Moore describes it. That self-identity comes to us in moments of mystical awareness and self-surrender. "We lie in the lap of immense intelligence," he says, "which makes us receivers of its truth and organs of its activity. When we discern justice, when we discern truth, we do nothing of ourselves, we allow a passage to its beams." Too often we check and doubt ourselves. We hesitate to "allow a passage to its beams." Our rationality—what Emerson calls the Understanding—gets in the way. We are told to pay no attention to such flights of fancy. Rather than drink from our own "internal ocean," we go "abroad to beg a cup of water of the urns" of others.[17]

With self-trust comes a new lease on life. Freed from everything that held us back, we feel a sense of relief and excitement. There is a power, Emerson asserts, that "resides in the moment of transition from a past to a new state, in the shooting of the gulf, in the darting to an aim." "Shooting the gulf" is an expression that was used to describe Sir Francis Drake's 1578 passage from the Atlantic to the Pacific oceans through the treacherous Strait of Magellan at the tip of South America.[18] It conveys the exhilaration of breaking out into something quite new, a whole new world. When we keep a job that we hate or stay in a relationship that is oppressive, we feel powerless and drained of vitality. When we are with someone we love or doing meaningful work, we feel just the opposite.

For Emerson, "shooting the gulf" describes the ecstatic nature of life itself. As products of nature, human beings are a manifestation of the ecstatic naturalism at the heart of things. We have within us, at an unconscious level, a power that is capable of releasing pent-up energy, enabling us to flow with the course of nature. The identity of the aboriginal self and the original self, or the oversoul and the individual soul, is revealed to us in moments of ecstasy. Self-reliance, then, is trust in the self-evident truth of this vision. "Inasmuch as the soul is present, there will be power not confident but agent," Emerson tells us. "To talk of reliance, is a poor external way of speaking. Speak rather of that which relies, because it works and is."[19]

Social conservatives, such as Robert Bellah and New York Times columnist David Brooks, say that self-reliance is harmful to institutions and human community.[20] But healthy institutions and communities require healthy, self-reliant individuals, not compliant, obedient ones. Emerson does not remove the individual from society, as these critics allege—quite the opposite. "For Emerson . . . genuine individualism was not narcissism, monomania, or isolation," Emerson scholar, Wesley T. Mott, explains. "Indeed, it was the *answer* to these diseases of the self as well as the remedy for the 'existing evils' of institutional and social life."[21]

"COMPENSATION"

In several of the essays in the *First Series*, "Compensation," "Spiritual Laws," and "Circles," Emerson offers spiritual principles useful in guiding us how to live our lives and resolve spiritual dilemmas that are as relevant today as they were when he wrote them. In "Compensation" he addresses justice and retribution, telling us that he was disturbed to hear a preacher say that justice is not executed in this world, but that sin would be punished in the afterlife. Emerson was not satisfied to let sinners off the hook in this way. Justice, he believed, is done now, in this world.

He based his argument on what he called the "law of Compensation." This law was validated, in part, by another law, that of polarity: for every action there is an opposite and equal reaction. Applying this law to the human condition, he says that "every excess causes a defect; every defect an excess; every evil its good." There is a leveling effect "that puts down the overbearing, the strong, the rich, the fortunate, substantially on the same ground with all others."[22]

This is a provocative claim. Many crimes obviously go unpunished. But Emerson argues, "This Law writes the laws of cities and nations. It is vain to build or plot or combine against it. Things refuse to be mismanaged long," he insists. "Though no checks to a new evil appear, the checks exist and will appear." Here he introduces another spiritual principle, that of the macrocosm and microcosm. The universe (macrocosm) is represented in every one of its parts (microcosm). "Everything in nature consists of all the powers of nature. Everything is made of one hidden stuff."[23]

Because nature is suffused with moral laws, these same laws are in us and hold us to account. "Every secret is told, every crime is punished, every virtue rewarded, every wrong addressed, in silence and certainty," he writes. "What we call retribution, is the universal necessity by which the whole appears wherever a part appears." While people may appear to evade the consequences of their actions, they pay the price with their peace of mind. "All infractions of love and equity in our social relations are speedily punished," he says. "They are punished by Fear." That we pay a price for our misdeeds does not mean that we must also pay a price for the good that we do. These do not cancel each other out. "There is no penalty to virtue; no penalty to wisdom; they are proper additions of being."[24]

Emerson did not believe in personal immortality or the last judgment. The challenge was how to address the problem of evil without recourse to the traditional remedy, namely, sinners paying a price for their misdeeds in the next life. All actions have consequences, whether immediately or in the long term, in this world, not the next. Some readers have likened Emerson's notion of compensation to that of *karma*, the Hindu belief that no one escapes the consequences of his or her actions. In the popular view, karma plays out in the course of one's lifetime. Strictly speaking, it affects the outcome of one's reincarnation. Thus karma, too, envisions a form of punishment in the next life for transgressions in this one. "The reward or the punishment is instead in the very nature of the act itself," as David Robinson describes Emerson's position. "Emerson emphasizes that no act can be separated from the integrated chain of relations that constitutes the unified whole of reality. It is our conventional ideas of 'reward' and 'punishment' that are superficial and falsifying."[25]

Is Emerson too naive and too optimistic in believing that each of us pays a price for our bad actions? Perhaps. Even if we don't get caught, we may still feel guilt, remorse, and fear. These emotions gnaw at the soul and erode our character. But they do not bring justice for the harm we caused to the offended party. Justice requires, at the least, contrition and public acknowledgment of the injury we have caused. There is, however, one area in which Emerson is absolutely correct, where injurious actions exact harsh consequences: nature. We have a collective responsibility to care for the well-being of this planet, which is our home. As a species, we cannot pollute our air and water, put carbon in the atmosphere, remove trees from our forests, and eradicate entire species of wildlife without paying a mortal price. Nature will always extract its toll. Or, as the saying goes, "Nature bats last."

"SPIRITUAL LAWS"

The essay "Spiritual Laws" introduces another set of provocative spiritual principles. The first: "The soul will not know either deformity or pain," as Emerson puts it. "All loss, all pain is particular; the universe remains to the heart unhurt." People are preoccupied with imagined problems and anxious when they need not be. "These are the soul's mumps and measles, and whooping-coughs, and those who have not caught them, cannot describe their health or prescribe the cure. A simple mind will not know these enemies." What he means is that difficulties, both imagined and real, confront us in our everyday lives. We envision our existence as a struggle to be overcome by acts of will. But if we will "live the life of nature" we will find tranquility and peace of mind.[26]

To "live the life of nature" is a central tenet of Stoic philosophy and another of Emerson's spiritual principles. It means to live simply and in harmony with nature. The Stoics held that we cannot control what happens to us, but we can choose how we will respond. Emerson admired the writings of Stoic philosophers Epictetus, Seneca, and Marcus Aurelius. In his essay "The Happy Life," Seneca wrote, "I follow the guidance of Nature—a doctrine upon which all Stoics are agreed. Not to stray from Nature and to mould ourselves according to her law and pattern—this is true wisdom." He further asserted, "The happy man is one who is freed from both fear and desire because of the gift of reason."[27] Through reason, by which Seneca means cultivating a simple mind, we are able to transcend or rise above both fear and desire.

The will is a stumbling block to spiritual growth. Emerson did not believe we could lift ourselves by our own bootstraps, as the saying goes. "The lesson is forcibly taught," Emerson writes, "that our life might be much easier and simpler than we make it; that the world might be a happier place than it is; that there is no need of struggles, convulsions, and despairs, of the wringing of the hands and the gnashing of the teeth; that we miscreate our own evils." In a passage strongly suggestive of Taoism, Emerson advises the following: "Let us draw a lesson from nature, which always works by short ways. When the fruit is ripe, it falls. When the fruit is dispatched, the leaf falls. The circuit of the waters is mere falling. The walking of man and all animals is a falling forward. All our manual labor and works of strength, as prying, splitting, digging, rowing, and so forth, are done by dint of continual falling, and the globe, earth, moon, comet, sun, star, fall forever and ever."[28]

The way of nature is simple and spontaneous. Our strained efforts are unnecessary. Only in "our own easy, simple, and spontaneous actions are we strong," he says. Letting go is the key. "The whole course of things goes to teach us faith. We need only obey. There is guidance for each of us, and by lowly listening we shall hear the right word. . . . For you there is a reality, a fit place and congenial duties. Place yourself in the middle of the stream of power and wisdom which animates all whom it floats, and you are without effort impelled to truth, to right, and a perfect contentment."[29]

Every person has a calling, a vocation he or she is best suited for. Like a boat on a river, we run into obstructions on all sides, except the one that is open to us. On that side we sweep "serenely over a deepening channel into an infinite sea." All too often people fit themselves as best they can into a trade and tend it as oxen grind wheat in a mill. We become part of the machine we operate. Instead, Emerson is saying we should heed our own genius, the thing that makes us unique. Our genius is a guiding spirit or inner voice that knows us better than we know ourselves. We succeed when we let our native genius guide us. We may admire others, but we should not try to copy them. "The fact that I am here, certainly shows me that the soul had need of an organ here," Emerson writes. "Shall I not assume the post?"[30]

Once again, Emerson's claim is provocative. Is it true that there is but one way open to us and that by acquiescing or letting go we may find truth, right, and "a perfect contentment"? He is not alone in offering such advice. Twentieth-century Taoist scholar Alan Watts writes, "The essence of Lao-tzu's philosophy is the difficult art of getting out of one's own way—of learning to act without forcing conclusions, of living in skillful harmony with the processes of nature instead of trying to push them around."[31]

Their advice isn't quite the same as following one's passions. Passions can be misguided and willful. They are a form of desire. Finding happiness in life requires both detachment and discernment. This is the function of what Emerson terms the daimon, the voice within. The ancient Greek term for happiness, *eudaimonia*, consists of *eu* (good) and *daimon* (guiding spirit or inner voice) and is usually translated as "flourishing." Thus, to flourish means trusting one's inner voice.

Emerson felt he was following the only course that was open to him, but it took some trial and error to discover it. We must find the current before we can go with it. He knew he wasn't cut out to be a doctor or lawyer. He tried teaching and preaching and found them unsatisfactory. The life of a writer and public speaker wasn't easy, but it was his true calling. To become unstuck in an unrewarding pursuit, whether an occupation or a relationship, one must first let go and listen to one's inner voice. Success is never guaranteed, but letting go is surely the best way to achieve it.

"CIRCLES"

The essay "Circles" examines the spiritual principle of impermanence. "Our life is an apprenticeship to the truth," Emerson writes, "that around every circle another can be drawn; that there is no end in nature, but every end is a beginning; that there is always another dawn risen on mid-noon, and under every deep a lower deep opens." This is a new twist on the absolute. It is not static but dynamic and open-ended. He describes it as "the Unattainable, the flying Perfect, around which the hands of man can never meet, at once the inspirer and the condemner of every success." This is consistent with his philosophy of ecstatic naturalism. "There are no fixtures in nature. The universe is fluid and volatile. Permanence is but a word of degrees."[32]

All things—ideas, institutions, inventions, people, nature itself—are in a constant state of change. Yet each time a change occurs or a new truth is revealed, we have a natural tendency to resist it. Only by embracing change is there hope for us. "If the soul is quick and strong," he says, "it bursts over that boundary on all sides and expands another orbit on the great deep, which also runs up into a high wave, with attempt again to stop and to bind. But the heart refuses to be imprisoned; in its first and narrowest pulses it already tends outward with a vast force and to immense and innumerable expansions."[33]

This is true for our spiritual life. Spiritual growth is a succession of enlargements of the soul. It is a process of transformation or metamorphosis—like a pupa into a butterfly. It brings us renewed vitality and an increase of personal power. Yet we hesitate to embrace the new. We cling to the old and the customary. We are fearful of change and feel threatened by it. We cling to stability and what we know. But we should neither fear nor resist change. Life is lived in the transitions between periods of stasis. It is an experiment with no final result. "But lest I should mislead any when I have my own head, and obey my whims," he writes, "let me remind the reader that I am only an experimenter. Do not set the least value on what I do, or the least discredit on what I do not, as if I pretended to settle anything as true or false. I unsettle all things. No facts are to me sacred; none are profane. I simply experiment, an endless seeker, with no Past at my back."[34]

Nature has no use for the past. "In nature every moment is new, the past is always swallowed up and forgotten; the coming only is sacred. Nothing is secure but life, transition, the energizing spirit," Emerson writes. "Life is a series of surprises." We can never know where these growths and movements of the soul might take us, but we do know that they require us to let go of surety. He concludes the essay with this observation: "The one thing which we seek with insatiable desire is to forget ourselves, to be surprised out of our propriety . . . and to do something without knowing how or why; in short to draw a new circle. Nothing great was ever achieved without enthusiasm. The way of life is wonderful; it is by abandonment."[35]

This essay is a considerable achievement for someone who, only a few years earlier, had lost his wife, his career, and his health. It is not remarkable simply because Emerson had recovered and moved on. By letting go of the past, he made a successful transition into something new. Despite the pain he had undergone, he could now say that the way of life is wonderful. He is speaking from personal experience when he writes, "Nothing is secure but life, transition, the energizing spirit." With transition comes renewed energy and a new lease on life. But in the depths of his despair, whether he would succeed in making it was never clear.

Twentieth-century writer Anne Morrow Lindbergh also talked about the constancy of change in *Gift from the Sea*: "We insist on permanency, on duration, on continuity; when the only continuity possible, in life as in love, is in growth, in fluidity—in freedom." It is a paradox Emerson himself recognized: the only way to hold on to life is to let go. The very things we most want to hold on to are the result of change themselves: a new baby, a new job, a new home. Change then seemed just as daunting as it does now. No matter how comforting the status quo feels today, it was once new and uncertain. "People wish to be settled," Emerson concluded; "only as far as they are unsettled, is there any hope for them."[36]

Some of the readers of this essay—Stephen Whicher, for example, in his book, *Freedom and Fate*—have concluded that it reflects a fall from grace, a sign of Emerson's disillusionment with the notion that transcendent experiences can be summoned or sustained.[37] But Emerson never succumbed to the skepticism of Wordsworth or Coleridge in their old age. He recognized the ebb and flow of life, but he never gave up hope. There is something heroic in Emerson's assertion in this essay: "We grizzle every day. I see no need of it. Whilst we converse with what is above us, we do not grow old, but grow young. Infancy, youth, receptive, aspiring, with religious eye looking upward, counts itself nothing and abandons itself to the instruction flowing from all sides. But the man and woman of seventy assume to know all, they have outlived their hope, they renounce aspiration, accept the actual for the necessary, and talk down to the young. Let them then become organs of the Holy Ghost; let them be lovers; let them behold truth; and their eyes are uplifted, their wrinkles smoothed, they are perfumed again with hope and power. This old age ought not to creep on a human mind. In nature, every moment is new; the past is swallowed up and forgotten; the coming only is sacred."[38] His life was an unbroken arc. He suffered tragedy, but he never surrendered to fatalism. As Emerson wrote in his journal in 1842, "There ought to be no such thing as Fate. As long as we use this word, it is a sign of our impotence and that we are not yet ourselves. . . . I am *Defeated* all the time; yet to Victory I am born."[39]

"THE OVER-SOUL"

In the winter of 1838–39, Emerson gave a lecture series called Doctrine of the Soul. In the opening lecture he announced, "The thought that is now awakening the minds of all men and appearing in all the arts, in the laws, in the manners, countenances, and actions of men is a faith in the Soul. . . . A new spirit characterises the men and works of this age." The new movement, he says, "will be religious but it will not be a religious history."[40] Today we might say that it will be spiritual but not religious.

Emerson recognizes a spiritual yearning that outworn religious institutions do not satisfy. Despite growing skepticism and secularization in American society, he declares that "the central hope of nature is on that somewhat miraculous and divine which always remains in man. Always there is in man somewhat incalculable, a presiding, overseeing, imparting, unexhausted soul." He confesses that he is unable to clearly express the doctrine of the soul. But he is convinced of this: "The end of all Culture is to establish its dominion by removing checks and impediments from it."[41]

Emerson's fullest expression of the doctrine of the soul is his essay "The Over-Soul." It is one of the most profound expositions on the subject in all of literature. He starts by referring to the two modes of consciousness he described in "The Transcendentalist": everyday experience and mystical insight. Naturally, most of our life is spent in the world of everyday experience. But from time to time we may have an experience of an entirely different kind, when we feel we transcend everyday experience and intuitively understand the true nature of reality. "There is a depth in those brief moments," Emerson says, "which constrains us to ascribe more reality to them than to all other experiences." For six thousand years, philosophers have pondered this dilemma but have been unable to resolve it. "Man is a stream whose source is hidden," he tells us. "Our being is descending into us from we know not whence." Mystical vision cannot be summoned by an act of will but only through "the attitude of reception."[42]

Mystics and poets have struggled to describe the character of these revelations. Although Emerson admits his own words "fall short and cold," he captures their essence better than most: "We live in succession, in division, in parts, in particles. Meantime within man is the soul of the whole; the wise silence; the universal beauty, to which every part and particle is equally related; the eternal one. And this deep power in which we exist, and whose beatitude is all accessible to us, is not only self-sufficing and perfect in every hour, but the act of seeing and the thing seen, the seer and the spectacle, the subject and the object, are one. We see the world piece by piece, as the sun, the moon, the animal, the tree; but the whole, of which these are the shining parts, is the soul."[43]

Speaking about the soul is difficult because the Understanding—the mode of consciousness where we spend most of our time—cannot comprehend it. The soul cannot be empirically verified. It cannot be weighed, measured, or quantified. It is not a *form* of being. It is being itself. "All goes to show that the soul in man is not an organ, but animates and exercises all the organs; is not a function, like the power of memory, of calculation, of comparison, but uses these as hands and feet; is not a faculty, but a light; is not the intellect or the will, but the master of the intellect and the will; is the background of our being, in which they lie—an immensity not possessed and cannot be possessed." We mistake our true self for our everyday self, or the soul for the ego. Only by transcending the ego can we embrace the soul. "All reform aims," Emerson says, "to let the soul have its way through us, in other words, to engage us to obey."[44]

On some level, we know that this is true. Though subtle, it is undeniable. "We know that all spiritual being is in man," even if not always clear to us. In moments of transcendence, "the walls are taken away," and we find that "we lie open on one side to the deeps of spiritual nature." In a similar vein, the philosopher and psychologist William James, in his chapter on mysticism in *The Varieties of Religious Experience*, writes that "our normal waking consciousness, rational consciousness as we call it, is but one special type of consciousness, whilst all about it, parted from it by the filmiest of screens, there lie potential forms of consciousness entirely different."[45] James notes four characteristics of mystical experiences: first, ineffability, the difficulty of describing such experiences in discursive language; second is transiency, the fleeting and evanescent quality of the revelation of the Reason; third, passivity, the sense in which one's will must be held in abeyance; and fourth, a noetic quality, consisting of insights "into the depths of truth unplumbed by the discursive intellect."[46]

As for the noetic quality of the mystical experiences, Emerson offered four observations on what we can learn from them. One is transcending space and time. "Before the revelations of the soul, Time, Space and Nature shrink away." For the duration of the experience we live in an eternal now. Second, "the soul's advances are not made by gradation, such as can be represented by motion in a straight line; but rather by ascension of state, such as can be represented by metamorphosis,—from the egg to the worm, from the worm to the fly." Third, each person is an individual incarnation of the soul, yet we share a common nature. "The mind is one." Fourth, "the soul is the perceiver and revealer of truth." Intuition, not discursive reason, is the gateway to spiritual knowledge.[47]

The revelation of the soul represents "an influx of the Divine mind into our mind," Emerson says. "It is an ebb of the individual rivulet before the flowing surges of the sea of life." It agitates us with awe and delight. "Every moment when the individual feels himself invaded by it, is memorable." The nature and duration of the experience varies with the state of the individual, from ecstasy and trance "to the faintest glow of virtuous emotion, in which form it warms, like our household fires, all the families and associations of men, and makes society possible."[48]

These revelations have nothing to do with fortune-telling or prophesying; they are of the Reason, not the Understanding. They cannot give us names, dates, places, or any predictions of the future. "The only mode of obtaining an answer to these questions of the senses is, to forego all low curiosity, and, accepting the tide of being which floats us into the secret of nature, work and live, work and live, and all unawares, the advancing soul has built and forged for itself a new condition, and the question and the answer are one." They come to those who are able to set the ego aside and surrender to them. "This energy does not descend into individual life, on any other condition than entire possession," Emerson writes. "It comes to the lowly and simple; it comes to whomsoever will put off what is foreign and proud; it comes as insight; it comes as serenity and grandeur."[49]

The soul gives itself to anyone who is open to receive it. Its reception makes us one with "the universal mind." In its presence we feel "the surges of everlasting nature." We come "to live in thoughts and act with energies that are immortal." In the rapture of the soul we "will come to see that the world is the perennial miracle which the soul worketh"; that the world is not profane but sacred; and that "the universe is represented in an atom, in a moment of time." Most important, we will be transformed. We "will weave no longer a spotted life of shreds and patches, but . . . will live life with a divine unity."[50]

The roots of Emerson's doctrine of the soul are difficult to trace. Many readers of the essay have noted the similarity between Emerson's concept of the oversoul and the distinction between the *atman* and *Brahman* in Hinduism. For Emerson, the individual soul is a manifestation of the oversoul. Likewise, in the Vedanta teaching of Hinduism, the atman, or individual self, is an incarnation of Brahman, or Supreme Self. Emerson had been curious about Hinduism since his youth. When he was nineteen, he wrote to his Aunt Mary that he wished to read "your Hindu mythologies" and "the treasures of the Brahmins."[51] As a student at Harvard he wrote a poem titled "Indian Superstition" for a school exhibition and consulted several anthologies of Hindu literature; these made a favorable impression on him, even though he still had a Western bias at the time, as the title of the poem suggests.

During the 1820s and 1830s he continued to read what he could find of translations from Hindu literature, but there is little evidence of its influence until after *Essays: First Series* was published. Until then, his primary influence had been Neoplatonic philosophy, which dated from the third century CE and also had considerable influence on Christian thought, the humanism of the Italian Renaissance, the Cambridge Platonists of the seventeenth century, and Romanticism.

Plotinus, the principal figure of Neoplatonism, introduced a threefold schema of spiritual reality: first, the One; second, the Divine Mind, or Intellect; and finally, the World Soul—or as Emerson termed it, the Over-Soul. The One is absolute and unknowable. All of creation is an emanation from the One, flowing down through the Divine Mind, which acts as a mediator between creation and the One. It contains the archetypes or forms of existing things. The oversoul is the vital principle of nature. All things share a common nature because they are contained in it. Having descended from the One, individuals seek to return to the source through spiritual practices or exercises.

Emerson's writing and that of Plotinus have many parallels. Take, for instance, this passage from "The Over-Soul":

> The heart in thee is the heart of all; not a valve, not a wall, not an intersection is there anywhere in nature, but one blood rolls uninterruptedly, an endless circulation through men, as the water of the globe

is all one sea, and truly seen, its tide is one. Let man then learn the
revelation of all nature, and all thought to his heart; this namely; that
the Highest dwells with him; that the sources of nature are in his own
mind.[52]

Compare it with this passage from Plotinus:

This All is one universally comprehensive living being, encircling all
the living beings within it, and having a soul, one Soul which extends
to all its members; every separate thing is an integral part of this All
by belonging to the total material fabric, while, in so far as it has participation in the All-Soul, it possesses spiritual membership as well.
Each several thing is affected none the less by all else in virtue of the
common participation in the All.[53]

As with all his reading, Emerson took what he wanted from Plotinus
and left the rest. He considered Plotinus one of the greatest philosophers,
and his opinion of him never wavered. He took the terminology but
conflated Plotinus's hierarchical model. He often used the words "the
One," "Divine Mind," "Intellect," and "Over-Soul" interchangeably. Also,
he subtlety shifted the locus of the oversoul. Like Plotinus, he writes
of the "influx of the Divine mind into our mind," but Emerson says we
share a common nature not because individual souls are in the oversoul
but because the oversoul is in us. That is to say, the oversoul is not in
any sense external to us, as Plotinus suggests.[54] More precise, there is an
identity between the individual soul and the Universal Soul. Emerson
believed that "in reality there is only One Soul, that the individual soul
in essence is also the subjective Universal Soul," according to Emerson
scholar David Lyttle. "Deep in the well of privateness, in the pure ground
water, Emerson found the universal identity of all individuals. Hence,
each individual has 'potential access' to the unconscious depth of his
or her own subjectivity where originates religious, artistic, and moral
inspiration—not to mention the entire external world."[55]

Emerson viewed Plotinus's philosophy—as he also did Hindu scriptures, Confucian writings, Sufi poetry, and other spiritual literature—as
an expression of the *perennial philosophy*, a term coined by German philosopher Gottfried Wilhelm Leibniz (1646–1716). This is a worldview
embraced by some of the world's greatest spiritual teachers and philosophers. Contemporary psychologist and author Ken Wilber summarizes
this worldview: "One, Spirit exists. Two, Spirit is found within. Three,

most of us don't realize this Spirit within, however, because we are living in a world of sin, separation, and duality—that is, we are living in a fallen or illusory state. Four, there is a way out of this fallen state of sin and illusion, there is a Path to our liberation. Five, if we follow this Path to its conclusion, the result is a Rebirth or Enlightenment, a *direct experience* of Spirit within, a Supreme Liberation, which—six—marks the end of sin and suffering, and which—seven—issues in social action of mercy and compassion on behalf of all sentient beings."[56]

Because society today places such an emphasis on empiricism and scientific verification, scholars have been reluctant to defend Emerson's subjective notion of the soul.[57] The soul cannot be verified, quantified, measured, or weighed. It defies description for the fact that it cannot be comprehended by the Understanding. It simply is. It is its own evidence. It must be experienced to be believed. "Every man's words, who speaks from that life, must sound vain to those who do not dwell in the same thought on their own part," Emerson recognized. "My words do not carry its august sense; they fall short and cold. Only itself can inspire whom it will, and behold! their speech shall be lyrical, and sweet, and universal as the rising of the wind."[58]

Emerson's teaching is itself an expression of the perennial philosophy. A month after the publication of his first series of essays, Emerson wrote the following in his journal: "For this I was born and came into the world, to deliver the self of myself to the Universe from the Universe [the Universal]; to do a certain benefit which Nature could not forego, nor I be discharged from rendering, and then immerge again onto the holy silence and eternity, out of which as a man I arose . . . . When I wish, it is permitted me to say, these hands, this body, this history of Waldo Emerson are profane and wearisome, but I, I descend not to mix myself with that or with any man. Above his life, above all creatures, I flow down forever a sea of benefit into races of individuals. Nor can the stream ever roll backward, or the sin or death of a man taint the immutable energy which distributes itself into men as the sun into rays, or the sea into drops."[59]

7

LABYRINTH

Despite the brilliance of *Essays: First Series*, with such classics as "Self-Reliance" and "The Over-Soul," Emerson's writing did not always go over well with his readers. Some took issue with the content, especially orthodox Christians who condemned the *Essays* as "a godless book."[1] Others found his writing enigmatic and disjointed. Even his friends had trouble with his style. Thomas Carlyle said his paragraphs resembled a "bag of buckshot held together by canvas."[2] His nineteenth-century diction and obscure references are still obstacles for today's readers in understanding Emerson's message. Yet, those who persist may come to agree with his friend Orestes Brownson, who wrote, "He who reads [the essays] will find, that he is no longer what he was. A new and higher life has been quickened in him, and he can never again feel, that he is merely a child of time and space, but that he is transcendental and immortal."[3]

Emerson likened his book to a raft—"only boards and logs tied together."[4] Although he intended it as a self-deprecating remark, the word is nevertheless an apt metaphor for conveying his intentions as a writer. The Buddha also likened his own teachings to a raft for carrying his followers across the stream from the everyday world of *samsara* to *nirvana*, a state that is "transcendental and immortal." In effect, what the Buddha was saying is, Don't get hung up on my words. The goal is not to parse or analyze them but look to them as signposts to your own enlightenment.

In 1844, exhausted from the push to get *Essays: Second Series* into print, Emerson resumed writing articles for the *Dial* magazine and preparing his annual series of winter lectures. He found respite tending to his vegetable garden and fruit orchard, with the assistance of Henry

David Thoreau, who had moved into the Emerson house as a handy-man. His normal routine was tragically disrupted in January 1842, when five-year-old Waldo suddenly died from scarlet fever. Emerson was dev-astated. As he confided to his journal, "The sun went up the morning sky with all his light, but the landscape was dishonored by this loss. For this boy in whose remembrance I have both slept and awaked so oft, decorated for me the morning star, and the evening cloud. . . . Every tramper that ever tramped is abroad, but the little feet are still. He gave up his little innocent breath like a bird."[5]

This personal tragedy marked a turning point in Emerson's spiritual life. From this time on, the polarities between fate and freedom and between skepticism and faith predominated in his thinking and writing. The self-confident mood in his first series of essays gave way to a more sober appraisal of the human condition. Critics have commonly char-acterized Emerson as naively optimistic. And Emerson did believe that nothing was to be gained by pessimism or negative thinking. But neither did he ignore the dark side of life. In an essay for the *Dial* magazine titled "The Tragic," he wrote: "He has seen but half the universe who never has been shown the House of Pain. As the salt sea covers more than two thirds of the surface of the globe, so sorrow encroaches on man on felicity. . . . In the dark hours, our existence seems to be a defensive war, a struggle against the encroaching All, which threatens surely to engulf us soon, and is impatient of our short reprieve."[6]

"EXPERIENCE"

The pain over the loss of his son moved Emerson to write perhaps his greatest and most personal essay, "Experience." The death of his child left him feeling numb and disoriented, drained of what he called "the affirmative principle." He imagined himself on a staircase, with steps above and below, lost in a fog of lethargy. "All things swim and glimmer," he writes. "Ghostlike, we glide through nature, and should not know our place again."[7] The opening lines of Dante's *Inferno* also speak to this feeling of being lost:

> Midway in our life's journey, I went astray
> from the straight road and woke to find myself
> alone in a dark wood.

. . . .
> How I came to it I cannot rightly say,
> so drugged and loose with sleep had I become
> when I first wandered there from the true Way.[8]

Emerson was lost in the labyrinth of his perceptions and struggled to find his way out. Grief had banished him there, confused and bereft of feeling. "In the death of my son, now more than two years ago, I seem to have lost a beautiful estate,—no more. I cannot get it nearer to me."[9]

His return to sanity took him through a succession of moods: "Dream delivers us to dream, and there is no end to illusion. Life is a train of moods like a string of beads, and, as we pass through them, they prove to be many-colored lenses which paint the world their own hue, and each shows only what lies in its focus."[10] In "Experience," Emerson describes his journey through seven moods or stages that he passed through, starting with this hazy groundlessness he calls "illusion." While this essay is deeply personal, Emerson believed his own experience was a template for others finding themselves in a similar situation. He begins the essay with the question, "Where do we find ourselves?," and throughout the essay he moves from "we" to "I" and back again.

He wonders, is there something that we can rely on? He finds it initially in temperament, which "prevails over everything of time, place, and condition." This is the idea that we are what we are and always will be. "Given such an embryo, such a history must follow." Temperament locks us into a determinism from which there seems to be no way out. But there's always an opening. "Into every intelligence there is a door which is never closed, through which the creator passes," as Emerson puts it. Or as the late Canadian songwriter Leonard Cohen writes in "Anthem," "There is a crack . . . in everything / That's how the light gets in."[11]

From temperament we pass into a stage he calls "succession." "Our love of the real draws us to permanence," Emerson observes, "but health of body consists in circulation, and sanity of mind in variety or facility of association. We need change of objects. Dedication to one thought is quickly odious." Temperament precludes growth, which requires openness to change. But there is a limitation to succession also. He compares change to "a bird which alights nowhere, but hops perpetually from bough to bough." It leads to sense of "indifferency" in which one thing seems to be as good as any other. The difficulty of making choices "ends in headache."[12]

From succession we transition to what Emerson names "surface." "We live amid surfaces," he tells us, "and the true art of life is to skate well on them." He describes a life that is balanced and serene:

> To finish the moment, to find the journey's end in every step of the road, to live the greatest number of good hours, is wisdom. It is not the part of men, but of fanatics, or of mathematicians, if you will, to say, that, the shortness of life considered, it is not worth caring whether for so short a duration we were sprawling in want, or sitting high. Since our office is with moments, let us husband them. . . . Without any shadow of doubt, amidst this vertigo of shows and politics, I settle myself ever the firmer in the creed, that we should not postpone and refer and wish, but do broad justice where we are, by whomsoever we deal with, accepting our actual companions and circumstances, however humble or odious, as the mystic officials to whom the universe has delegated its whole pleasure for us.

Who wouldn't wish to live this sort of life, free from anxiety and emotional nitpicking? We should relish "the pot-luck of the day" and be "thankful for small mercies" and "moderate goods," notes Emerson. Such a life is not achieved by dissection and overanalysis. "Everything good is on the highway. The middle region of our being is the temperate zone. We may climb into the thin and cold realm of pure geometry and lifeless science, or sink into that of sensation. Between these extremes is the equator of life, of thought, of spirit, of poetry,—a narrow belt."[13]

But Emerson does not want to linger here. It is the life of opium-eaters, all surface and no depth. "How easily, if fate would suffer it, we might keep forever these beautiful limits, and adjust ourselves, once for all, to the perfect calculation of the kingdom of known cause and effect." That is not to be. Sooner or later comes "an angel-whispering" that disrupts everything. Thus, we pass from surface to "surprise." "Power keeps quite another road than the turnpikes of choice and will, namely, the subterranean and invisible tunnels and channels of life." Those who always choose the prudent path are foolish. "Life is a series of surprises," Emerson says, "and would not be worth taking or keeping, if it were not."[14] Everything good comes from spontaneity, throwing caution to the winds. This is the method of nature, fluid and impulsive.

We, too, are subject to fits and pulses. "We thrive by casualties," he says, purposely using the word in two senses: unexpected losses and chance events. We cannot know what the future holds. Everything is impossible until we see it happen. We live by grace. "I would gladly be moral, and keep due metes and bounds, which I dearly love, and allow the most to the will of man," Emerson writes, "but I have set my heart on honesty . . . and I can see nothing at last, in success or failure, than more or less of vital force supplied from the Eternal. The results of life are uncalculated and uncalculable. The years teach much which the days never know."[15]

Surprise opens the way to reality. From time to time we see "flashes of light" revealing scenes of beauty and repose, as if clouds had parted and we can briefly see the world as it truly is. In one of his most extravagant statements, Emerson describes the experience in this way: "But every insight from this realm of thought is felt as initial, and promises a sequel. I do not make it; I arrive there, and behold what was there already. I make! O no! I clap my hands in infantine joy and amazement, before the first opening to me of this august magnificence, old with the love and homage of innumerable ages, young with the life of life, the sunbright Mecca of the desert. And what a future it opens! I feel a new heart beating with the love of the new beauty. I am ready to die out of nature, and be born again into this new yet unapproachable America I have found in the West." Before the U.S. Census Bureau announced the closure of the frontier in 1890, the West was a symbol both of the unknown and a new life. Emerson is not speaking of the literal West but rather "the subterranean and invisible tunnels and channels of life" he mentioned earlier in the essay. The "unapproachable America" is the reality we seek but which always seems to recede from our grasp.[16]

This reality has been called by many names: "Fortune, Minerva, Muse, Holy Ghost," all terms for "the ineffable cause," he says. For Thales of Miletus, it was water; for Anaximenes, air; for Anaxagoras, thought; for Zoroaster, fire; for Jesus, love. In Emerson's view, the Confucian philosopher Mencius comes closest to describing the ineffable cause as "vast-flowing vigor," which is the method of nature. Still, no explanation can encompass reality, he says. We do not arrive at a wall "but interminable oceans." Always the ideal journeys are before us, slightly out of reach. "Onward and onward! In liberated moments, we know that a new picture of life and duty is already possible," he says, "of a doctrine of life which shall transcend any written record we have. The new statement will comprise the skepticisms, as well as the faiths of society, and out of unbeliefs a creed shall be formed."[17]

Finally, Emerson arrives at the realization that reality is subjective. It is a projection of our consciousness. But this does not mean that it is *merely* subjective, as though it is a figment of our imagination. "Thus inevitably does the universe wear our color, and every object fall successively into the subject itself," Emerson says. "As I am, so I see; use what language we will, we can never say anything but what we are."[18] We may be like kittens chasing our tails, but we cannot get outside of our consciousness. We must cultivate the virtue of self-trust. Wisdom lies in holding hard to our own truth, realizing that other people have theirs also.

Still, a doubt remains. The world we live in is not the world we *think*. This is the dilemma of double consciousness: how to reconcile the actual world with the real one. The answer to this problem cannot be forced or figured out. We must be patient. "We dress our garden, eat our dinners, discuss the household with our wives, and these things make no impression, are forgotten next week, but in the solitude to which every man is always returning, he has a sanity and revelations, which in his passage into new worlds he will carry with him," Emerson concludes. "Never mind the ridicule, never mind the defeat: up again, old heart!—it seems to say,—there is victory yet for all justice; and the true romance which the world exists to realize, will be the transformation of genius into practical power."[19]

What are we to make of this essay? It is obviously heartfelt and describes the path that Emerson took to find his way out of the pain of a personal tragedy. In "Self-Reliance" he had written: "To believe your own thought, to believe that what is true for you in your private heart is true for all men—that is genius."[20] Is he right in this instance? Is his experience a universal pattern?

During the 1970s, the Swiss American psychiatrist Elizabeth Kübler-Ross described in *On Death and Dying* five sequential stages of grief: denial, anger, bargaining, depression, and acceptance.[21] While some elements of the Kübler-Ross paradigm may be found in "Experience," the essay as a whole does not conform to it. Emerson's model is illusion, temperament, succession, surface, surprise, reality, and subjectiveness.

It seems more unique to his experience than to that of Kübler-Ross's patients.

Those who have suffered the loss of a loved one sometimes experience both dissociation and neurasthenia. Dissociation is detachment from one's feelings, as when Emerson says of his son's death, "I cannot get it nearer to me." Neurasthenia is a condition of physical and mental exhaustion, commonly known today as chronic fatigue syndrome. "Sleep lingers all our lifetime about our eyes, as night hovers all day in the boughs of the fir-tree," he writes. "We are like millers on the lower levels of a stream, when the factories above them have exhausted the water."[22] Young Waldo's death induced both these conditions in his father, and Emerson courageously and honestly dealt with them. His essay also speaks to the human condition more universally.

First, every life has a tragic dimension that is usually hidden beneath the surface of daily life. In "Spiritual Laws," Emerson describes gloomy thoughts as "the soul's mumps and measles, and whooping-coughs," not worth being troubled about. In his reflective mood while writing this essay, he now acknowledges the shadow side of human existence. Second, we all experience the ebb and flow of life. Sometimes we feel the ebb more strongly than the flow. Depression and doubt eclipse self-confidence and creativity. We cannot see how to restore our sense of vitality. The only way out is through, as the saying goes. Emerson shows us in this essay how he found his way out of the labyrinth of despair. He models for his readers the truth of what he said in "The Transcendentalist," that "the path which the hero travels alone is the highway of health and benefit to mankind."[23] But each of us must find our own path.

"THE POET"

Although Emerson is most often thought of as a prose writer, he preferred to be known as a poet. In an 1835 letter written to his future wife, Lydia Jackson, he wrote the following: "I am born a poet, of a low class without doubt yet a poet. That is my nature and vocation. My singing be sure is very "husky," and is for the most part in prose. Still am I a poet in the sense of a perceiver and dear lover of the harmonies in the soul and in matter, and specially of the correspondences between these and those. A sunset, a forest, a snowstorm, a certain river-view, are more to me than many friends and do ordinarily divide my day with my books."[24] His poetry was published in three editions: *Poems* in 1847, *Mayday and Other Pieces* in 1867, and *Selected Poems* in 1876. He also wrote manuscript poems for most of his essays, as well as poetry that appears in his journals but did not find its way into print until much later. Adding together his published poems and those from his journals and essays, they amounted to more than five hundred altogether. His poetry deserves more appreciation than it has received. Victorian critics, such as Matthew Arnold, considered his poetry interesting but not of the highest caliber. Until recently, Arnold's assessment seems to have stuck.

In comparison with the popular American poets of his day—Henry Wadsworth Longfellow, James Russell Lowell, and Edgar Allan Poe, for example—Emerson's poetry seems enigmatic and philosophical. His critics called his prosody awkward and his rhymes strained. But his best poems—"The Sphinx," "Days," Brahma," "Threnody," "Hamatreya," and many others—elevate him as a poet above most of his contemporaries. He was a Romantic poet, influenced by Wordsworth and Coleridge, whose poetry was symbolic, subjective, and conveyed "a Feeling of the Infinite," as Emerson put it in "Thoughts on Modern Literature."[25]

For Emerson, the poet is a bard who enjoys "an original relation to the universe" and draws inspiration directly from the font of wisdom, as he says in "Thoughts on Modern Literature." The irony is that he worked and reworked his poems until he felt them ready for publication. He applied the word "poetry" to every kind of writing that he found inspiring, even to philosophical prose. In his "Divinity School Address" he had admonished preachers to be "a newborn bard of the Holy Ghost."[26] To Emerson, all inspired expression is oracular and, in this sense, poetic.

His poetry explores a wide variety of themes. Some of it is personal, such as "Threnody," a poem about his son's death. Nature is another common theme, as in "Woodnotes I & II." Some poems address social and political issues, as in "Boston Hymn," celebrating the Emancipation Proclamation. As with "Each and All," others are mystical in nature. Some of his poems, like "Brahma," express his religious cosmopolitanism, while others, such as "The Problem," recount his rift with the church and historical Christianity.

On the second floor of the Emerson House in Concord hangs a large print, yellowed with age, of one of his own favorite poems, "Days."

"Emerson was haunted for most of his life by the sense that the days were slipping past him, one by one, in an irrevocable procession. He seldom felt he had made the fullest possible use of a day," according to literary historian, Robert D. Richardson Jr.[27] He expressed this feeling in the most spiritual of all his poems:

> Daughters of Time, the hypocritic Days,
> Muffled and dumb, like barefoot dervishes,
> And marching single in an endless file,
> Bring diadems and fagots in their hands.
> To each they offer gifts after his will,
> Bread, kingdoms, stars, or sky that holds them all.
> I, in my pleached garden, watched the pomp,
> Forgot my morning wishes, hastily
> Took a few herbs and apples, and the Day
> Turned and departed silent. I, too late,
> Under her solemn fillet saw the scorn.[28]

Emerson begins "The Poet" by observing that much of what passes for criticism in the arts is shallow. Most critics judge individual works of art by comparing them with ones that are commonly admired. "It is a proof of the shallowness of the doctrine of beauty, as it lies in the minds of our amateurs, that men seem to have lost the perception of the instant dependence of form upon soul," he says. "There is no doctrine of forms in our philosophy." This is a reference to Plato, who argued that ideal forms and not the material world are the ultimate reality. Our criticism does not rise to that level. Instead we judge things on a material basis. "We are not pans and [wheel] barrows, nor even porters of the fire and torch-bearers, but children of the fire, made of it, and only the same divinity transmuted, and at two or three removes, when we know least about it."[29] The poet is a child of the fire, who, like Prometheus, brings that fire to the rest of us.

We may be able to perceive the "supersensual" reality of the material world, but most of us cannot adequately express it. "The poet is the sayer, the namer, and represents beauty." It is the poet who sees beauty in the world and gives it expression. We "hear those primal warblings, and attempt to write them down," but fail to do them justice. The poet, "of more delicate ear," writes "down these cadences more faithfully." He is a prophet who "announces that which no man foretold."[30]

Emerson famously says that "it is not metres, but a metre-making argument that makes a poem." Thought precedes form. Another way of expressing this idea is the distinction Emerson often makes between genius and talent. Genius is inspiration and imagination; talent is craft and technique. "Talent may frolic and juggle," he says, but "genius realizes and adds." True poetry is a work of genius, transporting us "above these clouds and opaque airs" in which we live, giving us knowledge of what is really real.[31]

"The Universe is the externalization of the soul," Emerson says. Through the objects of the natural world, which the poet uses as symbols and signs, we are acquainted with the soul. The poet has better perception than do we and stands nearer to the essence of things. This keener insight is called "imagination," "a very high sort of seeing which does not come by study, but by the intellect being where and what it sees, by sharing the path, or circuit of things through forms, and so making them translucid to others." It is by abandonment, "suffering the ethereal tides to roll and circulate through him," that the poet's words become "universally intelligible." It is only when the poet "speaks somewhat wildly, or, 'with the flower of the mind,'" thereby liberating the intellect, that he speaks adequately.[32]

Emerson has a bardic theory of poetry. The poet is a conduit or mouthpiece of the spirit, announcing truths revealed as if in a trance. This is why bards love such stimulants as wine, incense, and drugs. They seek to ravish the intellect in order to come nearer the source of inspiration. "These are auxiliaries to the centrifugal tendency of a man, to his passage out into free space, and they help him to escape the custody of that body in which he is pent up." But intoxicants are only a trick, he says. They produce a counterfeit excitement. "The sublime vision comes to the pure and simple soul in a clean and chaste body."[33]

The imagination that intoxicates the poet is latent in the rest of us. The poet's use of symbols can emancipate and excite us, as though touched by a magic wand. "We are like persons who come out of a cave or cellar into the open air," Emerson observes. "This is the effect on us of tropes, fables, oracles, and all poetic forms. Poets are thus liberating gods." If poetry is not "transcendental and extraordinary," it has little value. We are like a poor shepherd, who, blinded by a blizzard, perishes within a few feet of his cottage. "On the brink of the waters of life and truth, we are miserably dying."[34] We revere the poet who can inspire us and awaken our slumbering spirits.

The mystic uses a symbol in just one sense, which is true for a moment perhaps but soon becomes false. "Mysticism consists in the mistake of an accidental and individual symbol for an universal one." Religion suffers from making symbols too literal and rigid. Emerson compares symbols to ferries, "for conveyance," rather than farms, "for homestead." Poetic language should be "vehicular and transitive."[35] For the poet, the imagination must flow, not freeze.

Emerson long searched in vain for this bardic type of poet. As he said in his "American Scholar" address, he wanted American writers to find their own voices and reflect their own experiences, not always look to European literature for models. In 1855, a little-known poet named Walt Whitman sent him a copy of *Leaves of Grass*. The book had been published a few months earlier, with thirty-two poems in the first edition. (The number grew to more than four hundred in the last edition, published in 1892.) Emerson was impressed. In a letter to Whitman, he wrote, "I find it the most extraordinary piece of wit and wisdom that America has yet contributed. I am very happy in reading it, as great power makes us happy. It meets the demand I am always making of what seemed the sterile and stingy nature, as of too much handiwork, or too much lymph in the temperament, were making our western wits fat and mean. . . . I greet you at the beginning of a great career."[36]

In his preface to the first edition of *Leaves of Grass*, Whitman writes, "The greatest poet has less a marked style and is more the channel of thoughts and things without increase or diminution, and is the free channel of himself. . . . I will not have in my writing any elegance or effect or originality to hang in the way between me and the rest like curtains." Given all that Emerson had written about ecstasy, abandonment, and "shooting the gulf," he must have nodded in approval when he read in Whitman's preface that the grandeur of nature and human existence is "something in the soul which says, Rage on, Whirl on, I tread master here and everywhere, Master of the spasms of the sky and of the shatter of the sea, Master of nature and passion and death, And of all terror and all pain."[37]

In the conclusion of "The Poet," Emerson urges the aspiring poet to find symbolism in everything. "Nothing walks, or creeps, or grows, or exists, which must not in turn arise and walk before him as exponent of his meaning." He has the whole world to choose from: "Wherever snow falls, or water flows, or birds fly, wherever day and night meet in twilight, wherever the blue heaven is hung by clouds, or sown with stars, wherever are forms with transparent boundaries, wherever are outlets into celestial space, wherever is danger, and awe, and love, there is Beauty, plenteous as rain, shed for thee, and though thou shouldst walk the world over, thou shalt not be able to find a condition inopportune or ignoble."[38] Nothing escaped Whitman's attention or failed to symbolize spiritual reality. He, like Emerson, sought the miraculous in the common, as shown in these lines from *Leaves of Grass*:

> I believe a leaf of grass is no less than the journeywork of the stars,
> And the pismire is equally perfect, and a grain of sand, and the egg of
> the wren,
> And the tree-toad is a chef-d'ouvre for the highest,
> And the running blackberry would adorn the parlors of heaven,
> And the narrowest hinge in my hand puts to scorn all machinery,
> And the cow crunching with depressed head surpasses any statue,
> And a mouse is miracle enough to stagger sextillions of infidels,
> And I come home every afternoon of my life to look at the farmer's girl
> boiling her iron tea-kettle and baking shortcake.[39]

In Whitman, Emerson found the poet he had been looking for.

"NEW ENGLAND REFORMERS"

For one whose reformist impulses have often been questioned, Emerson lectured a lot about reform. He returned to this subject in the last essay in the second volume, titled "New England Reformers." As in previous lectures on the subject, he notes the wide variety of reform efforts of the time: temperance, nonresistance, abolition, socialism, and more. "What a fertility of projects for the salvation of the world," Emerson remarks. "One apostle thought all men should go to farming; and another, that no man should buy or sell: that the use of money was the cardinal evil; another, that the mischief was in our diet, that we eat and drink damnation. These made unleavened bread, and were foes to the death of fermentation."[40] The list goes on and on. The fervor that moral people once devoted to the church they now directed toward social change.

Emerson welcomes the scrutiny of existing institutions and societal structures. He observes a contest between what he calls "mechanical and spiritual methods" and notes "a steady tendency of the thoughtful and virtuous to a deeper belief and reliance on spiritual facts."[41] He offers the example of capitalism, which widens the disparity between wealth and poverty. When society is organized around accumulating money, it creates false relations between people of greater and lesser means. Similarly, when we base our educational system around accumulating knowledge, much of it useless, rather than the cultivation of character, the soul is lost.

Emerson approves of those who reject materialism in favor of a spiritual approach to improving both institutions and human relations. But he worries that the reformers are not up to the task. "They are partial," he says, "they are not equal to the work they pretend." Consumed by their singular focus, they lose their way and fail in the effort. "The criticism and attack on institutions which we have witnessed, has made one thing plain, that society gains nothing whilst a man, not himself renovated, attempts to renovate things around him: he has become tediously good in some particular, but negligent or narrow in the rest."[42]

Too often reformers try to solve a problem by forming an association. Emerson questions the influence of communitarian social theorists, such as Henri de Saint-Simon (1760–1825), Charles Fourier (1772–1837), and Robert Owen (1771–1858), who sought to establish human community on an egalitarian basis. He fears associations privilege compliance over freedom. If they consist of people not themselves renovated, they are doomed to fail. The assumption seems to be, he observes, "I have failed, and you have failed, but perhaps together we shall not fail. Our housekeeping is not satisfactory to us, but perhaps a phalanx, a community, might be." Group effort is only effective when it is made up of self-reliant individuals: "What is the use of the concert of the false and disunited? There can be no concert in two, where there is no concert in one. When the individual is not individual, but is dual; when his thoughts look one way, and his actions another; when his faith is traversed by his habits; when his will, enlightened by reason, is warped by his sense; when with one hand he rows, and with the other backs water, what concert can be?"[43]

Both the evils of society and the failure of reforms to correct them follow from a lack of faith in self-culture. "We do not think we can speak to divine sentiments in man, and we do not try," Emerson tells us. "We renounce all high aims. We believe that the defects of so many perverse and so many frivolous people, who make up society, are organic, and society is a hospital of cripples." People seek comfort in churches and amusements in society. "Having settled ourselves into this infidelity, our skill is expended to procure alleviations, diversions, opiates." But the remedy is spiritual. "Life must be lived on a higher plane. We must go up to a higher platform, to which we are always invited to ascend; there, the whole aspect of things changes." The materialists and educated elites may doubt that people generally are capable of doing this, but Emerson pushes back on their skepticism: "I do not believe that the differences of opinion and character [in people are] organic."[44] We are all capable of discerning and responding to the intuitions of Reason.

The truth is, we want to be shaken out of our sense of complacency. "We are weary of gliding ghostlike through the world," Emerson observes, "which is itself so slight and unreal. We crave a sense of reality, though it come in strokes of pain." We all wish to be convicted of our error and come to ourselves. We want to be lifted to that higher platform so we may see, beyond our current fear, the "transalpine good." We cling to our possessions, "although we confess, that our being does not flow through them." Unbeknownst to us, "there is a power over and behind us, and we are the channels of its communications." Opening a channel to this reality is the answer to our unbelief and the awakening of our powers. "Shall not the heart which has received so much, trust the Power by which it lives? May it not quit other leadings, and listen to the Soul that has guided it so gently, and taught it so much, secure that the future will be worthy of the past?"[45]

Reading the highly introspective essay "Experience" alongside the outward-looking "New England Reformers" in the same volume may feel incongruous. But there is no dichotomy between introspection and social action. They are integrally related. The dis-ease we feel in ourselves is both a reflection and a cause of the dis-ease we witness in society. The solution to both is opening a channel to the soul and living life on a higher plane. The two essays are linked by a sense of alienation from both self and society. Emerson uses the word "ghostlike" in both essays to describe this condition. In both he welcomes a jolt of pain to make us realize that we are alive. In the face of the death of his child and a growing realization of the enormity of slavery, he has suffered the loss of "the affirmative principle."

Many of Emerson's readers see the essays in the second series—"Experience," especially—as a turning point in his spiritual journey from the "Saturnalia of Faith" of his earlier years to a benign surrender to skepticism and the power of fate.[46] Others have described it as a transition from idealism to pragmatism. Still others have claimed it marks the passage from Emerson, the scholar, to Emerson, the reformer.[47] For all of us the ecstasies of our youth fade with age. In Emerson's case, these ecstatic moments became increasingly rare. But he never gave up hope. "Up again, old heart!" he says, "there is victory yet."

Rather than pragmatism, what these essays highlight is Emerson's Stoicism. In youth his Aunt Mary had introduced him to the aphorisms of Marcus Antoninus, otherwise known as Marcus Aurelius, author of *Meditations*, a book that was never far from his desk. Antoninus was an ethical philosopher of the Stoic school. In a series of lectures on literature given in the winter of 1835, Emerson called attention to "a class of writers who carry an antidote against oblivion in the very direction of their thought, who address certain feelings and faculties in us which are alike in all men and which no progress of arts and no variety of institutions can alter; those writers, namely, who have not to do with opinions but with Principles; those who write not upon local institutions or particular men and to particular ends but to the general nature of man."[48] The Stoics, including Epictetus, Seneca, Antoninus, and others, were of this class of writers.

Contrary to popular belief, Stoicism does not teach resignation. It is not a surrender to fate but a response to fate. It will not let fate have the last word. The Stoics were guided by two principles: act according to nature, and the present only is our happiness. All things proceed from the same source, including what appear to be the accidents of fate. Antoninus says, "Be mindful at all times of the following: the nature of the whole universe, the nature of the part that is me, the relation of the one to the other, the one so vast, the other so small. No one can ever prevent me from saying and doing what is in complete conformity with the whole of which I am so small yet integral a part." Of the second principle, Antoninus writes: "Were you to live three thousand years, or even thirty thousand, remember that a man can lose only the life he is living, and he can live no other life than the one he loses. Whether he lives a long time or a short time amounts to the same thing, for the present moment is of equal duration for everyone, and that is all any man possesses."[49]

In his perceptive review of *Essays: Second Series* in the *Christian Examiner*, Frederic Hedge wrote, "What pleases us best in this chapter ['Experience'], is the strong emphasis which it gives to the present momentary life. This is not an article peculiar to the Emersonian philosophy. It is one, perhaps the only one, in which all philosophies unite. . . . But we have met no statement of this doctrine so adequate to our conception of it, as Mr. Emerson's in this essay."[50] Faced with his personal losses and mindful of the transience of life, Emerson sought solace in Stoicism. In his journal many years earlier, he said of Stoicism that it is for nothing if it "cannot set the soul on an equilibrium when it leans to the earth under the pressure of calamity."[51] I believe he found that it did.

Emerson never gave up trying to reconcile the dilemma of double consciousness, knowing those attempts would always be incomplete. Nor did he succumb to skepticism or resignation. He acknowledged the claims of science, the advance of materialism, the brutality of civil war, and the pain of personal tragedy, but he always viewed events from the perspective of the Reason. He never ceased to be, at heart, a Transcendentalist.

8

AN EASTERN EDUCATION

One of Emerson's many legacies to those who came after him was a spiritual cosmopolitanism that enriched and enlarged on the Western religious tradition he had inherited. His interest in other faiths and philosophies went much deeper than mere curiosity. He studied them, not as a scholar might—although he understood and appreciated them better than most of his contemporaries—but as a spiritual seeker, looking for insight and inspiration wherever he could find it. He believed the spiritual teachings of India, China, and the Middle East were part of a perennial wisdom, growing out of shared truths. As he said in his "Divinity School Address" in 1838: "This thought dwelled always deepest in the minds of men in the devout and contemplative East: not alone in Palestine, where it reached its purest expression, but in Egypt, in Persia, in India, in China."[1] As time went on, he became even more convinced that every religion was rooted in a common spiritual impulse.

HINDU TEACHINGS

In July 1840, Emerson wrote the following in a letter to his friend Samuel Gray Ward: "In the sleep of the great heats there was nothing for me but to read the Vedas, the bible of the tropics, which I find I come back upon every three or four years. It is sublime as heat and night and a breathless ocean. It contains every religious sentiment, all the grand ethics which visit in turn each noble and poetic mind. . . . It is of no use to put away the book: if I trust myself in the woods or in a boat upon the pond, nature makes a Bramin of me presently: eternal necessity, eternal compensation, unfathomable power, unbroken silence—this is her creed."[2] His early curiosity about Hinduism had turned into a passion. He was reading everything he could get his hands on: the Upanishads, the Laws of Manu, the Bhagavad Gita, and extracts from the *Rig-Veda*. He copied out passages from these into his journal and quoted them in his lectures and essays.[3]

Emerson first encountered some of this literature at age seventeen in preparation for the Harvard senior class poem he delivered in 1821, titled "Indian Superstition." He also referenced Hinduism in his Bowdoin Prize dissertation, "The Present State of Ethical Philosophy," the same year. Even though he showed his youthful Western prejudice by referring to the "superstitions" of Indian society, he already ranked their moral teachings superior to the petty penances of medieval Catholicism. "The Hindoo had gone far beyond them in his moral estimates," he wrote in his student dissertation. "'If thou be not,' says the lawgiver Menu, 'at variance, by speaking falsely, with Yama, the subduer of all, with Vaivaswata, the punisher, with that great divinity who dwells in the breast, go not on a pilgrimage to the river Ganga, nor to the plains of Curu, for thou hast no need of expiation.'"[4] In other words, the pure of heart have no need of penances.

The reference to Menu (usually spelled Manu) is especially significant for the fact that *The Institutes of Hindu Law, Or, The Ordinances of Manu*, translated by English philologist Sir William Jones in 1794, was one of the first Indian books Emerson read. He mentioned it often in his journals, lectures, and essays. He cited several passages in his 1836 lecture series The Philosophy of History as examples of the universality of the moral sentiment. He also copied fifty-two verses from the work into his 1840 notebook. The ones he selected praise humility, nonviolence, simplicity, solitude, detachment, conscience, equanimity, virtuous living, and the study of the scriptures. One entry perhaps influenced his concept of the oversoul, which he wrote about the following year: "The man who perceives in his own soul the supreme soul present in all creatures, acquires equanimity toward them all, and shall be absorbed at last in the highest essence, even that of the Almighty himself."[5]

Some scholars, including Frederic Ives Carpenter, have argued that Emerson's acquaintance with these Hindu scriptures actually followed the publication of "The Over-Soul" and did not greatly influence it. Plotinus was the more likely source. But judging from Emerson's notes on his reading prior to writing "The Over-Soul," we know he was familiar with the concept, if not to the extent he later came to learn.[6]

Over time, other Hindu scriptures became more influential on Emerson's thinking, but the Laws of Manu initially attracted Emerson's attention because it is a treatise largely about moral self-cultivation. Dating to sometime between the second century BCE and the third century CE, the book is a compendium of duties, rites, conduct, and ethical precepts essential to virtuous living. Emerson would have dismissed many of the injunctions regarding gender and class in the book, but the emphasis on moral self-cultivation was in line with the Unitarian program of self-culture.

Emerson was especially drawn to the Vedanta school of philosophy, one of the six schools of classical Hindu thought—and the monistic, nondualistic perspective of the Advaita tradition within that school. The principal texts of the Vedanta school are the Upanishads, *Brahma Sutras*, and the Bhagavad Gita. Emerson was familiar with them all, especially the Gita. In Vedanta teachings he found confirmation of his own beliefs relating to the oversoul (Atman/Brahman), compensation (karma), and illusion (maya).

The Advaita Vedanta school of Indian philosophy has both theoretical and practical principles, as do other philosophies of self-cultivation. On the theoretical side, it is a fundamental teaching of Vedanta that the true self of the individual (Atman) is identical with the highest metaphysical reality (Brahman). Enlightenment is achieved through knowledge of one's true nature, the identity of Atman and Brahman. The illusion of maya—that is, mistaking empirical reality, or the world of appearances, for ultimate reality, or Brahman—hinders us from this realization. In the Advaita teaching, the everyday world is not illusory or a dream but a lower order of knowledge and experience. It is the realm in which our spiritual self-development takes place.

Our self-development is aided by the practice of *jnana* yoga, the pathway of knowledge, or self-realization. This consists of attitudes and behaviors, the goal of which is *moksha*, or spiritual liberation—the annihilation of the ego and the realization of the true self. The enlightened person continued to live in the world but was no longer ensnared by the delusions of maya. "The wise man beholds all beings in the Self, and the Self in all beings," according to the *Isa-Upanishad*. "To the seer, all things have verily become the Self: what delusion, what sorrow, can there be for him who beholds that oneness?"[7]

The Bhagavad Gita occupied a central place in Emerson's library of Hindu texts. Composed sometime between the fifth and second centuries BCE, it is part of a much longer work, the *Mahabharata,* an epic tale of the conflict between two ruling families. In the Gita, Arjuna, a great warrior, has family on both sides and is therefore reluctant to join the battle between them. His charioteer Krishna, a Hindu god in disguise, tells Arjuna that victory and defeat are one and the same. "He who considers this Self as a slayer or he who thinks that this Self is slain, neither of these knows the Truth. For It does not slay nor is It slain."[8] No doubt, Emerson was thinking of this verse when he wrote one of his most famous poems, "Brahma":

> If the red slayer think he slays,
> Or if the slain think he is slain,
> They know not well the subtle ways
> I keep, and pass, and turn again.[9]

Throughout the Gita, Krishna's discourses with Arjuna illustrate Vedanta teachings and practices.

Emerson's essay "Plato" comes closest to expressing his deep attraction to Indian spirituality. It is one of seven essays in his book *Representative Men*, published in 1850, based on a series of lectures from the winter of 1845. Each of the essays profiles a historical figure who exemplifies a way of being in the world. "Plato is philosophy, and philosophy is Plato," Emerson writes. More specifically, Plato is the voice of the monistic point of view, the idea that the mind, or soul, and the body are one. At the base of philosophy are "two cardinal facts," Emerson says, "the One; and the two. 1. Unity or Identity; and 2. Variety."[10] Plato is the philosopher of unity.

Emerson presents Plato's thought in the context of a perennial philosophy, the view that all the world's spiritual traditions share a common origin or core set of beliefs. Hindu thought exemplifies this perennial wisdom: "In all nations, there are minds which incline to dwell in the conception of the fundamental Unity. The raptures of prayer and ecstasy of devotion lose all beings in one Being. This tendency finds its highest expression in the religious writings of the East, and chiefly in the Indian scriptures, in the Vedas, the Bhagavat Geeta, and the Vishnu Purana. Those writings contain little else than this idea, and they rise to pure and sublime strains in celebrating it." All things share a common identity. They are of one stuff. Quoting the *Vishnu Purana* in "Plato," Emerson writes, "The whole world is but a manifestation of Vishnu, who is identical with all things, and is to be regarded by the wise as not differing from, but as the same as, themselves. I neither am going or coming, nor is my dwelling in any one place, nor art thou, thou, nor are others, others; nor am I, I."[11]

The one and the many, monism and dualism, represent two modes of thought. Emerson identifies the first with the East and the second with the West, and he suggests that Plato was influenced by Eastern thought. "Plato, in Egypt and in Eastern pilgrimages, imbibed the idea of one Deity, in which all things are absorbed. The unity of Asia and the detail of Europe, the infinitude of the Asiatic soul, and the defining, result-loving, machine-making, surface-seeking, operagoing Europe, Plato came to join, and, by contact, to enhance the energy of each."[12]

In a reference to Plato's *Phaedrus*, in which a charioteer must control two charging horses, one Beauty and the other Chaos, with the reins in his hands, Emerson writes, "The two poles appear, yes, and become two hands to grasp and appropriate their own."[13] Plato presents a bipolar unity, in Emerson's view. The two elements do not represent a dualism but a hybrid monism. He seeks balance between the two, rather than diametrical opposition.

Emerson, too, habitually strives to reconcile opposites—Reason and Understanding, solitude and society, repose and action—but in a dynamic way. He does not seek equilibrium. Energy is produced in their alteration, or undulation, passing from one to another, as in his favorite image, "shooting the gulf." The reconciliation is never final or complete. "So it fares with all," he says, "so it must fare with Plato. In view of eternal Nature, Plato turns out to be philosophical exercitations. He argues on this side, and on that."[14] And so does Emerson.

His Indian studies confirmed for him the notion of identity: *tat tvam asi*, in the Vedanta teaching, translated as "that art thou" or "you are that." They also reinforced the distinction between appearance and reality. The Hindu goddess, Maya, was responsible for the appearance of variety. As Emerson observed in a journal entry, "In the history of intellect no more important fact than the Hindoo theology, teaching that the beatitude or supreme good is to be attained through science; namely by the perception of the real and unreal, setting aside matter, and qualities, and affections or emotions and persons, as Maias or illusions, and thus arriving at the contemplation of the one eternal Life and Cause, and a perpetual approach and assimilation to Him, thus escaping new births or transmigration."[15] Maya is often understood as illusion, although not in the sense that the world does not exist or is simply a figment of the imagination. The infinite is hidden behind the finite. We confuse what is *real* (spiritual reality) with what is *actual* (the phenomenal world). Saying the phenomenal world is an appearance, or *maya*, does not mean the phenomenal world does not exist. Rather, it is to assert that the spiritual takes precedence over the material, just as the Reason takes precedence over the Understanding. Emerson's own view aligned closely with the Vedanta teaching that reality is spiritual: "In our definitions, we grope after the *spiritual* by describing it as invisible. The true meaning of *spiritual* is *real*."[16]

Similarly, his own idea of compensation aligned closely with the Hindu concept of karma. The doctrine of karma teaches that our actions have consequences, for good or ill. Like the Hindus, Emerson believed self-enforcing moral laws govern the universe. We reap what we sow, as the Bible puts it. However, while Emerson believed evildoers are punished in this life, Hinduism says that retribution is enacted in the next one, through reincarnation. Emerson believed the soul is eternal but did not believe in a personal afterlife. Criminals do sometimes get away with their crimes, and to suggest that they are punished by feelings of remorse does not achieve justice, nor does it comfort their victims. But in our personal everyday lives we often suffer for our mistakes, and retribution does occur through the attitudes other people, including our loved ones, take toward us. In a psychological sense, karma, like compensation, does govern our behavior.

Finally, Vedanta reinforced Emerson's idea of nature as a dynamic, self-generating process. In 1851 he recorded a Hindu fable into his journal illustrating "the flying force" that propels all creation: "As Vishnu in the Vedas pursues Maya in all forms, when to avoid him, she changes herself into a cow, then he into a bull; she into a doe, he into a buck; she into a mare, he into a stallion; she into a hen, he into a cock, and so forth;

so our metaphysics should be able to follow the flying force through all transformations, and name the new pair, identical thro' all variety."[17] Vedanta teaching emphasized the vitalism of nature. The nondualistic Advaita school located that vitalism within nature itself. In doing so it validated subjective idealism in contrast to objective idealism, which was also an important development in Emerson's own thinking.

By the 1840s Emerson had left Christian theism far behind. His search for answers to life's perennial questions—Who are we? Where do we find ourselves? What is expected of us?—led him eastward to discover wisdom beyond his Unitarian heritage. His reading of Indian scriptures, as well as Chinese and Middle Eastern literature, enriched his spiritual life and infused his writing from that point on.

CONFUCIAN TEACHINGS

Confucius (551 BC–479 BC), like Emerson, was a moral philosopher who believed that character is developed through the practice of self-culture. Benevolence was the highest virtue, in the Confucian view. A person who exhibited benevolence was known as a sage. Benevolence was not a given, however. It was attained through the practice of rites and knowledge of the Four Books comprising the core teachings of Confucius: *The Analects of Confucius*, *The Great Learning*, *The Doctrine of the Mean*, and the *Book of Mencius*.

Some scholars have been dismissive of the influence of Confucianism on Emerson. An example is again Frederic Ives Carpenter, who observes that Chinese literature epitomized formalism and lacked "the progressive element," in contrast to Emerson's philosophy. Although Emerson gained much from his reading, Carpenter concludes that "his prevailing attitude is decidedly not one of enthusiasm."[18] Yet Emerson, in his own words, tells a different story. In a speech given at the reception for the Chinese Embassy in Boston in 1868, Emerson said, "Confucius has not yet gathered all his fame. . . . [W]hat we call the Golden Rule of Jesus, Confucius had uttered in the same terms, five hundred years before. His morals, though addressed to a state of society utterly unlike ours, we read with profit to-day. His rare perception appears in his Golden Mean, his doctrine of Reciprocity, his unerring insight,—putting always the blame of our misfortunes on ourselves."[19]

Scholars have often failed to distinguish between the teachings of Confucius himself and the modifications of his teachings by a succession of followers in the Confucian tradition. Emerson first encountered Chinese philosophy in 1830 in Joseph-Marie de Gérando's encyclopedia of philosophy. He read *The Analects of Confucius* in 1836, a complete version of the Four Books in 1843, and then James Legge's translation of them in 1863. Emerson quoted passages from these books in several of his essays, but the similarity between the views of Emerson and Confucian philosophy is deeper and more extensive than that.

Zhu Xi ([or Chu Hsi] 1130–1200) was an interpreter and compiler of the Confucian classics and is considered the second most influential thinker in Chinese history. His commentaries on the classics were influential in establishing the examination system in China. Confucianism had undergone major modifications between its beginnings in the fifth century BCE and the Song dynasty (960–1279 CE), when Zhu Xi lived. In its earlier period, Confucianism centered on the study of a different set of books, called the Five Classics: *The Book of Changes*, *The Book of Odes*, *The Book of Documents*, *The Book of Rites*, and *The Spring and Autumn Annals*. The Five Classics "describe in detail how one should conduct oneself in life's various objective situations; and prescribe at length the ritualistic practices for maintaining a well-ordered society," according to Chinese scholar Daniel K. Gardner. In this respect, their function is similar to that of *The Ordinances of Manu* in Hinduism.

Zhu Xi altered the focus of Confucian philosophy by promoting the study of the Four Books over of the Five Classics. The Four Books are less concerned with formalism and rituals, emphasizing instead "the nature of man, the springs or inner source of his morality, and his relation to the larger cosmos," Gardner writes. This move away from the Five Classics to the Four Books "thus represents an 'inward' shift on the part of the literati toward texts in the canon that treat more deliberately the inner realm of human morality."[20]

In the preface to his study of the *Conversations of Master Chu* [Zhu Xi], Gardner notes, "Chu's central concern was how man could learn to be a sage, that is, to be fully moral." He believed that all human beings were innately moral, but that morality required cultivation for one to be fully human. He developed a systematic, step-by-step program for perfecting the self. The first step in this program was "establishing the principle in things," which involved the study of nature and human knowledge, including the Four Books. "Since man shared the moral principle with everything else in the world, study of other things and apprehension of the principle inhering in them would lead to an understanding of the same principle inhering in oneself. Study was thus the road to self-awakening, the process of returning to one's true self; for Chu Hsi its aim was never the acquisition of knowledge for its own sake."[21] Clearly, there is a similarity between Chu's teaching and Emerson's idea that the moral sentiment is innate and that character is developed through self-culture.

Many people view morality as following rules or laws laid down by religion or the state, that is, by some exterior authority. Both Emerson and Zhu rejected this idea. In one of his later essays, "Character," Emerson relates this story from *The Analects*: "Confucius said one day to Ke Kang: 'Sir, in carrying on your government, why should you use killing at all? Let your evinced desires be for what is good, and the people will be good. The grass must bend, when the wind blows across it.' Ke Kang, distressed about the number of thieves in the state, inquired of Confucius how to do away with them. Confucius said, 'If you, sir, were not covetous, although you should reward them to do it, they would not steal.'"[22]

Character, for Emerson, acts in a similar manner as it does for Confucius. "There is no end to the sufficiency of character," Emerson says.[23] Confucianism also says that character developed through self-cultivation is sufficient or efficacious because one has power (*de*) to affect others by setting an example for them to follow.[24] This power is a kind of charisma—such as Nelson Mandela and Mahatma Gandhi had—that inspires others to practice benevolence, compassion, courage, and justice. In the passage just above that Emerson cited, the grass/wind metaphor ("the grass must bend, when the wind blows across it") illustrates the influence the sage has over others. It is one of the most famous passages in the Confucian tradition.[25] Ultimately, this power comes from being in accord with the Way, or the *Tao*, of the universe.

One of the selections from the Four Books that Emerson and Henry David Thoreau chose for their Ethical Scriptures column in the *Dial* magazine discusses the influence of the sage: "The superior man's nature consists in this, that benevolence, justice, propriety, and wisdom, have their root in his heart, and are exhibited in his countenance. . . . Wherever the superior man passes, renovation takes place. The divine spirit which he cherishes above and below, flows on in extent and influence with heaven and earth."[26] Another example is a passage from the *Book of Mencius*, one of the Four Books, which Emerson quotes in "Experience": "'I fully understand language,' [Mencius] said, 'and nourish well my vast-flowing vigor.'—'I beg to ask what you call vast-flowing vigor?'—said his companion. 'The explanation,' replied Mencius, 'is difficult. This vigor is supremely great, and in the highest degree unbending. Nourish it correctly, and do it no injury, and it will fill up the vacancy between heaven and earth. This vigor accords with and assists justice and reason, and leaves no hunger.'"[27]

Mencius (372 BCE–289 BCE), who lived about two hundred years after Confucius, was a humanist who believed, as Emerson did, in the innate goodness of human nature. His primary concern was also moral self-cultivation. In Emerson's case, this meant the cultivation of the soul. Mencius expressed it as cultivating *qi*, translated as "vigor" in this passage. Qi is the vital energy that constitutes the entire universe and everything in it. Human beings are endowed with this "vast-flowing" energy, but if we fail to nurture it, we become spiritually malnourished. Given what Emerson has written about self-culture, the writings of Mencius would undoubtedly have appealed to him.[28]

The focus of later Confucian philosophers on the inner source of morality and the vitalism of nature plainly contrasts with the rules and rituals of early Confucianism. Many Western readers think of Confucianism as only the formalism of the Five Classics and are not familiar with the dynamism of the Four Books, which may account for the mistaken views of Carpenter and others that Emerson's philosophy does not align with Confucianism. In fact, Emerson repeatedly returned to his library of Confucian literature for inspiration throughout his career.

SUFI TEACHINGS

Many scholars have commented on Emerson's attraction to Persian poetry. Some have noted that this poetry is an expression of Sufi Muslim teaching. But few have examined the nature of its influence on Emerson's thinking. In all fairness, there isn't much to go on, not only because Emerson did not study it to the extent that he did Vedantism and Confucian philosophy, both of which offered him numerous scriptures to read and ponder, but also because he pursued Sufism primarily through its poetry, not its prose.

His introduction to the subject was *The Practical Philosophy of the Muhammadan People*, a fifteenth-century treatise on Islamic philosophy in which the English translator described Sufism as the "practical pantheism of Asia" and a pure form of idealism, "holding all visible and conceivable objects to be portions of the divine nature."[29] In addition, he read numerous anthologies of Persian poetry, including Joseph von Hammer's two-volume German-language edition of Hafiz's poetry, from which he translated many of the poet's works; Saadi's *The Gulistan; or Rose Garden*; *The Desatir, or Sacred Writings of the Ancient Persian Prophets*; and *Specimens of the Popular Poetry of Persia*.

Emerson relished the imagery of Persian verse, taken from nature and everyday life. He especially loved the exuberance and joy of living he found in the spiritual poetry of Saadi (1210–92) and Hafiz (1315–90). Both came from the city of Shiraz in Persia. Emerson wrote the essay "Saadi," which was published in the *Dial*, and another essay "Persian Poetry" for *Letters and Social Aims*. He translated from German anthologies many poems of Persian poets and often echoed Persian themes and prosody in his own poems.

Sufism is difficult to describe. It is more a kind of spirituality than a religion. It is commonly thought of as a third branch of Islam, along with Sunni and Shia. Like the others, it is rooted in the Koran and the teachings of Mohammad, but it became a religious movement centered in Persia (Iran) during the Islamic Golden Age, dating from the eighth to the fourteenth century. "The inner, mystical dimension of Islam, Sufism is a way of thinking and living that has some elements of what is sometimes called the perennial philosophy," writes Emerson scholar Robert D. Richardson Jr. "Sufis believe that the individual can draw closer to God and embrace the divine presence experientially in *this* life."[30]

Sufism is best expressed by a succession of poets, not only Saadi and Hafiz, but also Omar Khayyam (1048–1131), Rumi (1207–73), Attar of Nishapur (ca. 1145–ca. 1220), and many others. As Sufis, these poets resisted conforming to Islamic laws and customs, believing "that the mind suffers no religion and no empire but its own," as Emerson notes in his essay "Persian Poetry." He cites this verse as an example:

> Ask me not, as Muftis can,
> To recite the Alkoran;
> Well I love the meaning sweet,—
> I tread the book beneath my feet.[31]

Sufism was of two kinds: drunk and sober. Drunken Sufism was the revelation of an all-embracing unity and the imminence of God. Sober Sufism, on the other hand, was a vision of differentiated multiplicity and God's transcendence. The Persian poets were drunken Sufis, whose poetry appealed to Emerson's own antinomian streak. Like him, they believed that religion is neither law nor theology, neither creed nor ritual. Rather, it is the means by which one transcends the ego and becomes one with the Absolute. Omar Khayyam, author of the *Rubaiyat*, in his treatise "On the Knowledge of the Universal Principles of Existence," describes Sufis as knowers "who do not seek knowledge intellectually or discursively, but by the cleansing of their inner self and through purgation of their morals, they have cleansed their rational soul from the impurities of nature and incorporeal body. . . . For all that man lacks is due to the impurities of nature, for if the [spiritual] veil is lifted and the screen and the obstacle is removed, the truth of things as they really are becomes apparent."[32]

Classical Persian poetry consisted of, in Emerson's words, "gnomic verses, rules of life, conveyed in lively image, especially in an image addressed to the eye, and contained in a single stanza." The stanza was a quatrain: the first three lines set the scene, and the last conveys the message. Emerson himself translated some of these poems, including this one written by Hafiz:

> See how the roses burn!
> Bring wine to quench the fire!
> Alas! the flames come up with us,—
> We perish with desire.[33]

In this quatrain, roses symbolize desire, and wine symbolizes abandonment. Although both are earthly elements, they convey a spiritual message. We desire oneness with the Absolute. Through abandonment, we reach that oneness. Longer poems were often built from quatrains joined together, as in another of Hafiz's poems:

Drink wine, and the heaven
New lustre diffuses,
And doubt not that sinning
Has also its uses.

The Builder of heaven
Has sundered the earth,
So that no footway
Leads out of it forth:

On turnpikes of wonder
Wine leads the mind forth,
Straight, sideways & upward,
Southward, and north.

Stands the vault adamantine
Until the last day;
The wine-cup shall ferry
Thee o'er it away.[34]

Emerson was especially attracted to Persian poetry because it appealed to a side of him that yearned for release, not only from religious conformity but also from the constraints of his own typically reserved personality. The Persian poets celebrated ecstasy and self-reliance, cardinal virtues for Emerson himself. There is also a seize-the-day quality to their poetry, which he took to heart. In both essays, "Saadi" and "Persian Poetry," and in numerous journal entries he quotes the Koran: "To all men is their day of death appointed, and they cannot postpone or advance it one hour."[35] How precious, then, are the days we are given to enjoy and not to waste in worry, regret, or forgetfulness? The Persian poets were a constant reminder to Emerson of this wisdom from the East.

Emerson's education in Eastern religions and philosophies was extensive for his day, but it also had its limitations. For example, he mentions Buddhism in his journals, letters, and essays, but he often confuses it with Hinduism. In an 1843 letter to his close friend Elizabeth Hoar, he wrote, "The only other event is the arrival in Concord of the Bhagavat Gita, the much renowned book of Buddhism, extracts from which I have often admired, but never before held in my hands."[36] The Gita, of course, is a work of Hindu Vedic literature, not Buddhist.

To be fair, Buddhism received comparatively little attention in America before the 1860s, notes historian Thomas A. Tweed.[37] If mid-nineteenth-century Americans' knowledge of Buddhism was scant, information about Taoism was virtually nonexistent. The concept of the Tao, or the Way, was common to Confucianism and Taoism but was understood differently by the two traditions. For Confucius and his followers, the Tao was the highest ideal for human society, according to Japanese scholar Yoshio Takanashi. For the Taoists, it was the hidden source and shaping force of the natural order of things.[38] No doubt the Taoists would have intrigued Emerson, especially their emphasis on spontaneity and living according to nature.

Despite the gaps in his Eastern education, Emerson was deeply appreciative of the texts that were available to him. He, along with others in the Transcendentalist circle, including Lydia Maria Child, James Freeman Clarke, Elizabeth Peabody, Samuel Johnson, and Henry David Thoreau, set the stage for the explosion of American interest in world religions in the later nineteenth and twentieth centuries. Emerson studied these teachings and drew on them in the course of his own spiritual development.

9

A HIGHER LAW

Many have called Emerson a reluctant reformer. Although he often lectured on reform, he distanced himself from reformers and often denied pleas to join their causes. Single-issue activism was too limited, he said, and reformers were too strident. He believed, like Unitarians generally, that moral suasion and education were the best approaches to social change. The reform of society must begin with the reform of individuals, he stated in his lectures, and hearts must change before laws can be effective. "Society gains nothing whilst a man, not himself renovated, attempts to renovate things around him," he said in his lecture "New England Reformers."[1] As moralists, Emerson and the Unitarians insisted that only the total renovation of society, not piecemeal remedies, could rectify social evils. It is true that Emerson felt unsuited to the role of social reformer. He resented the intrusion of current events on his studies and writing. But two issues in particular called out for a response: abolition and women's rights.

ABOLITION

The evil of slavery was the more immediate issue. On a visit to Saint Augustine, Florida, in 1827 Emerson was horrified to witness an auction of enslaved persons. At a meeting of the local Bible Society, he could hear from outside the hall the auctioneer's voice: "'Going, gentlemen, Going!' And almost without changing our position we might aid in sending the scriptures into Africa or bid for 'four children without the mother who had been kidnapped therefrom.'"[2] He condemned the practice in his first sermon as a young minister. In 1836, when British author Harriet Martineau gave an antislavery speech that caused a furor in Boston, Emerson invited her to stay with him in Concord. Following the murder of abolitionist publisher Elijah P. Lovejoy in 1837, Emerson gave a speech in outrage. In an 1834 journal entry he wrote, "Democracy/Freedom has its root in the Sacred truth that every man hath in him the divine Reason." That is "the equality and the only equality of all men," and "because every man has within him somewhat really divine, therefore slavery is the unpardonable outrage it is."[3]

Several national events drove him to action. Beginning in 1836 Congress passed a series of "gag rules" that automatically tabled any petitions related to slavery without hearing them. Then in 1837, Texas, a vast slaveholding territory, petitioned for annexation to the United States. Texas annexation would upset the balance of slave and free states negotiated in the 1820 Missouri Compromise, which limited the spread of slavery and gave slave states control of Congress. The "three-fifths rule" in the U.S. Constitution—counting those enslaved as three-fifths of a person to determine legislative representation—already gave Southern slave states an unjust advantage, which they threatened to use to kill the compromise altogether.

EMANCIPATION IN THE BRITISH WEST INDIES

In 1844, at the urging of his wife, Lidian, Emerson accepted an invitation from the Concord Female Anti-Slavery Society to deliver an address commemorating the tenth anniversary of "Negro emancipation in the West Indies." The abolition movement was driven, to a significant degree, by female antislavery societies throughout New England. The one in Concord was especially influential because it was close to Boston and was led by Concord resident Mary Merrick Brooks, who was effective in attracting notable abolitionist speakers, such as Wendell Phillips and Frederick Douglass, to speak at local antislavery events. Lidian Emerson was a member of this group, as were Emerson's daughter Ellen, along with Abigail and Louisa May Alcott, and Henry Thoreau's mother, Cynthia, and sister, Helen.

The churches in Concord, fearful of controversy, were unwilling to host the event, so the crowd gathered in the Middlesex County courthouse in town. In defiance of church leaders, Henry Thoreau rang the bell of the Unitarian meetinghouse, summoning the town to come out to hear the address. Abolitionists William Lloyd Garrison and Frederick Douglass, who also spoke, agreed that Emerson's address was a great success.[4] From that point on, Emerson fully committed himself to anti-slavery activism.

Emerson began the address by describing the terrible conditions of servitude and the slow process by which the conscience of lawmakers was stirred to abolish slavery throughout the British colonies. In 1833 England passed the Slavery Abolition Act, which went into effect the following year, giving American abolitionists hope of a similar victory. Emerson's address stirred that hope further. He described the peaceful implementation of the policy and the backlash that followed. Sadly, he said, "the habit of oppression was not destroyed by a law and a day of jubilee. It soon appeared in all the islands, that the planters were disposed to use their old privileges . . . and exert the same licentious despotism as before."[5]

He blamed the market economy of Britain and America, "which streams into our ways of thinking, our laws, our habits, and our manners," for the resilience of slavery and the difficulty of abolishing it for good. Enslaving Africans was a boon to trade, making merchants rich and providing the citizens of slave-owning countries with a wonderfully comfortable, though massively unjust, standard of living: "We found it very convenient to keep them at work, since, by the aid of a little whipping, we could get their work for nothing but their board and the cost of whips. What if it cost a few unpleasant scenes on the coast of Africa? . . . The sugar they raised was excellent: nobody tasted blood in it. The coffee was fragrant; the tobacco was incense; the brandy made nations happy; the cotton clothed the world. What! all raised by these men, and no wages? Excellent! What a convenience! They seemed created by providence to bear the heat and the whipping, and make these fine articles." He was not talking only of the British. He was speaking to an American audience just as complicit in the slave trade as they were. "The rich men may walk in State-street [Boston's financial district], but they walk without honor; and the farmers may brag their democracy in the country, but they are disgraced men."[6] The British Slavery Abolition Act signaled a moral revolution. An appeal to conscience, not violence, brought it about. The same is possible here, Emerson insisted. Despite all he had previously said about associations, he praised the work of antislavery societies and urged his listeners to join in their actions.

"Not the least affecting part of this history of abolition, is, the annihilation of the old indecent nonsense about the nature of the negro," Emerson remarked. Their oppressors have propagated this myth: "The white has, for ages, done what he could to keep the negro in this hoggish state. His laws have been furies. It now appears, that the negro race is, more than any other, susceptible of rapid civilization." He concluded with this declaration: "The civility of no race can be perfect whilst another race is degraded. It is a doctrine alike of the oldest, and of the newest philosophy, that, man is one, and that you cannot injure any member, without a sympathetic injury to all the members."[7]

THE FUGITIVE SLAVE LAW

After his 1844 speech, Emerson became increasingly outspoken on the evil of slavery, the need for emancipation, and the dignity and worth of African Americans. He felt yet even more urgency after Congress passed the Fugitive Slave Act in 1850. The new law required Northern law enforcement officials and citizens to report and help return escaped enslaved persons to the South. Anyone who aided such a runaway with food or shelter could be fined and imprisoned. The act was part of a compromise worked out by Daniel Webster in hopes of preserving the Union. Emerson condemned the law in two important speeches.

In the first of these, in Concord in 1851, Emerson angrily denounced "Mr. Webster's treachery," forcing Massachusetts to abet slavery. He decried his fellow citizens' passive acceptance of it. This latest outrage, like "the illuminating power of a sheet lightning at midnight," will reveal the truth of the moral crisis this country faces, he said. "The whole wealth and power of Boston,—200,000 souls, and 180 millions of money,—are thrown into the scale of crime; and the poor black boy, whom the fame of Boston had reached in the recesses of a rice-swamp, on in the alleys of Savanna, on arriving here, finds all this force employed to catch him. The famous town of Boston is his master's hound. The learning of the Universities, the culture of elegant society, the acumen of lawyers, the majesty of the Bench, the eloquence of the Christian pulpit, the stoutness

of Democracy, the respectability of the Whig party, are all combined to
kidnap him."[8]

He listed the reasons the act was immoral. First, the right to liberty
is as inalienable as the right to life. A higher law supersedes an immoral
law. Our duty is to break it, he said, "at every hazard." Second, he said,
the law offends our compassion for the oppressed. "How can a law be
enforced that fines pity, and imprisons charity? As long as men have
bowels, they will disobey." Third, the act is contravened by existing laws.
In 1807 Congress had outlawed the importation of those enslaved, pun-
ishable with death. If it is a crime to import enslaved persons, it should
also be a crime to reenslave them and export them South. Fourth, it
requires citizens to commit immoral deeds. "Every person who touches
this business is contaminated." Finally, it does not achieve what Senator
Webster intended. Instead of preserving the Union, the Compromise of
1850 has driven a wedge between moral individuals and the law. It has
stirred dissent. "It has turned every dinner-table into a debating club,
and made every citizen a student of natural law."[9]

Webster had been considered "the best head in Congress, and the
champion of the interests of the northern seaboard." But he dishonored
himself with this act, Emerson charged. Those who once admired him
"have torn down his picture from the wall" and "thrust his speeches
into the chimney." Lacking compassion, Webster has acted as though
government exists only for the protection of property, enslaved persons
included. As Emerson graphically put it, "All the drops of his blood have
eyes that look downward."[10] Webster could not see that this law is sui-
cidal. It cannot be obeyed. It invites disunion.

"What shall we do?" Emerson asked. "First, abrogate this law; then
proceed to confine slavery to the slave states, and help them effectually
to make an end of it." Everything pleads for emancipation, either sending enslaved persons who had been freed to Liberia, an African nation
founded by the American Colonization Society, or simply purchasing
their freedom directly. The expense would not be too much, Emerson
asserted: "Every man in the world might give a week's work to sweep
this mountain of calamities out of the earth." Massachusetts may be
small, but so were Greece and Judea. They have furnished "the mind and
heart by which the rest of the world is sustained." Moral rectitude is an
immense power. The Fugitive Slave Law must be repealed, he exhorted

his listeners. And while it exists, it must be disobeyed. "Let us not lie, nor steal, nor help to steal; and let us not call stealing by any fine names, such as 'union' or 'patriotism.' Let us know, that not by the public, but by ourselves, our safety must be bought."[11]

By the time Emerson delivered his second speech on the Fugitive Slave Law in 1854, Congress had passed the Kansas-Nebraska Bill, which nullified the Missouri Compromise of 1820 and allowed new Western states to decide for themselves whether to allow slavery. The need to abolish slavery became even more urgent. People must now choose which side they will take, Emerson said: the side of principles, humanity, and justice, or the side of abuse, oppression, and chaos. Sadly, Webster chose the latter.

The law and the courts have failed, Emerson charged. "What is the use of guarantees provided by the jealousy of ages for the protection of liberty,—if these are made of no effect?" Churches have failed as well. One would expect that Christians would not keep enslaved persons, he said, but they do. "No forms, neither Constitutions nor laws nor covenants nor churches nor bibles, are of any use in themselves; the devil nestles comfortably into them all." None of these guarantees are of any use without honest people to obey them. Only if we are determined to do right, will justice be done. "For the Eternal constitution of the universe is on [our] side. It is of no use to vote down gravitation or morals. What is useful will last; whilst that which is hurtful to the world will sink beneath all the opposing forces which it must exasperate."[12]

To exploit the labor of others is to lose our humanity, he went on. To say "the negro is an inferior race" is an abomination. It "cuts out the moral eyes" and puts the lie to the good we think we do. Slavery will not persist forever, he prophesied, noting that "the spasms of nature are centuries and ages and will tax the faith of short-lived men. Slowly, slowly the avenger comes, but surely." We are the agents of that Providence, and we cannot stand on the sidelines. Our scholars and literary men "are lovers of liberty in Greece, and in Rome, and in the English Commonwealth, but they are very lukewarm lovers of the specific liberty of America in 1854." The lovers of liberty must be aggressive, not passive. He closed by praising the Anti-Slavery Society and urging his listeners to join its cause. "I hope we have come to the end of our unbelief," he said, and "have come to a belief that there is a Divine Providence in the world which will not save us but through our own co-operation."[13]

Emerson and his fellow antislavery activists were frustrated, not only by actions of the federal government but also by local opposition to their cause. In Boston, a vigilance committee assisted fugitive enslaved persons who had settled in the city or were on their way to Canada with food, clothing, shelter, work, or whatever they needed. Committee members also acted as bodyguards to protect antislavery speakers from unruly mobs. In May 1854 Anthony Burns, an enslaved person who had escaped, was arrested in the city. Those who escaped were still considered property of their owners and had no legal right to take their case to court, even in the North. The committee hatched an elaborate plan to break Burns out of his custody in the federal courthouse. Unfortunately, the effort failed, and Burns was sent back to the South.

At this point Emerson was spending a great deal of his time giving antislavery speeches and actively campaigning for an abolitionist candidate running for Congress. He delivered yet another lecture on slavery in Boston in 1855, which he subsequently delivered in New York, Philadelphia, and other cities. He started by acknowledging the exhaustion the abolitionists were feeling. "An honest man is soon weary of crying 'Thief!'" Yet, on slavery "one must write with a red hot iron to make any impression." Emerson lamented the complicity of the courts and the Boston elites in slavery. It had drained the moral pulse of society and eroded the norms on which democracy is based.[14]

The lecture was largely a reprise of his speeches on the Fugitive Slave Act. But where once he had criticized reformers, now he praised them. Where once he had counseled patience, now he urged action. Where once he had advocated social change through the reform of individuals, he now realized that ending slavery would require collective action. "Whilst I insist on the doctrine of independence and the inspiration of the individual, I do not cripple but exalt the social action."[15]

JOHN BROWN

After the Kansas-Nebraska Act passed in 1854, New Englanders flocked to these territories to fight to keep them free. Pro-slavery activists from neighboring Missouri made repeated violent attacks on these Eastern settlers. In May 1856, a pro-slavery gang led by the local county sheriff ransacked the Kansas capital of Lawrence, destroying the hotel and shutting down two newspapers. Abolitionists led by Rev. Henry Ward Beecher raised funds for purchasing rifles—dubbed "Beecher's bibles"—to arm the Free State settlers. Emerson spoke at a Kansas Relief Meeting in Concord later that year. In an appeal for funds to aid the imperiled settlers, he declared that force must be met with force and made a generous contribution himself.

An antislavery settler in Kansas named John Brown had also concluded that the time had come to use force. Furious at the Lawrence raid and threats against his family, Brown, together with several others, attacked two farms of pro-slavery activists, killing several men with their swords. The South vilified Brown as a terrorist, and the North celebrated him as a heroic man of action. Emerson first met Brown in March 1857, when he came to Concord seeking donations in support of the antislavery effort in Kansas. Emerson held a reception for Brown at his home and invited him to spend the night. They met again when Brown returned to Concord in May 1859, this time to raise funds to arm enslaved persons to revolt against their enslavers, though Emerson knew nothing about his intentions at that point.

That October, Brown and his men raided the federal arsenal at Harpers Ferry, Virginia (now part of West Virginia). The assault was a failure. Brown was wounded, and several of his men were killed. The survivors were jailed to await trial for treason. Back in Concord, Brown's supporters were shocked at the news. In Emerson's eyes, Brown was a romantic hero "and seems to have made this fatal blunder only to bring out his virtues."[16] In a lecture on "courage" on November 8, Emerson spontaneously added a few lines in praise of Brown, comparing him to Jesus on the cross: "that new saint, than who, none purer or more brave was led by love of men into conflict and death,—the new saint awaiting his martyrdom, and who, if he shall suffer, will make the gallows like the cross."[17]

Later that month, Emerson spoke at a meeting to aid Brown's family. He declared that Brown's daring raid "eclipses all others which have occurred for a long time in our history." He welcomed the "sudden interest in the hero of Harper's [sic] Ferry" and described Brown as "the rarest of heroes, a pure idealist, with no by-ends of his own," guided only by the Golden Rule and the Declaration of Independence. Frustrated by the pacifism of many abolitionists, Brown put his ideals into action.

"He did not believe in moral suasion;—he believed in putting the thing through." Those who are now making him suffer will find themselves on the wrong side of history. There is "no other citizen as worthy to live, and as deserving of all public and private honor, as this poor prisoner."[18]

Brown was executed on December 2, 1859. After the failed raid on Harpers Ferry, only a small number of people in New England sympathized with him. Most thought him a fanatic who got what he deserved. In January 1860, Emerson eulogized Brown in a speech in Salem. He expressed shock at "the easy effrontery with which political gentlemen, in and out of Congress, take it upon them to say that there are not a thousand men in the North who sympathize with John Brown. It would be far safer and nearer the truth to say that all people, in proportion to their sensibility and self-respect, sympathize with him. For it is impossible to see courage, and disinterestedness, and the love that cast out fear, without sympathy." "Who makes the Abolitionist?" Emerson demanded of those who complained of sympathy for John Brown. "The Slaveholder," he insisted. "The sentiment of mercy is the natural recoil which the laws of the universe provide to protect mankind from destruction by savage passions."[19]

Emerson was correct to say that Brown's detractors would find themselves on the wrong side of history. The words of Emerson, along with those of Thoreau and Julia Ward Howe (who wrote "The Battle Hymn of the Republic" to the tune of "John Brown's Body") and other Transcendentalists, turned Brown into a martyr.[20] As soon as Emerson made those impromptu remarks likening Brown's execution to the crucifixion of Jesus, newspapers around the country printed and reprinted them. Celebrated as the foremost lecturer and public intellectual in America, Emerson was nationally known, and his comments caused outrage in the South. Emerson's repeated defense of him rescued Brown's reputation and changed Northern public opinion. "Emerson was as well positioned as anyone in America to accomplish such a rescue," says historian David S. Reynolds, author of *John Brown, Abolitionist*. "Thoreau was eloquent about Brown, but he didn't come close to having Emerson's clout. When Emerson spoke, America listened. A pithy phrase from him could create shock waves."[21]

Reynolds insists that Emerson played a pivotal role in the presidential election of 1860. Emerson's endorsement of Brown and his violent actions split the Democratic Party in two, resulting in Northern and Southern slates. Except for the split, a Democratic candidate would likely have won, as the Democratic Party was much larger than the newly formed Republican Party. And Lincoln would not have become president.[22]

Emerson gave at least thirteen widely publicized and reprinted antislavery addresses. He urged disobedience of the Fugitive Slave Act that required Northern officials to return enslaved persons who had escaped to their enslavers. He raised funds for rifles for antislavery settlers in Kansas. He praised and financially supported John Brown's radical and violent actions seeking to end slavery. He solicited funds for Brown's defense and compared him to Jesus Christ when many Northerners had turned against Brown. When the Civil War came, he welcomed it as an opportunity to rid the nation of the curse of slavery and pressed Lincoln to emancipate those enslaved. After the war he called for Black enfranchisement and reparations to be paid to former enslaved persons.[23]

Emerson paid a price for his activism. Abolitionism was not popular in the North. And when the South seceded from the Union, endangering the Northern economy, abolitionists were blamed for it. The mobs that pummeled antislavery activists in Boston included State Street businessmen and Harvard college students, as well as local working people. In January 1861, Wendell Phillips, one of the foremost abolitionist leaders, invited Emerson to speak at the annual meeting of the Massachusetts Anti-Slavery Society. The event was described years later by Emerson's son, Edward: "The meeting . . . was interrupted by a well-dressed mob of 'Union-at-any-price' citizens of Boston and the suburban towns. Hearing of the probable danger, Mr. Emerson felt bound to go, and sat upon the platform. The jeers and howls of the mob drowned his attempt at earnest speech."[24] This was not the first time he had been shouted down. As reported in the *Liberator*, a popular abolitionist newspaper, when he delivered his address on the Fugitive Slave Law in Cambridge in 1851, "a considerable body of students from Harvard College did what they could to disturb the audience and insult the speaker, by hisses and groans. . . . Mr. Emerson's refinement of character, scholarship, and mild and dignified deportment, could not save him from their noisy, yet feeble, insults." He also suffered financial losses from lectures canceled in Philadelphia and elsewhere as a result of his public support of John Brown.[25]

Readers and critics have often made assumptions about Emerson's views on reform looking only at his earlier essays, in which he argued that reform begins with the self. However, his thinking changed as he encountered the obstacles to abolition and then caught fire with the urgency of the antislavery movement. Self-reliance was "the key to collective efforts at social reform," according to Emerson scholar Len Gougeon. "For him, and for other Transcendentalists, social reform begins with the individual, but it does not end there."[26] Emerson came to realize that to be truly self-reliant, individuals must fight for freedom—the precondition for self-reliance—for all Americans.[27]

The idea that Emerson stood for apolitical individualism is a myth, which recent scholarship and the publication of Emerson's antislavery writings have put to rest.[28] He may initially have been reluctant to engage in activism, but ultimately he staked his reputation as a public intellectual on defending the rights of African Americans, women, and native peoples. Individual change of heart, while necessary, would never abolish slavery, he realized. In the same way, Civil War, constitutional amendments, and civil rights laws have not been sufficient to abolish the racism and the discrimination that have persisted to the present day. Overcoming racism, homophobia, misogyny, and other forms of prejudice requires a change of heart as well as the passage of laws.

WOMEN'S RIGHTS

Women propelled the antislavery movement during the 1840s and 1850s. It was not long before they began to turn the critical lens of civil rights on themselves and their own situation. Up to this point, women had few rights. With limited exceptions they were prohibited from inheriting property, signing contracts, serving on juries, and voting. Men controlled almost every aspect of their personal lives. Few were allowed to speak publicly, even on the issue of slavery. The deeper they involved themselves in the antislavery crusade, the more they came to view their own status as a form of servitude.

The issue of women's rights was brought to the fore by Elizabeth Cady Stanton and others in calling for a convention on women's rights to be held in Seneca Falls, New York, in July 1848. This convention was followed by similar ones, including a series of annual National Women's

Rights Conventions beginning in 1850. At this time female suffrage was but one of many concerns. More generally, the issue was one of empowerment and self-reliance, which Margaret Fuller forcefully addressed in her essay "The Great Lawsuit," published in the *Dial* magazine in 1843. The essay was expanded into the book *Woman in the Nineteenth Century*, the first American feminist manifesto, a year later.

"A new manifestation is at hand, a new hour in the day of man," Fuller declared in this groundbreaking work. "While [the condition of] any one is base, none can be entirely free and noble." For too long, women have been subjugated by men and denied the opportunity to freely and fully flourish as human beings in their own right. "We would have every arbitrary barrier thrown down," she wrote: "We would have every path laid open to woman as freely as to man. . . . [T]hen and only then, will mankind be ripe for this, when inward and outward freedom for woman as much as for man shall be acknowledged as a right, not yielded as a concession. As the friend of the negro assumes that one man cannot by right, hold another in bondage, so should the friend of woman assume that man cannot, by right, lay even well-meant restrictions on woman."[29]

Fuller's argument was grounded in the theory of self-culture, of which she was a prominent exponent. "Margaret's life *had an aim*," James Freeman Clarke wrote in his account of her in the *Memoirs of Margaret Fuller Ossoli*. "This aim, from first to last, was Self-culture."[30] Gendered "conversations" in Boston from 1839 to 1844 were a primary means or praxis by which Fuller sought to raise women's consciousness, develop their self-reliance, and empower them.[31] Her tragic death from a shipwreck in 1850 prevented her from having a greater impact on the women's movement in its formative years.

Emerson approached women's issues in much the same way. Both Fuller and Emerson were inclined to believe that souls have no sex and thus women and men had an equal right to self-development. But in the case of women there was limited opportunity to exercise that right. When he received an invitation to address the Women's Rights Convention in 1850, he politely declined. He acknowledged "the political and civil wrongs of women" and said he would "vote for every franchise for women,—vote that they should hold property, and vote, yes and be eligible to all offices as men." But, he continued, "I should not wish women to wish political functions, nor, if granted assume them."[32] He considered politics a grubby affair and hated to see women get involved in it. He also turned down an invitation to speak the following year, begging off because he was working on Fuller's *Memoirs*. But his views were beginning to change. When asked again in 1855, he agreed to address the convention in September of that year.

WOMAN

"Woman is the power of civilization," Emerson declared in his speech before the delegates to the convention. "Here, at the right moment, when the land is full of committees examining election frauds and misdeeds, woman asks for her vote. It is the remedy at the moment of need." Men and women possess different but complementary attributes. "Man is the will, and woman the sentiment. In this ship of humanity, the will is the rudder, and sentiment the sail."[33] Both are necessary, but by virtue of their experience as educators and caregivers, women play a civilizing role in society.

The Quakers, Emerson says, were the first to establish equality in the sexes. Another important step in the empowerment of women was their involvement in the antislavery crusade. "One truth leads in another by the hand," he observes; "one right is an accession of strength to take more. And the times are marked by the new attitude of woman urging, by argument and by association, her rights of all kinds, in short, to one half of the world: the right to education; to avenues of employment; to equal rights of property; to equal rights in marriage; to the exercise of the professions; to suffrage." There are misogynists who make light of women's abilities. Others argue that women are too sensitive and sentimental. It is also the case that many women do not wish these things, considering such changes to be "irksome and distasteful." In spite of these objections, he asserts that "if the woman demand votes, offices, and political equality with men . . . it must not be refused."[34]

Additional objections were that women would become "contaminated and unsexed" from involvement in politics, that they were naive and lacked "practical wisdom." But, in Emerson's view, they are just as capable of voting wisely as men are. "As for the unsexing and contamination," he continues, "that only accuses our existing politics, shows how barbarous we are, that our policies are so crooked, made up of things not to be spoken, to be understood only by wink and nudge, this man is to be coaxed, and that man to be bought, and that other to be duped." He doesn't think women wish as yet for an equal share in public affairs: "But it is they, and not we, that are to determine it. Let the laws be purged of every barbarous remainder, every barbarous impediment to women. Let the public donation for education be equally shared by them. Let them enter a school, as freely as a church. Let them have, and hold, and give their property, as men do theirs. And, in a few years, it will easily appear whether they wish a voice in making the laws that are to govern them." Women are as competent and well-qualified to vote as men are. History is a record of growth and "the expanding mind of the human race." What is popular will be adopted. "The aspiration of this century [for women's equality] will be the code of the next."[35]

If it appears that Emerson is giving less than a full-throated endorsement of women's right to vote, it is because he was being given conflicting advice and because he was reluctant to prescribe women's duties. Although his wife, Lydian, was in favor of suffrage, his daughter Ellen was adamantly opposed. In a letter to his friend Caroline Sturgis Tappan in 1868, he wrote, "It is of course for women to decide this question! the part of men, if women decide to assume the suffrage, is simply to accept their determination and aid in carrying it out."[36]

Caroline Healey Dall, an organizer of the convention, said newspapers were puzzled, uncertain whether Emerson was, as she put it, "for us or against us." But, she noted, it was Emerson's strategy "to lure the Conservatives on over his flowers, till all of a sudden their feet were pierced with the thorns of reform."[37] Paulina Wright Davis, another of the convention's organizers, felt the women got what they hoped for. "More than a disquisition on the slavery of sex," writes historian Phyllis Cole in summarizing Davis's opinion, "they looked for idealism from Emerson, the high-philosophical and poetic words of all his essays they knew he could use to argue for the empowerment of women."[38]

Emerson's importance to the women's movement had less to do with whether he supported woman's right to vote—this he surely did—than with the emphasis he, along with Margaret Fuller, placed on self-culture as a means of personal empowerment and social reform. Drawing on the ideas of Emerson and Fuller, feminists in the women's movement, according to historian Tiffany K. Wayne, "addressed the

Transcendentalist's paradox of securing both individual and universal reform by focusing on the development of women's individual *selves* as the foundation of larger social change for women as a *class*. They translated the Transcendentalist philosophy and rhetoric of *self-culture* into a reform agenda to promote women's education and 'right to think.' They formulated a cultural critique aimed at altering public opinion about gender and removing obstacles to women's pursuit of selfhood, and they voiced their critique within the emerging women's rights movement of the same period."[39]

In a time when women were denied economic and political rights, Emerson's position was very progressive. "Viewing the time line . . . of the development of Emerson's thoughts on women, and particularly on their right to political equality," historian Armida Gilbert argues, "Emerson was already, at the beginning of the American suffrage movement in the 1850s, convinced of and speaking out for its necessity."[40] Len Gougeon, mentioned previously in relation to Emerson's involvement in the abolition movement, notes a similarity with respect his support of women's rights: "Both began with a troubled concern, moved to a reserved commitment, and culminated in unambiguous support."[41] In the decade following the 1855 convention, Emerson regularly attended women's rights meetings and in 1869 was even listed as a vice president of the New England Woman Suffrage Association.

10

THE ART OF LIFE

In 1824, when Ralph Waldo Emerson was only twenty-one years old, he wrote in his journal: "I propose to look philosophically at the conduct of life."[1] From then on, everything he wrote and lectured about was on this subject. From his first book, *Nature*, to his late lectures he was addressing the question, How shall we live? While many of his topics seem abstract—divinity, reform, poetry, beauty, success, power, and so forth—he examined each according to its impact on our lives and the cultivation of our souls.

Emerson's earlier work had an exuberance that waned to some degree in his later lectures and essays. He found that the ecstasies of youth became less frequent with age and the muses more difficult to summon. But with age comes wisdom. As Emerson said, "The years teach much which the days never know."[2] In his later works, *The Conduct of Life* and *Society and Solitude*, for example, he revisits many of the issues he raised in his earlier ones. In some cases, he revises or adds to what he said previously; in other instances, he underscores or emphasizes these views.

In his midlife Emerson became widely known and influential as a public philosopher and as an opinion maker on the social and political issues of the day. He kept up a vigorous schedule of lecture tours, venturing farther and farther from New England. "Emerson is perhaps the only lecturer in the movement who could unhesitatingly be called great," historian Carl Bode writes in his book on the lyceum movement, the public adult education programs that flourished in mid-nineteenth-century America. "The amazing thing is that he was also enormously popular. He did not entertain audiences; on the contrary he sometimes irritated them. . . . Yet the demand to hear him remained at a peak for nearly twenty years."[3]

In October 1847, at the invitation of a Scottish friend, he left on a whirlwind speaking tour of Britain. On his first trip to England, in 1833, he had traveled as an unknown. Now he was greeted as a celebrity. Accompanied at times by his friend Thomas Carlyle, he delivered lectures and sermons in Manchester, Birmingham, London, Edinburgh, and other cities before moving on to France. After his return in July 1848, his American followers were curious about his trip. He delivered a series of lectures about it, later published as *English Traits* in 1856. Emerson's trip to England, historian Wallace E. Williams writes, not only "became a turning point in his popularity, but it also matured him, deprovincialized him, and brought him current with the intellectual tides of the mid-nineteenth century as his own study in Concord, the Boston Athenaeum, and New York could not."[4] In this same period Emerson finished another book, *Representative Men*, published in 1850, featuring six thinkers he admired throughout history—Plato, Swedenborg, Montaigne, Shakespeare, Napoleon, and Goethe—from a series of lectures he had given in 1845, prior to his travels. Plus, he prepared a collection of poetry, published as *Poems* in 1846.

In the midst of all this productivity, his personal well-being suffered a terrible blow with the death of his close friend Margaret Fuller at age forty in 1850. The two first met in 1836 when Emerson invited her for a visit to his home in Concord after reading her translation of Goethe's *Torquato Tasso*. She stayed for three weeks. She and Emerson had long conversations, went for walks together, and quickly became intellectual and spiritual soul mates. Emerson was reserved toward most people, but Fuller drew him out. They gossiped and quipped. She slid notes under his door. Recalling that visit in an 1852 memoir that friends compiled about her, he wrote that her eyes "swam with fun and drolleries, and the very tides of joy and superabundant life. . . . she made me laugh more than I liked." It's no wonder that their relationship aroused jealousy in Emerson's wife, Lidian.[5]

Fuller and Emerson worked together closely coediting the *Dial* magazine during the four years of its publication. Their lives often intertwined. When Emerson was on tour in Britain in 1847, Fuller was in Italy, actively supporting the drive toward Italian independence from

France and Austria. She met a young aristocratic revolutionary, Giovanni Ossoli, with whom she had a child. After the fall of the short-lived democratically elected government, she and her family sailed for America. Their ship ran aground in a hurricane, and all three drowned. Learning of the shipwreck, Emerson sent Henry Thoreau to Long Island in search of their bodies and personal effects. The only trace was a jacket belonging to Ossoli, from which Thoreau removed a button. Lamenting her death in his journal, Emerson wrote, "I have lost in her my audience."[6]

The Conduct of Life was published in 1860. It represents his mature thinking on issues he had wrestled with his entire adult life. It consists of nine essays, the most important of which are "Fate," "Worship," "Considerations by the Way," and "Illusions."

"FATE"

The midcentury was a time of many transitions in Emerson's life: in his personal life, in his growing activism, and also in his spirituality. His essay "Experience," in *Essays: Second Series*, marked a turning point in his spiritual life, notes Stephen E. Whicher in *Freedom and Fate: An Inner Life of Ralph Waldo Emerson*. "If the keynote of his early thought is revolution, that of his later thought is acquiescence and optimism," Whicher writes. "From an intense rebellion against the world in the name of the Soul, he moved to a relative acceptance of things as they are, world and Soul together; from teaching men their power to rise above fate, he turned to teaching them how to make the best of it."[7] In other words, Whicher is saying, Emerson's revolt against social conformity and institutional rigidity subsided into skepticism and resignation.

There is no disputing the change of tone and mood in Emerson's later writing, but was this change acquiescence or was it something else? The difference between the earlier Emerson and the later one, according to Gertrude Reif Hughes, another Emerson scholar, was more a distinction between affirmation and confirmation: "The promises Emerson offers do not reassure, they make demands. As he warned throughout his career, it can be costly to believe in individuals' essential divinity. The cost confirms the value, not the foolishness, of such a belief. Thus, the supposed capitulations of later works like 'Experience' and *The Conduct of Life* do not recant the bold faith of earlier works like 'Self-Reliance,'

'Compensation,' and *Nature*; rather the later essays articulate those earlier affirmations more fully."[8] Other scholars, such as David Robinson, attribute the difference between earlier and later Emerson writings to a growing pragmatism about the nation's social turmoil leading up to the Civil War: "The decade following the second English journey of 1847–48 is perhaps the most crucial for Emerson's testing and enactment of the public role of the intellectual. Not only was his public stature higher then, but his concerns were fundamentally directed toward the moral questions of social life. His increasing orientation toward the ethical and pragmatic, catalyzed . . . by the antislavery crisis, became the focus of his lecturing in the 1850s."[9]

My own view is that Emerson experienced both renewed determination and growing wisdom as a result of his own maturity and the social and spiritual challenges he and the nation were facing. He was, indeed, less naive and more realistic about the nature of these challenges and their potential outcomes. This was a battle, as he puts it in "Fate," the first essay in *The Conduct of Life*, between fate and freedom. Many scholars have read this essay, like "Experience," as a retreat from Emerson's earlier bold calls to listen to one's inner voice, in defiance of convention, toward an acceptance of the existing order of things. But Robert D. Richardson Jr. views the essay differently, noting that "despite its title, [it is] a vigorous affirmation of freedom, more effective than earlier statements because it does not dismiss the power of circumstance, determinism, materialism, experience, Calvinism, and evil, and because Emerson now had a much subtler grasp of the interrelation of fate and freedom, involving processes vastly more complex than that of simple compensation."[10] Furthermore, Richardson says, the essay needs to be read in light of Emerson's growing involvement in the antislavery cause.

In previous essays and lectures, Emerson had put forth an ideal of the self-reliant individual. But with maturity, he learned firsthand that human beings experience tragedy and suffering and that social problems, such as slavery, can be intractable. These seemed to undermine his self-confident assertions about the unlimited potential of human nature.

The times we live in—whether the tumultuous years leading up to the Civil War or the early divisive decades of the twenty-first century—always feel besieged by forces, ideas, and events that seem too complex to comprehend, much less resolve. "We are incompetent to solve the times," he says in the essay; the only question that matters is "How shall I live?"[11]

The dilemma we face in every era is how to reconcile freedom and fate. There are always forces beyond our control. At the same time, we human beings have agency and free will. "If we must accept Fate," Emerson says, "we are not less compelled to affirm liberty, the significance of the individual, the grandeur of duty, the power of character."[12] If the one is true, so is the other. How to reconcile them is the question Emerson seeks to answer.

The problem is not easy to solve. Fate seems to preclude freedom. But if liberty is real, then there must be some limit to necessity. Each of us must figure out this dilemma for ourselves. Other people and other nations in other times have coped with the terrors of life by adopting a fatalistic attitude. For the Greeks, the Muslims, the Hindus, and even the Calvinists, a belief in fate gave them dignity and strength. The wise have always felt, Emerson writes, "that the weight of the universe held them down to their place. . . . [T]here is something which cannot be talked or voted away—a strap or belt which girds the world."[13]

If those religions and cultures believed that humans must obey the decrees of the gods, Emerson believed the same about the laws of nature. Many people to this day believe in a benign Providence. But Emerson writes, "Nature is no sentimentalist—does not cosset or pamper us. We must see that the world is rough and surly, and will not mind drowning a man or a woman, but swallows your ship like a grain of dust." Diseases, the elements, fortune, and the forces of nature are no respecters of persons. "The way of Providence is a little rude," he says. "The habit of snake and spider, the snap of the tiger and other leapers and bloody jumpers, the crackle of the bones of his prey in the coil of the anaconda—these are in the system, and our habits are like theirs."[14]

Emerson cites a litany of natural disasters that wiped out human life—the 1755 earthquake in Lisbon, a recent volcanic eruption in Naples. We cannot deny Nature's indiscriminate destructiveness. "Providence has a wild, rough, incalculable road to its end," Emerson insists, "and it is of no use to try to whitewash its huge mixed instrumentalities, or to dress up that terrific benefactor in a clean shirt and white neckcloth of a student in divinity."[15] Heredity and upbringing also determine who we are. We cannot escape from our ancestry. We are born with certain qualities, and "all the privilege and all the legislation in the world cannot meddle or help to make a poet or prince" of us. Religions and philosophies have put forth notions such as karma, destiny, and predestination to account for their effects.

Life has its limitations. "Once we thought positive power was all," Emerson says. "Now we learn that negative power, or circumstance, is half."[16] He makes a solid case for determinism. Nature is tyrannous as well as beneficial, he says. There is no turning back from the course of evolution. The advance of civilization favors one group and then another. The science of statistics makes everything a matter of fixed calculation. Even disease and death are subject to the mathematics of actuarial tables. There is no escaping the conclusion that we are hemmed in by circumstances beyond our control. "The force with which we resist these torrents of tendency looks so ridiculously inadequate that it amounts to little more than a criticism or protest made by a minority of one, under compulsion of millions," Emerson writes.[17] Our view of life can have no validity unless we acknowledge such troublesome facts.

Fate is limitation, whether we see it as blind forces or as religious doctrines. We are bound, like the wolf Fenris in Norse mythology, by the fetters of necessity. Nothing can escape it. Fate is the great leveler, bringing down the high, lifting up the low, impossible even for God to resist. Fate is at work everywhere—in matter, mind, and morals—but it, too, has limits. Emerson says that "though Fate is immense, so is Power, which is the other fact in the dual world, immense."[18]

If fate limits power, power thwarts fate: "We must respect Fate as natural history, but there is more than natural history. Man is not order of nature, sack and sack, belly and members, link in a chain, nor any ignominious baggage; but a stupendous antagonism, a dragging together of the poles of the Universe. He betrays his relation to what is below him. . . . But the lightening which explodes and fashions planets, maker of planets and suns, is in him." If there is matter, there is also mind. If there is fate, there is also freedom. We can no more deny free will than we can ignore necessity. We have the ability to choose and to act. "Intellect annuls Fate," Emerson concludes.[19] Insofar as we think, we are free.

We should not blame fate for our circumstances. We should not use it as an excuse. Those who cite destiny or astrology for their misfortune "invite the evils they fear."[20] If fate is powerful, so are human beings, for we are part of it. Between our will to survive and to make sense of the world and put it in order, we can confront fate with the power we do have over our own individual fates. We can resist the forces of entropy and annihilation.

Emerson does not envision a standoff between fate and freedom, as though the two cancel each other out. In the end, freedom vanquishes fate by "the noble creative forces," the first of which is thought. By thought, Emerson does not mean mere mental activity but rather vision or insight that liberates us from paying attention only to our day-to-day needs: "The day of days, the great day of the feast of life, is that in which the inward eye opens to the Unity in things, to the omnipresence of law—sees that what is must be and ought to be, or is the best. This beatitude dips from on high down to us and we see. It is not so much in us as we are in it. If the air come to our lungs, we breathe and live; if not, we die. If the light come to our eyes, we see; else not. And if truth come suddenly to our mind we suddenly expand to its dimensions, as if we grow to worlds. We are as lawgivers; we speak for Nature; we prophesy and divine."[21]

In such moments we see ourselves as a part of the universe. What is true of the universe is true of us as well. We are made strong by its power, immortal by its timelessness. Insight is liberating, and the knowledge that comes from insight is a form of power. Those who see through the design preside over it. A divine inevitability, "a permanent westerly current," carries us and everything else along with it: "A breath of will blows eternally through the universe of souls in the direction of the Right and the Necessary. It is the air which all intellects inhale and exhale, and it is the wind which blows the worlds into order and orbit."[22]

The second "noble creative force" is the moral sentiment, or conscience. We gravitate toward what we believe to be true. We wish to see the truth prevail. The feeling that we are aligned with "the universal force," or the way of things, gives us great strength. As Emerson says, "The pure sympathy with universal ends is an infinite force, and cannot be bribed or bent. Whoever has had experience of the moral sentiment cannot choose but believe in unlimited power."[23] Courage in the face of obstacles that once seemed insurmountable disproves a fatalistic approach to human history.

"The one serious and formidable thing in nature is a will," Emerson insists. Will is where thought and conscience—the two "noble forces"

—coalesce. Neither by itself is enough. "Perception is cold, and good-ness dies in wishes." The two must fuse to create will, without which there can be no driving force. For want of it, society languishes and looks to "saviours and religions."[24]

Many people compartmentalize power and fate, believing that they have free will in their personal relations with others, but in the world of nature and politics and commerce, "they believe a malignant energy rules." But fate can be turned into freedom through deeper insight. "Every jet of chaos which threatens to exterminate us is convertible by intellect into wholesome force." Water may drown a ship or a sailor, but "trim your bark" or learn to swim and you have mastered this elemental force.[25] We are not helpless in the face of fate. Disease may kill thousands, but we can vaccinate and treat it. Steam can burn us, but it can be harnessed into power. So it is with politics. Human unrest can lead to positive change. The tendency of the universe is progressive. Behind us is fate that has been ameliorated. Before us are human freedom and a better world.

It is hard to know where fate leaves off and freedom begins. Everything is interconnected. "This knot of nature is so well tied that nobody was ever cunning enough to find the two ends," Emerson says. There is a bal-ance between fate and freedom that makes everything—inanimate as well as animate—seem suited to its environment: eyes in light, feet on land, wings in air, and so on, "each creature where it was meant to be, with a mutual fitness." A certain kind of intelligence works in the interplay of these natural forces and, "as soon as there is life," becomes self-directing.[26] This applies to the human world as well. Our fortunes are the fruit of our character, as Emerson puts it. All of history is the action and reaction of nature and thought, which he compares to "two boys pushing each other on the curbstone of the pavement. Everything is pusher or pushed; and matter and mind are in perpetual tilt and balance, so."[27]

This intricate interaction accounts for the "wonderful constancy in the design this vagabond life admits." The key to solving the mysteries of the human condition and "the old knots" of fate and freedom lies in the propounding of "the double consciousness." Our life swings between outside forces and inner states of being, or nature and thought. When we seem to be victims of fate, we need "to rally on [our] relation to the Universe, which our ruin benefits."[28]

These two opposites—nature and thought—comprise a "Blessed Unity" that is ultimately providential. In the closing paragraphs of the essay, Emerson writes: "Let us build altars to the Blessed Unity which holds nature and souls in perfect solution and compels every atom to serve an universal end. I do not wonder at a snow-flake, a shell, a summer landscape, or the glory of the stars; but at the necessity of beauty under which the universe lies; that all is and must be pictorial; that the rainbow and the curve of the horizon, and the arch of the blue vault are only results from the organ of the eye. . . . How idle to choose a random sparkle here or there, when the indwelling necessity plants the rose of beauty on the brow of chaos, and discloses the central intention of Nature to be harmony and joy."[29]

"Let us build altars to the Beautiful Necessity," Emerson says. Human freedom is not a license to alter the order of things. "If in the least particular one could derange the order of nature—who would accept the gift of life?" Everything is made of one piece. We should not fear nature. There is no danger that we are not equipped to face. There are no contingencies or exceptions. The law of nature rules throughout the universe. This law, in Emerson's words, "is not intelligent, but intelligence; not personal nor impersonal—it disdains words and passes understanding; it dissolves persons; it vivifies nature; yet solicits the pure in heart to draw on all its omnipotence."[30]

Freedom is an undeniable fact of experience. But Emerson is no longer talking about the total freedom he had envisioned in his earlier essays. "Fate" is another demonstration of Emerson's Stoicism. He gives fate its due, but not the last word. Acknowledging fate and limitation does not mean acquiescence. We are free to rise above them, free to determine how we shall live in their shadow. Our freedom, like everything else in life, is limited. Although our freedom is conditional, as Emerson writes in his journal, there is an *"eternal tendency to the good of the whole, active in every atom, every moment."*[31]

Emerson's viewpoint is a spiritual one. As he says at the beginning of the essay, the solution to the problem of fate lies in the answer to the question, "How shall we live?" As in so many of his essays, he is trying to find a middle path between credulity and despair. Do we live in a world presided over by a supernatural being or forces that are totally random and capricious? Emerson's answer is a religious naturalism, finding religious meaning in the natural world. Joseph Campbell describes it this way:

> The first step to the knowledge of the wonder and mystery of life is the recognition of the monstrous nature of the earthly human realm as well as its glory, the realization that this is just how it is and that it cannot and will not be changed. Those who think they know—and their name is legion—how the universe could have been had they created it, without pain, without sorrow, without time, without death, are unfit for illumination.
>
> So if you really want to help this world, what you will have to teach is how to live in it. And that no one can do who has not themself learned how to live in the joyful sorrow and sorrowful joy of life as it is.[32]

This is essentially what Emerson means by building dual altars to "Blessed Unity" and "Beautiful Necessity," the belief that all things are of a piece and serve universal ends.

"WORSHIP"

In his "Divinity School Address" in 1838, Emerson was speaking to a small group of candidates for the Unitarian ministry. In "Worship," another essay in *The Conduct of Life*, he is addressing a much larger secular audience. In comparing the two, we see an example of the pattern of affirmation and confirmation Hughes described as characteristic of his mature writing: "The relationship between affirmation and confirmation is subtle and volatile. Temporally of course, affirmation comes first. Without affirmation there can exist no confirmation, for where nothing has been projected nothing can be verified. Functionally, affirmation and confirmation work as complements each to the other. Without confirmation, what has been affirmed, believed, hoped, announced, or promised remains incompletely known. Confirmation not only validates existing belief or thought, it also constitutes a revelation of what the original thought or belief entailed."[33] If the "Divinity School Address" is Emerson's affirmative statement on religion—that nature, not scripture or church teaching, is the foundation of worship—"Worship" is his confirmation of earlier views. It also represents an advance in his thinking about the nature and function of religion.

In "Fate," as we have seen, Emerson concludes that fate limits freedom but does not cancel it. In "Worship" he takes a similar approach to skepticism. In a century rife with religious revivals, camp meetings, and emotional preaching, Emerson is prophetic in describing the coming rise and consequences of secularism. He searches for a third way between atheism and sectarian religion. "Sect" is usually defined as a small religious movement that has broken away from a larger, more established religious group. But in Emerson's use of the word, "sectarianism" refers to the distinguishing features of every religious group, differentiating them from all others by virtue of doctrines and rituals. In a letter to his brother William in 1835, Emerson said he wished "to write and print a discourse upon Spiritual and Traditional Religion, for Form seems to be bowing Substance out of the World and men doubt if there be any such thing as spiritual nature out of the carcass in which once it dwelt."[34] Doctrines and rituals are the forms of religion, while spirituality is its substance. Three years later he addressed this theme in his "Divinity School Address," and he returns to it again in "Worship" in 1860.

Emerson isn't worried about losing his faith as he explores skepticism. "I dip my pen in the blackest ink, because I am not afraid of falling into my inkpot." Faith is innate. "We are born believing," he says. "A man bears beliefs, as a tree bears apples." Some people believe that without some form of religion, moral anarchy would result, but such is not the case. Emerson observes that "the stern old faiths have all pulverized" and that there's "a whole population of gentlemen and ladies out in search of religions." But faith adheres to every soul and cannot be expunged. "God builds his temple in the heart on the ruins of churches and religions."[35]

Other essays in the collection examine power, wealth, culture, and behavior in light of the need for self-culture. In "Worship" he is saying self-culture is a form of religion, or worship: "The whole state of man is a state of culture; and its flowering and completion may be described as Religion, or Worship. . . . But the religion cannot rise above the state of the votary [an adherent or follower]."[36] Self-culture is the means by which he or she—and thus religion too—may be elevated.

Previous ages were savage, superstitious, and intolerant. Now, he is saying, "we live in a transition period, when the old faiths which comforted nations . . . seem to have spent their force." Religions have lost their moral and intellectual credibility. Their followers have fallen into doubt and despair. "In our large cities, the population is godless, materialized,—no bond, no fellow-feeling, no enthusiasm. These are not men, but hungers, thirsts, fevers, and appetites walking. How is it people manage to live on,—so aimless as they are?" Their faith is in technology and materialism, not in "divine causes."[37] They have substituted superstition and seances for creeds. What better proof of religious decline than slavery?

This lack of faith is so commonplace that people have begun to take it for granted. But, as Emerson says, "the multitude of the sick shall not make us deny the existence of health." Despite the infidelity of so many, to say there is no basis for faith is "like saying in rainy weather, there is no sun, when at the moment we are witnessing one of its superlative effects." Behind or beneath the distortions of religion exists the possibility of living a spiritual life, if we will but wait for the clouds to clear: "There is a principle which is the basis of things, which all speech aims to say, and all action to evolve, a simple, quiet, undescribed, undescribable presence, dwelling very peacefully in us, our rightful lord: we are not to do; not to work, but to be worked upon; and to this homage there is a consent of all thoughtful and just men in all ages and conditions. To this sentiment belong vast and sudden enlargements of power. 'Tis remarkable that our faith in ecstasy consists with total inexperience of it. It is the order of the world to educate with accuracy the senses and the understanding; and the enginery at work to draw out these powers in priority, no doubt, has its office. But we are never without a hint that these powers are mediate and servile, and that we are one day to deal with real being,—essences with essences."[38]

We must free ourselves from religious systems of the past, he says. Faith suffers from conformity. "Religion must always be a crab fruit, it cannot be grafted and keep its wild beauty." New sects may break off, adding on their creeds and practices to get closer to the truth as they see it, but none can deliver the transcendence of spiritual ecstasy. The only cure for the "false theology" of decayed forms of religion is living a moral and spiritual life, according to the laws that "pervade and govern" the universe, omnipresent in every atom in nature. When we learn to act out of an intuition of moral laws and not out of a fear of being cheated or caught, then everything goes well. We have changed our "market-cart into a chariot of the sun."[39]

Worship, Emerson says, is "the source of intellect." By "intellect," Emerson means insight into what he calls Universal Mind, rather than reasoning. Intellect and morals are interdependent, and those who cultivate the moral sentiment are "nearer to the secret of God than others; are bathed by sweeter waters; they hear notices, they see visions, where others are vacant."[40] The moral sense is the measure of our spiritual well-being, the health of which is threatened when we accept wealth as a measure of our worth.

Human beings have learned to weigh and measure the sun, trace the path of a star, and predict the next eclipse. We must also discover the laws of the moral universe. Worship is the attitude of those who have insight into these laws and see that "the nature of things works for truth and right forever." We see cause and effect in the moral universe just as we do in the physical world. "A man does not see, that, as he eats, so he thinks; as he deals, so he is, and so he appears; . . . that fortunes are not exceptions but fruits; that relation and connection are not somewhere and sometimes, but everywhere and always; no miscellany, no exception, no anomaly,—but method, and an even web; and what comes out, that was put in." These laws operate in nature and in the human mind. They form the basis of what we experience as the moral sentiment. They hold sway everywhere. "The dice are loaded," Emerson declares; "the colors are fast because they are the native colors of the fleece."[41]

We will always be known by our work and our actions. We can't hide our character. "Society is a masked ball, where everyone hides his real character, and reveals it by hiding," Emerson quips. Character affects not only how the world sees us, but also how we view the world. "If we meet no gods, it is because we harbor none," Emerson says. "If there is grandeur in you, you will find grandeur in porters and sweeps."[42]

The qualities we value in human life—love, humility, and faith—are in the very atoms, he continues. Because we are part of a moral universe, we are "equal to every event" that transpires.[43] We are protected from danger so long as our actions are consistent with the life that nature has ordained for us. Thus, our task is our life preserver. There is a moral quality to our work. When we perform it well, the world is on our side.

Traditional Christianity discourages us from this task because it tells us we are unworthy sinners. But the truth is that we are suited to our work and it is essential that we do it. "The weight of the Universe is pressed down on the shoulders of each moral agent to hold him to his task," Emerson writes. "The only path of escape known in all the worlds of God is performance. You must do your work, before you shall be released." This is a spiritual truth written into law by "the government of the universe": "The last lesson of life, the choral song which rises from all elements and all angels, is a voluntary obedience, a necessitated freedom. Man is made of the same atoms as the world is, he shares the same impressions, predispositions, and destiny. When his mind is illuminated, when his heart is kind, he throws himself joyfully into the sublime order, and, does with knowledge, what the stones do by structure."[44]

A religion that "is to guide and fulfil the present and coming ages," Emerson says, "must be intellectual," meaning it must acknowledge the "moral science" he is describing. A new church will be founded on ethical law, he predicts. It may lack the outward signs of traditional religion, "but it will have heaven and earth for its beams and rafters."[45] Its self-reliant adherents will be motivated by moral law rather than the approval of others.

In this essay, Emerson inquires into the foundation of morality. Anticipating the demise of historical Christianity, he wanted to establish morality on another basis. Some believe morality is dictated by divinely inspired religious scriptures and teachings, divinely sanctioned. Emerson came to believe that the Bible is riddled with errors and that churches are flawed institutions. He grounded morality in nature and human nature. The laws that govern nature apply to humans, who are, after all, part of nature. We know this by virtue of an innate moral sensibility. What Emerson proposes is virtue ethics on the basis of religious naturalism. Morality is aspirational and humanistic rather than duty-bound and rule based. The way to moral development is self-culture.

"Before about the middle of the nineteenth century, atheism or agnosticism seemed almost palpably absurd," writes historian James Turner in *Without God, without Creed: The Origins of Unbelief in America*. "Shortly afterward unbelief emerged as an option fully available within the general contours of Western culture, a plausible alternative to the still dominant theism." Emerson's essay on "Worship" marks this dramatic shift in religious consciousness. Many people were beginning to question their Christian inheritance because of increasing historical criticism of the Bible, growing religious cosmopolitanism, and declining respect for religious authority. Emerson, Turner says, "provided a bridge between Christianity and undoctrinal theism; his essays made it easier for a young man or woman raised in an Evangelical home to realize that one could abandon Christianity without losing morality, spirituality, reverence, and the larger hope."[46]

"CONSIDERATIONS BY THE WAY"

In this essay Emerson returns to the spiritual practices of self-culture. He confirms and adds to previous advice on the subject, such as that of the Human Culture lecture series delivered in the winter of 1837. He begins by saying he hesitates to give advice because "life is rather a subject of wonder, than of dialectics." He would rather celebrate life than lay down rules for living it. Yet he recognizes that "fine society, in the common acceptation, has neither ideas nor aims. . . . It is an unprincipled decorum; and affair of clean linen and coaches, of gloves, cards, and elegance in trifles. . . . Society wishes to be amused. I do not wish to be amused. I wish that life should not be cheap, but sacred. I wish the days to be as centuries, loaded, fragrant." It seems that most people are content with matters the way they are "and have not yet come to themselves." But for those who wish to live a more "loaded, fragrant" way of life, he shares five rules for attaining it.[47]

Now in his late fifties, he recommends good health as the first rule. "No labor, pains, temperance, poverty, nor exercise, that can gain it, must be grudged." Healthy living makes everything else possible. And not just physical health, but mental health also, including cheerfulness, good temper, and a sense of contentment. Next, Emerson advises us to find fulfilling work. He notes that "the high prize of life, the crowning fortune of a man is to be born with a bias to some pursuit, which finds him in employment and happiness,—whether it is to make baskets, or broadswords, or canals, or statues, or songs."[48]

Conversation, his next rule, is one of the spiritual practices he mentions most frequently—for example, also in "The Transcendentalist," "The Over-Soul," and "Circles." He finds much of our conversation superficial, focusing on "politics, trade, personal defects, exaggerated bad news, and the rain." It is tedious. "Now, if one comes who can illuminate this dark house with thoughts, show them their native riches, what gifts they have, how indispensable each is, what magical powers over nature and men; what access to poetry, religion, and the powers which constitute character; he wakes in them the feeling of worth, his suggestions require new ways of living, new books, new men, new arts and sciences,—then we come out of our egg-shell existence into the great Dome, and see the zenith over and the nadir under us." Nothing, no book or pleasure in life, is comparable to it. Conversation elevates us to higher platforms of thought. "In excited conversation, we have glimpses of the Universe, hints of power native to the soul, far-darting lights and shadows of an Andes landscape such as we can hardly attain in lone meditation. Here are oracles sometimes profusely given, to which the memory goes back in barren hours."[49]

Emerson counts friendship as another rule of life. Friends stimulate virtue in us. They encourage us to do and be our best. "We take care of our health; we lay up money; we make our roof tight, and our clothing sufficient; but who provides wisely that he shall not be wanting in the best property of all,—friends?" How we dressed, what we ate, where we lodged, and whether we went around town in style five years ago matters little, but it "counts much whether we have had good companions, in that time."[50]

Emerson's last rule of life is to treat no one harshly or unfairly, and "to make yourself necessary to somebody." He says he could make more rules, but what is important is that we stick by them. Aspiration is one thing; the question is, "Will you stick?" Much of our energy for accomplishing our goals is dissipated. Those who succeed and can be relied on are those who are centered on their task. "The secret of culture is to learn, that a few great points steadily appear alike in the poverty of the obscurest farm, and in the miscellany of metropolitan life, and that these few are alone to be regarded,—the escape from all false ties; courage to be what we are; and love of what is simple and beautiful; independence, and cheerful relation, these are the essentials,—these and the wish to serve,—to add somewhat to the wellbeing of men."[51]

"ILLUSIONS"

Each of the essays in *The Conduct of Life* attempts to answer the question first posed in "Fate": How shall I live? In "Illusions" the question might be put this way: Given the shifting perceptions of everyday life, is there a moral ground for human action?

Emerson opens the essay with an account of his visit to Kentucky's Mammoth Cave in 1850. He must have had Plato's allegory of the cave from *The Republic* in mind, in which the observer views shadows cast on the wall of a cave, mistaking them for the real world rather than seeing them as the illusions they are. The source of the shadows, light, comes from outside the cave. On Emerson's visit, deep inside Mammoth Cave, the guide extinguished the lamps, and visitors were treated to what appeared to be a show of stars and "a flaming comet among them." The illusion reminded Emerson of actual experiences he'd had looking at the night sky, and it showed him how much imagination embellishes our experience of natural events, such as "sunset glories, rainbows, and northern lights."[52]

Imagination also shapes our experience of pleasure and pain. We are mistaken, he says, if we believe that "the circumstance gives the joy to which we give the circumstance." If life is sweet, it is because we ascribe a certain pleasure to the activities we are engaged in. We cherish our illusions, often preferring them to reality. "We live by our imaginations, by our admirations, by our sentiments," Emerson observes. "The child walks amid heaps of illusions which he does not like to have disturbed."[53]

We fantasize that we live better lives than we do. Society is a masquerade. Everyone wears the mask they want to show the world, and no one likes to be unmasked. We are all victims of illusion, "led by one bawble or another," leaving us confused: "All is riddle, and the key to a riddle is another riddle. There are as many pillows of illusion as flakes in a snow-storm. We wake from one dream into another dream. The toys, to be sure, are various, and are graduated in refinement to the quality of the dupe. . . . But everybody is drugged with his own frenzy, and the pageant marches at all hours, with music and banner and badge."[54]

Illusions affect our circumstances and our relationships. Even the scholar in his library is susceptible. A few see through the illusions, but "the enchantments are laid on very thick." We admire those who can "lift a corner of the curtain" to let us see what is behind. It helps to know that there are gradations in "the phantasms," from the lowest of masks to the most subtle and beautiful. There are the hallucinations of narcotics, but time is also an illusion, and life itself is a masquerade. What if the importance we attach to things radiates from ourselves or, as Emerson puts it "the sun borrows his beams?" Once we believed in magic. Now it has been dispelled, along with "all vestige of theism and beliefs."[55] From the deceptions of the senses to the illusions of the intellect, all of experience is subject to the workings of the imagination, so much so in fact that we delude ourselves as to our own role in it.

Science treats time and space as forms of thought and the material world as hypothetical. Every generalization yields to a larger one. Our estimates of things are loose and floating. "We must work and affirm," Emerson says, "but we have no guess of the value of what we say or do." The things which to us seem trivial—the activities of mundane, everyday life—are actually the most significant. In Emerson's view, "if we weave a yard of tape in all humility and as well as we can, long hereafter we shall see it was no cotton tape at all but some galaxy which we braided, and that the threads were Time and Nature."[56]

If we can't predict "the variable winds," how can we penetrate "the law of our shifting moods and susceptibility?" The firmament that once existed is gone and along with it the stars that might have signaled our destiny. We seem to be adrift: "From day to day the capital facts of human life are hidden from our eyes. Suddenly the mist rolls up and reveals them, and we think how much good time is gone that might have been saved had any hint of these things been shown. A sudden rise in the road shows us the system of mountains, and all the summits, which have been just as near us all the year, but quite out of mind." Yet we need not fear. Life may be a succession of dreams, but "the visions of good men are good." Only the undisciplined will is "whipped with bad thoughts and bad fortunes."[57]

"In this kingdom of illusions we grope eagerly for stays and foundations," Emerson observes. These prove to be quite simple and personal, really: honesty and truth—with ourselves and others—are what we must rely on. "Speak what you think, be what you are, pay your debts of all kinds." Cheats live for appearances, but "it is what we really are that avails with friends, with strangers, and with fate or fortune."[58] In other words, self-reliance is key to finding one's way among the clouds of appearance and clutter of triviality.

We think that having riches proves our value. But Native Americans do not think the white man, "with his brow of care, always toiling, afraid of heat and cold, and keeping within doors," has any advantage of them, Emerson points out. "The permanent interest of every man is never to be in a false position," he insists, "but to have the weight of nature to back him in all that he does." Riches and poverty are but a costume; the life of all of humankind is identical. We are all capable of transcending our circumstances and tasting the real quality of existence, seeing "God face to face every hour," and knowing "the savour of Nature."[59] We can all transcend our circumstances and taste the real quality of existence.

In Hindu philosophy, variety and separateness are illusory. Only the unity of things is real. The waves come and go, but the ocean remains the same. Although the intellect and the will are prey to deception, "the unities of Truth and Right are not broken by the disguise." We need not be confused about these. Beneath or behind the world of appearances is a reality we can be certain of and can rely on as a moral ground for human action. "There is no chance and no anarchy in the universe," Emerson says. He concludes the essay with an allegory of his own about the discovery of illusion and the affirmation of reality: "The young mortal enters the hall of the firmament: there he is alone with them alone, they pouring on him benedictions and gifts, and beckoning him up to their thrones. On the instant, and incessantly, fall snow-storms of illusions. He fancies himself in a vast crowd which sways this way and that, and whose movement and doings he must obey: he fancies himself poor, orphaned, insignificant. The mad crowd drives hither and thither, now furiously commending this thing to be done, now that. What is he that he should resist their will, and think or act for himself? Every moment, new changes and new showers of deceptions, to baffle and distract him. And when, by and by, for an instant, the air clears, and the cloud lifts a little, there are the gods still sitting around him on their thrones,—they alone with him alone."[60] All of us are subject to the "snow-storms of illusions," delusions that we are isolated and insignificant and incapable of thinking or acting on our own. Occasionally, however, "the air clears and the cloud lifts a little," and we see that our actual existence is among the gods, beckoning us to live a fuller, richer, deeper life.

The Conduct of Life comes closer to a manual of self-culture than any of Emerson's other books. Moral guidebooks, David Robinson observes, were "a flourishing form in mid-nineteenth-century America that answered the cultural need for authoritative rules of conduct and, more generally, a sense of the individual's place in the moral order of nature and the American social order."[61] Emerson is reluctant to be didactic in his rules for life. He wants to release the spirit rather than constrain it. As he says in "Worship," his intention is to elevate the votary, to raise us to a higher spiritual level and dispel the illusions that trap us in a world without wonder.

11

THE SOUND OF TRUMPETS

By 1860 Emerson had become famous far beyond New England. During the previous decade he had delivered as many as sixty-nine lectures a year on his tours. These trips were exhausting and hazardous. He traveled to major cities by train but often had to ride by horse and buggy for miles to smaller towns. During the winter of 1855 he crossed the frozen Mississippi River three times on foot! A year later, writing home from Dixon, Illinois, where it was fifteen degrees below zero, he wrote, "A cold raw country this, and plenty of night travelling and arriving at four in the morning, to take the last and worst bed in the tavern. Advancing day brings mercy and favor to me, but not the sleep." In January 1863, while staying in Niagara Falls, he was awakened at 3:00 a.m. by the sound of "Fire! within the house."[1] Emerson managed to throw on some of his clothes and make his way downstairs through the smoke and darkness. The hotel was a total loss. Despite all these hardships of travel, he retained an exuberant spirit, as shown in this 1859 journal entry: "The joy which will not let me sit in my chair, which brings me bolt upright to my feet, and sends me striding around my room, like a tiger in his cage, and I cannot have composure and concentration enough even to set down in English words the thought which thrills me—is not that joy a certificate of the elevation? What if I never write a book or a line? For a moment, the eyes of my eyes were opened, the affirmative experience remains, and consoles through all suffering."[2]

The decade of the 1860s was marked by war and loss for all of America. In January 1862 Emerson spoke at the Smithsonian Institution in Washington, D.C. While there he met with President Abraham Lincoln and government officials, pressing the case for emancipation. By this time, he was convinced that the war, however terrible, was the only way to end slavery. When he learned that Lincoln had signed the Emancipation Proclamation that September, he composed the poem "Boston Hymn," which he read at the great jubilee held in Boston's Music Hall on January 1, 1863, the day emancipation went into effect. An excerpt follows:

> Today unbind the captive,
> So only are ye unbound;
> Lift up a people from the dust,
> Trump of their rescue, sound!
>
> Pay the ransom to the owner,
> And fill the bag to the brim.
> Who is the owner? The slave is the owner,
> And ever was. Pay him.[3]

The decade was also one of great personal loss for Emerson. In June 1860 his friend and fellow Transcendentalist Theodore Parker died at age forty-nine in Florence. Parker had exhausted himself with his preaching, lecturing, and antislavery activism, and he was hoping to recover in sunny Italy. "He was willing to perish in the using," Emerson wrote in his journal. "He sacrificed the future to the present, was willing to spend and be spent, felt himself to belong to the day he lived in, and had too much to do than that he should be careful for fame."[4]

This was just the beginning. In May 1862, his dear friend Henry David Thoreau died at age forty-four after a lengthy bout of tuberculosis. They had first met when Thoreau was a student at Harvard. Fourteen years his junior, Emerson mentored his protégé as he developed as a writer, encouraging him to keep a journal, giving him use of his library, printing his contributions to the *Dial* magazine, allowing him to build a cabin on Emerson property at Walden Pond, and helping him find a publisher for his first book. Thoreau was practically a member of the Emerson family. He helped Emerson with his garden, built a wooden playhouse for the Emerson girls, and served as a live-in handyman when Emerson toured Britain in 1847–48. They shared many interests—walking, nature studies, and antislavery activism. As Thoreau lay dying, Emerson frequently visited his bedside. In his eulogy at Thoreau's memorial, Emerson spoke movingly of his friend's legacy: "The country knows not yet, or in the least part, how great a son it has lost. It seems an injury that he should leave in the midst of his broken task, which none else can finish,—a kind of indignity to so noble a soul, that it should depart out of nature before he has yet been really shown to his peers for what he is. But he, at least, is content. His soul was made for the noblest society; he had in a short life exhausted the capabilities of this world; wherever there is knowledge, wherever there is virtue, wherever there is beauty, he will find a home."[5]

Several other close relatives and friends also died that decade. Emerson's aunt Mary Moody Emerson died in 1863, and his aunt Sarah Alden Ripley, in 1867. The following year saw the deaths of his sister-in-law Lucy Brown; his brother, William; and William's wife, Susan. "When our friends die, we not only lose them," he wrote in his journal, "but we lose a great deal of life which in the survivors was related to them."[6]

Despite the rigors of travel, the calamity of the Civil War, and the deaths of family, friends, and colleagues, Emerson was far from slowing down. His literary output was, if anything, increasing. Following the success of *The Conduct of Life*, he focused his energies on another book of essays, *Society and Solitude*. This one, too, drew on his stock of lectures. Like those in *The Conduct of Life*, the essays in *Society and Solitude* were a reaffirmation of his earlier work. His major concern was the cultivation of the soul or, as he now expressed it, "the natural method of mental philosophy." As always, his intention was to provoke his audiences rather than merely edify them. The effect of these lectures was electric, as the poet James Russell Lowell attempted to describe in a letter to Charles Eliot Norton in 1867:

> Emerson's oration was more disjointed than usual, even with him. It began nowhere, and ended everywhere, and yet, as always with that divine man, it left you feeling that something beautiful had passed that way, something more beautiful than anything else, like the rising and setting of stars. Every possible criticism might have been made on it but one,—that it was not noble. There was a tone in it that awakened all elevating associations. He boggled, he lost his place, he had to put on his glasses; but it was as if a creature from some fairer world had lost his way in our fogs, and it was our fault, not his. It was chaotic, but it was all such stuff as stars are made of, and you couldn't help feeling that, if you waited awhile, all that was nebulous would be whirled into planets, and would assume the mathematical gravity of

system. All through it I felt something in me that cried, "Ha! ha!" to the sound of the trumpets.[7]

Society and Solitude was published in 1870, ten years after *The Conduct of Life*. Several of the essays in the book had previously appeared in the *Atlantic Monthly*, a magazine Emerson helped launch in 1857. Sales outpaced those of any of his previous books, prompting a wry note in his journal: "This is not for its merit, but only shows that old age is a good advertisement. Your name has been seen so often that your book must be worth buying."[8] Others were more effusive in their praise. In an *Atlantic Monthly* review, fellow Transcendentalist Thomas Wentworth Higginson commented, "It is not enough to say that essays such as these constitute the high water mark of American literature; it is not too much to say that they are unequalled in the literature of the age."[9] Perceptively, the short-story writer Bret Harte remarked that "from a secular pulpit he preaches better practical sermons on the conduct of life than is heard from two-thirds of the Christian pulpits of America."[10]

"SOCIETY AND SOLITUDE"

Emerson was an introvert. Solitude was his refuge as well as his source of inspiration. From his first lectures to his last, Emerson emphasized the importance of solitude in the pursuit of self-culture. In his early lectures on "human culture" in the 1830s, he advocated "the simple habit of sitting alone occasionally to explore what facts of moment lie in the memory [which] may have the effect in some more favored hour to open to the student the kingdom of spiritual nature."[11]

He begins the essay "Society and Solitude" with a parable about a man who felt unfit for society. Even in solitude he felt exposed and embarrassed. He sought anonymity in his mode of dress, but its very drabness betrayed him. Emerson's son Edward, in his notes on the essay, suggests his father's parable may have been autobiographical. "Mr. Emerson believed himself so unfitted for society, in his younger years, that his memories were mortifications, and he turned his face resolutely away from them. . . . In those days he was not strong, and perhaps memories of his awkwardness in his personal duties distressed him. . . . In Concord woods he found healing for body, and oracles for the soul."[12]

If Isaac Newton had been "fond of dancing, port, and clubs," we would never have had *Principia*, the foundation of all modern science. "Dante was very bad company, and was never invited to dinner," Emerson continued. "Michael Angelo had a sad, sour time of it. Ministers of beauty are rarely beautiful in coaches and saloons." But the significance of solitude is deeper. An important part of us is diminished in the company of others. We are born into and conditioned by society, but we must ask ourselves, "Which is first, man or men?"[13]

Solitude can feel alienating and unnatural. It seems so contrary to human nature that we feel it must be "corrected by a common sense" and "clothed with society." Living in isolation is difficult. The benefit of society is that "it is so easy with the great to be great; so easy to come up to an existing standard." But society should be taken in small doses. "If solitude is proud, so is society vulgar," given to gossip and social status-seeking. Thus, "we sink as easily as we rise." The remedy, Emerson says, is to reconcile the two. "Society we must have; but let it be society, and not exchanging news, or eating from the same dish."[14]

Society and solitude are a polarity, one of nature's "extreme antagonisms." Emerson says "our safety is in the skill with which we keep the diagonal line. Solitude is impractical, and society fatal. We must keep our head in the one, and our hands in the other. The conditions are met, if we keep our independence, yet do not lose our sympathy." Using one of his favorite images, he likens the effort to driving a pair of horses. "These wonderful horses need to be driven by fine hands. We require such a solitude as shall hold us to its revelations when we are in the street and in palaces." We derive our principles from insights gained in solitude and "accept society as the natural element in which they are to be applied."[15]

Solitude can be hard to come by in today's world. Work that demands us to always be on call, sprawling cities that never rest, ease of transporting ourselves from one event to another, technologies that lure our attention, and the very pace of our culture leave us few moments truly to ourselves. Solitude seems almost to be a luxury or a sign of indolence, a reproach to society's emphasis on practicality. As Anne Morrow Lindbergh observes in *Gift from the Sea*, "If one sets aside time for a business engagement, a trip to the hairdresser, a social engagement, or a shopping expedition, that time is accepted as inviolable. But if one says: I cannot

come because that is my hour to be alone, one is considered rude, ego-
tistical or strange. What a commentary on our civilization, when being
alone is considered suspect; when one has to apologize for it, make
excuses, hide the fact that one practices it—like a secret vice!"[16]

There is also resistance to Emerson's contention that solitude is the
source of spiritual insight and by implication the wellspring of religion.
Alfred North Whitehead expressed it as "religion is solitariness; and if
you are never solitary, you are never religious." All the rest—rituals,
scriptures, dogmas, and institutions—are, as Whitehead says, "the trappings of religion, its passing forms."[17] Emerson, Theodore Parker, and
other Transcendentalists, as well as philosophers such as William James
and John Dewey, all took this view. Certainly, religion has an important
social dimension, but it must be grounded in personal experience.

"WORKS AND DAYS"

One of Emerson's favorite poems, "Days," expresses a thought central to
Emerson's philosophy of life: that every day the world is laid out for us
in this garden that is our home. We are given the precious gift of time to
make the most of. But these priceless moments are for this day only. Any
that go unused are taken away. In this short poem that begins, "Daughters of Time, the hypocritic Days," Emerson has forgotten his morning
wishes—that is to say, his hopes and dreams and best intentions—and
settles only for a few herbs and apples. Too late, he realizes that he has
squandered the gifts that time has offered. This poem, appearing in
the Centenary Edition of Emerson's complete works, begins his essay
"Works and Days."[18]

The nineteenth century, Emerson says, is the age of tools, of machines.
But these instruments are only extensions of ourselves, our limbs and
senses. We humans are truly the measure of all things. To be sure, the
advances of science and technology are exciting: "so many inventions
have been added that life seems almost made over." One after another,
these inventions have transformed society on a scale previously unimaginable: "We ride four times as fast as our fathers did; travel, grind,
weave, forge, plant, till and excavate better. We have new shoes, gloves,
glasses and gimlets; we have the calculus, we have the newspaper,
which does its best to make every square acre of land give an account

of itself at your breakfast table; we have money, and paper money; we have language,—the finest tool of all, and nearest the mind. Much will have more." But Emerson is troubled by the incessant demand for ever more improvements. It is a thirst, like that of the wicked king Tantalus of Greek mythology—"vainly trying to quench his thirst with a flowing stream"—a thirst that cannot be quenched. No matter how many centuries of advances have gone before, no matter how many problems have been solved, "the new man always finds himself on the brink of chaos, always in a crisis."[19]

We have become a captive to our own tools. "We must look deeper for our salvation than to steam, photographs, balloons or astronomy," Emerson insists. "The weaver becomes a web, the machinist a machine. If you do not use the tools, they use you"[20] For all our mechanical inventions, we have not lightened anyone's toil. What have any of these inventions done for character or human worth? Are we the better for them? The pace of technological invention has outstripped moral progress. We have not made a wise investment. We were offered both works and days, and we took only works, he says.

The title of the essay is taken from a poem by the ancient Greek poet Hesiod, praising the simple virtues of farming and everyday life. Emerson tells us of a farmer who wanted to have all the land that joined his own, comparing him to Napoleon, who had the same appetite on a larger scale. But even if the farmer or Napoleon gained the whole world, he would still be a pauper. "He only is rich who owns the day," Emerson says. "There is no king, rich man, fairy or demon who possesses such power as that. The days are ever divine. . . . They are of the least pretension, and of the greatest capacity, of anything that exists."[21]

Some days are full of significance. Holidays, for example, are especially memorable: the Fourth of July, Thanksgiving, and Christmas. School days and college terms, when "life was then calendared by moments, [and] threw itself into nervous knots of glittering hours." Even the Sabbath offers "a clean page, which the wise may inscribe with truth." There are days when we feel close to greatness. "There are days which are the carnival of the year. The angels assume flesh, and repeatedly become available." But each day offers its gifts only to those who are ready to receive them: "The days are made on a loom whereof the warp and woof are past and future time. They are majestically dressed, as if every god brought a thread to the skyey web. 'Tis pitiful the things by which we are rich or poor,—a matter of coins, coats and carpets, a little more or less stone, or wood, or paint, the fashion of a cloak or hat." The treasures that nature offers—the earth, the sea, the air, the heavens, and the eye which beholds them—"these, not like a glass bead, or the coins or carpets, are given immeasurably to all."[22]

We seldom appreciate such gifts because we are "coaxed, flattered and duped from morn to eve, from birth to death." Where, Emerson asks, "is the old eye that ever saw through the deception?" Caught up in maya, we cling to the childish illusion that "a rattle, a doll, a horse, a gun" will make us happy. "Seldom and slowly the mask falls and the pupil is permitted to see that all is one stuff, cooked and painted under many counterfeit appearances."[23]

Illusion hides the value of the present moment. "Every man in moments of deeper thought is apprised that . . . an everlasting Now reigns in Nature." Everything we need is right here, not in the past or somewhere else, in this and not some other hour. "One of the illusions is that the present hour is not the critical decisive hour. Write it on your heart that every day is the best day in the year. No man has learned anything rightly until he knows that every day is Doomsday."[24]

As mythical gods sometimes appear in the guise of beggars, so the seemingly most trivial hour has everything to offer: "We owe to genius always the same debt, of lifting the curtain from the common, and showing us that divinities are sitting disguised in the seeming gang of gypsies and peddlers." Wisdom lies using the materials at hand rather than looking for better ones or those that others have used. "Do not refuse the employment which the hour brings you, for one more ambitious," Emerson admonishes us. "The highest heaven of wisdom is alike near from every point, and thou must find it, if at all, by methods native to thyself alone."[25]

We are often under the illusion that there is not enough time for our work. Emerson relates this anecdote: When someone remarked to a chief of the Six Nations of New York that he didn't have enough time, the chief replied, "Well, I suppose you have all there is." We always have all the time there is. It is up to us to make the best use of it. Another illusion that deceives us is that the longer the duration—a year, a decade, a century—the better. "God works in moments," as an old French saying goes. "We ask for long life, but 'tis deep life, or grand moments, that signify," notes Emerson. The measure of time should be qualitative, not quantitative. "Moments of insight, of fine personal relation, a smile, a glance,—what ample borrowers of eternity they are!" Eternity culminates in the present moment, or quoting Homer, "The gods ever give to mortals their appointed share of reason only on one day."[26]

We are measured by the appreciation of the day. The most learned scholar is not the one who unearths ancient history "but who can unfold the theory of this particular Wednesday." The minutes we have are not a way to *achieve* happiness. In fact, they *constitute* happiness and the only eternity we have. Understood in this way, we will move beyond a menial and dependent life, to one of riches and fulfillment. We must give up our habit of analyzing and dissecting experience. Emerson put it this way: "Life is good only when it is magical and musical, a perfect timing and consent, and when we do not anatomize it. You must treat the days respectfully, you must be a day yourself, and not interrogate it like a college professor. The world is enigmatical . . . and must not be taken literally, but genially. We must be at the top of our condition to understand anything rightly. You must hear the bird's song without attempting to render it into nouns and verbs. Cannot we be a little abstemious and obedient? Cannot we let the morning be?"[27]

Emerson remembers that in his youth he heard a visiting foreign scholar talk about the native Hawaiians, who "delight to play with the surf, coming in on top of the rollers, then swimming out again, and repeat the delicious manoeuvre for hours." The speaker concluded: "Well, human life is made up of such transits. There can be no greatness without abandonment. . . . Just to fill the hour,—that is happiness. Fill my hour, ye gods, so that I shall not say, whilst I have done this, 'Behold, also, an hour of my life is gone,'—but rather, 'I have lived an hour.'"[28] Like the Hawaiian surf riders, we should do what we do for the joy of it, rather than from a sense of duty. This advice applies to all areas of life and thought.

It is the quality of the moment and not its duration that counts. "It is the depth at which we live," Emerson insists, "and not at all the surface extension that imports." Time is but the flitting surface of life. With "the least acceleration of thought" we pierce through it to eternity and "make life to seem to be of vast duration." We call it "time," but when it is understood in this way, "it acquires another and higher name."[29]

He concludes "Works and Days" with this thought: "And this is the progress of every earnest mind; from the works of man and the activity of the hands to a delight in the faculties which rule them; from a respect to the works to a wise wonder at this mystic element of time in which he is conditioned; from local skills and the economy which reckons the amount of production *per* hour to the finer economy which respects the quality of what is done, and the right we have to the work, or the fidelity with which it flows from ourselves; then to the depth of thought it betrays, looking to its universality, or that its roots are in eternity, not in time."[30]

Emerson might as well have been speaking of the twenty-first century as the nineteenth. In our day as much as his, works supersede days. We need both, and we need to find a balance between a respect for works and a wise wonder at the mystic element of time in which we live and move and have our being. Emerson is not alone in conveying this perennial wisdom. As Joseph Campbell writes in *The Power of Myth*: "Eternity isn't some later time. Eternity isn't even a long time. Eternity has nothing to do with time. Eternity is that dimension of here and now that all thinking in temporal terms cuts off. And if you don't get it here, you won't get it anywhere. . . . [T]he experience of eternity right here and now, in all things . . . is the function of life." Similarly, the twentieth-century essayist Storm Jameson writes: "There is only one world, the world pressing against you at this minute. There is only one minute in which you are alive, this minute here and now. The only way to live is by accepting each minute as an unrepeatable miracle."[31]

"CLUBS"

For Emerson and his friends, clubs provided a venue for conversation, which they pursued as a spiritual practice. It is spiritual in the sense that good conversation elevates us. Fellow Transcendental Club member Bronson Alcott put it this way: "Good conversation is lyrical: a pentecost of tongues, touching the cords of melody in all minds, it prompts the best each had to give, to better than any knew they had, what none claims as his own, as if he were the organ of some invisible player behind the scenes."[32]

The nineteenth century was the great age of conversation in America. "Wise, cultivated, genial conversation is the last flower of civilization and the best result which life has to offer us," Emerson observes.[33] Elizabeth

Peabody's salon above her bookshop on West Street in Boston; the celebrated "conversations" of Margaret Fuller and Bronson Alcott; meetings of the Transcendentalist circle in Emerson's home in Concord—all of these offered intoxicating conversation. This was the age of "table talk," "parlor culture," and clubs.

Emerson belonged to at least five literary clubs at different times during his career: the Transcendental Club, the Saturday Club, the Town and Country Club, the Radical Club, and the Concord Social Circle, according to American studies scholar Alfred G. Litton. Most of these clubs included women.[34] Margaret Fuller, Julia Ward Howe, Elizabeth Peabody, and Caroline Healey Dall, among others, were active club members. Emerson's clubs also boasted of such literary luminaries as Henry Wadsworth Longfellow, Nathaniel Hawthorne, Robert Lowell, and Oliver Wendell Holmes. Emerson was a prime mover in these clubs, helping organize them and set the rules for discourse.

We need stimulation and variety in our lives to keep us going. Emerson finds that conversation with others is the best way to supply them. People seek conversation for different reasons—some for facts, some for love, some for debate. "But one thing is certain," he says, "at some rate, intercourse we must have."[35] In conversation we clarify our own thinking. The days we remember best are those spent with a companion sharing our thoughts. When we tire of reading, we seek out intelligent conversation with friends.

We are less when we are together than when we are alone, Emerson asserts, but in conversation we are enlarged. Talking with others brings out facts hidden in the recesses of memory. "Nothing seems so cheap as the benefit of conversation: nothing is more rare." Some people love to talk because they feel superior, rather than conversing with others on an equal basis. He calls these talkers "gladiators"; conversation is always a battle to see who wins. Rather than "conceited prigs," he advises, we should seek out those rare people of "genial temper" who dispose "all others irresistibly to good humor and discourse."[36]

Emerson traces the history of clubs through the ancient Greek and Roman periods to the Middle Ages and into nineteenth-century France, Germany, and Britain. They are most commonly found in cities and "are the compensation which these can make to their dwellers for depriving them of the free intercourse with nature."[37] In cities, people with similar educational background and social standing could easily find clubs, such as Boston's elite Saturday Club that Emerson was part of. But he was also a devoted member of the Concord Social Circle which included a cross section of the town's citizens. He and Bronson Alcott also founded the Town and Country Club to bring together thoughtful people from diverse backgrounds.

Some people, he allows, are not suited to club life and table talk. "There are those who have the instinct of a bat to fly against any lighted candle and put it out, marplots and contradictors." Some come only to talk, others only to hear. Neither is good for conversation. He also offers this rule: "Admit no man whose presence excludes any one topic."[38] In a later lecture titled "Table Talk," Emerson offers more guiding rules: "You shall not be leaky," that is, members must not share with others what was said in confidence. A second rule is, "You shall not be opinionative and argumentative." Third, "Beware of jokes." A little wit is fine, but ridicule is not. Finally, "You shall not be negative, but affirmative."[39] Dismal, negative views of life and politics are disheartening and are to be discouraged. In a club, everyone ideally has something to add to the conversation, and that contributes to the self-culture of all. "Wisdom," Emerson says, "is like electricity. There is no permanent wise man, but men capable of wisdom, who, being put into certain company, or other favorable conditions, become wise for a short time, as glasses rubbed acquire electric power for a while."[40]

Clubs like Emerson describes are uncommon today. There is certainly a wide variety of groups: book groups, support groups, discussion groups, meetups. And they do provide some of the benefits of the clubs in Emerson's day, but they are less formal and less focused on the art of good conversation. Although we communicate more frequently than ever—by text, messaging, and phone—we seldom engage in meaningful conversation, observes Sherry Turkle in *Reclaiming Conversation: The Power of Talk in a Digital Age*. Whether we are walking down the street or attending a dinner party, a meeting, or a lecture, we keep our phones always in view, sucking at our attention. The phone is a silent partner to every verbal exchange and, in Turkle's view, prevents us from going deeper into conversation. We can't use body language and tone to convey emotion, so we sprinkle in emoticons and use all caps. Sending a text is often easier than having a difficult conversation; signing an online petition is a quick and easy way of expressing one's opinion, an exercise in salvation by proxy.[41] At the same time, we lose the value of conversation as a means of self-culture. Most people remember times when they felt elevated by deep conversation of the kind that Emerson describes. Our lives today are busier and more complicated than were those who frequented clubs in the nineteenth century, and therefore we appear to have fewer opportunities for the kind of spiritual enrichment that comes from the exciting give-and-take exchange of ideas in a group setting.

"SUCCESS"

Corporate leaders, motivational speakers, college coaches, and writers of greeting cards have seized on Emerson's essays about such topics as wealth, success, and power for personal inspiration and advice to others. But most miss the very points Emerson is trying to make. He often brings his own meaning to common terms. For example, in the essay "Wealth" in *The Conduct of Life*, Emerson says that "man was born to be rich." By "rich," he does not mean the accumulation of money and power. The wealthy are not those who "hoard and conceal"; such people are, in Emerson's eyes, "the greater beggars." Rather, the wealthy are those "whose work carves out work for more, and opens a path for all." The essay goes on to assert that true thrift is not hoarding but spending on a higher plane. For Emerson, it means to invest with keener insight, so as to "spend in spiritual creation," and not merely on our material wants.[42]

Emerson's essay "Success" in *Society and Solitude* makes a similar statement. Americans are especially zealous of success, driven "by exclusion, grasping, and egotism," taking from all for the benefit of one. "I hate this shallow Americanism which hopes to get rich by credit," Emerson says, "to get knowledge by raps on midnight tables, to learn the economy of the mind by phrenology, or skill without study, or mastery without apprenticeship, or the sale of goods through pretending that they sell, or power through making believe you are powerful." People think they have succeeded, "but they have got something else,—a crime which calls for another crime, and another devil behind that; these are steps to suicide, infamy, and the harming of humankind."[43] We countenance puffery at the expense of excellence.

Each of us has an aptitude we are born with. Yet, instead of believing in ourselves, we too often defer to others' opinions of what we should do and whether we are doing it well. We must do our own work. "Self-trust is the first secret of success, the belief that, if you are here, the authorities of the universe put you here, and for cause, or with some task strictly appointed you in your constitution, and so long as you work at that you are well and successful."[44]

Next, Emerson says, success depends on maintaining a harmonious and receptive relationship with the world. He invites us to "remember when, in early youth the earth spoke and the heavens glowed; when any evening, grim and wintry, sleet and snow, was enough for us; the houses were in the air. Now it costs a rare combination of clouds and lights to overcome the common and mean." Once, the woods were full of "pomp and glory . . . garlanded with vines, flowers, and sunbeams."[45] Now the owner of the wood lot sees only trees ripe for harvesting.

The beauty that we see in the world comes from us. Is the home we grew up in only a piece of real estate? The church and school only a pile of wood and bricks? In addition to knowledge, we must have love to see the world aright. "A deep sympathy is what we require for any student of the mind." If we could be content to "live in the happy self-sufficing present, and find the day and its cheap means contenting"—which comes by receptivity rather than ambition—then we would be successful. "We are not strong by our power to penetrate, but by our relatedness," Emerson insists. "The world is enlarged for us, not by new objects, but by finding more affinities and potencies in those we have."[46]

Another key to success is spiritual health, which leads to wisdom. It comes, he says, when we understand that "the heart at the center of the universe with every throb hurls the flood of happiness into every artery, vein, and veinlet, so that the whole system is inundated with the tides of joy." It is the recognition that there is abundance to be found even in the poorest circumstance. A fourth trait of success is embracing the affirmative. We are sustained by a belief in the power of truth and goodness. "It is true there is evil and good, night and day:" Emerson says, "but these are not equal. The day is great and final. The night is for the day, but the day is not for the night."[47] Nothing is accomplished by negativity. Cynicism is easy and cheap, but it is not productive.

Emerson observes that "we live on different planes or platforms." On the one hand, there is the external, everyday life in which we are educated to get ahead, grasping all we can, making ourselves "useful and agreeable," in order to "shine, conquer, and possess." On the other hand, we have an inner life in which we do not value such accomplishments at all. It does not care about power or reputation. "It lives in the great present; it makes the present great. This tranquil, well-founded, wide-seeing soul is no express rider, no attorney, no magistrate: it lives in the sun, and broods on the world."[48]

Emerson's belief that our daily life should be lived on a higher plane of existence is easy to accept. Living happily in the "self-sufficing present" requires only receptivity, he says. But there is a fundamental paradox of the spiritual life. To sustain such awareness requires a commitment to a spiritual practice. We need daily reflection, which we can achieve by reading, journaling, walking, conversation, contemplation, or whatever practice speaks to us. Otherwise, we soon find ourselves back in our old harmful, socially conditioned ways.

"OLD AGE"

Emerson first delivered the final essay in *Society and Solitude*, "Old Age," as a lecture in 1861, when he was fifty-eight years old. Life expectancy at the time was approximately forty years. Two primary factors for the low average life expectancy were high infant mortality and tuberculosis. During his lifetime, tuberculosis was the leading cause of death in Concord. It afflicted many families, including his own. His first wife, Ellen, died from it at age nineteen, as did two brothers with whom he was very close. Henry Thoreau also died of the disease. Emerson himself suffered from symptoms of tuberculosis at various times of his life, although it was not the cause of his own death.

Emerson remained productive through the 1850s and 1860s, but his lecture tours, his antislavery activism, and the public's demand for more books must have exhausted him. Around 1850, he penned the poem "Terminus":

> It is time to be old,
> To take in sail:—
> The god of bounds,
> Who sets to seas a shore,
> Came to me in his fatal rounds,
> And said: "No more!"

. . . .

As the bird trims her to the gale,
I trim myself to the storm of time,
I man the rudder, reef the sail,
Obey the voice at eve obeyed at prime:
"Lowly faithful, banish fear,
Right onward drive unharmed;
The port, well worth the cruise, is near,
And every wave is charmed."[49]

At age sixty-three, just before setting out on his 1866 winter journey to the West, Emerson read the poem to his son Edward. "I was startled," Edward wrote in a memoir of his father, "for he, looking so healthy, so full of life and young in spirit, was reading his deliberate acknowledgement of failing forces and his trusting and serene acquiescence."[50]

Emerson's audience at the Salem Lyceum in 1861, hearing "Old Age" for the first and only time he read it publicly as a lecture, must also have wondered what was on Emerson's mind. The signs we associate with age, he notes, are deceptive: "dim sight, deafness, cracked voice, snowy hair, short memory." But these are masks, and not only of old age. Some younger people are old before their time, while many older people remain youthful. What counts is intellect, not time. Time is elastic. "The mind stretches an hour to a century, and dwarfs an age to an hour," writes Emerson.[51] What is inside us does not decay. Alone, by ourselves, we are not aware of the inroads of time. If we did not compare ourselves to those who are younger, we would hardly be aware of its passage.

But Emerson fears the public is dubious of the pleasures of aging, noting that "the estimate of age is low, melancholy, and skeptical." Next to alcohol and drugs, "the surest poison is time": "This cup, which Nature puts to our lips, has a wonderful virtue surpassing that of any other draught. It opens the senses, adds power, fills us with exalted dreams, which we call hope, love, ambition, science: especially, it creates a craving for larger draughts of itself. But they who take the larger draughts are drunk with it, lose their stature, strength, beauty, and senses, and end in folly and delirium. We postpone our literary work, until we have more ripeness and skill to write, and we one day discover that our literary talent was a youthful effervescence which we have now lost." The reader cannot help but wonder whether this essay is autobiographical. Age confers some respect in society, but accepting the personal ravages of time takes a Stoic attitude. Few envy the old. "We do not count a man's years," Emerson says, "until he has nothing else to count." Age may not be disgraceful, but it is seen as "immensely disadvantageous."[52]

In typical fashion, Emerson will have none of this skepticism. "We know the value of experience." Wisdom is cumulative, built over time through our accomplishments. "Skill to do comes of knowing; knowledge comes by eyes always open, and working hands; and there is no knowledge that is not power."[53] Look at the late-life contributions of such statesmen as Benjamin Franklin, Thomas Jefferson, and John Adams and of such intellectuals as Francis Bacon, Alexander Humboldt, and Goethe. All of these were elders when they made major contributions, but they were hardly considered old at the time.

One of the satisfactions of age is that we have less to fear after having weathered "the perilous capes and shoals in the sea whereon we sail." With age comes "a feeling of immense relief from the number of dangers" we have escaped. Another advantage is that we have already amassed a "fund of merit," and whether we have additional success means very little. "Every one is sensible of this cumulative advantage in living," Emerson observes. "All the good days behind him are sponsors, who speak for him when he is silent, pay for him when he has no money, introduce him where he has no letters, and work for him when he sleeps."[54]

A further advantage is that age "has found expression." Youth suffers from unrealized dreams, untested abilities, and visions of a career as yet uncertain. There is no "correspondence between things and thoughts." With the passage of time our life takes shape. "One by one, day after day," we learn to "coin [our] wishes into facts." With age we reconcile our wishes with their possession and experience "the satisfaction it slowly offers to every craving." The fourth advantage is that "age sets its house in order and finishes its works." In youth "every object glitters and attracts. . . . We leave one pursuit for another, and [our] year is a heap of beginnings." But the time we spend on what we start but don't finish is not wasted. We "hive innumerable experiences," as Emerson puts it.[55] Our unfinished beginnings may seem of little value at the time, but they contribute to our growth as a person. With age we have a sense of satisfaction and completion.

A life well lived is a kind of secular immortality. Emerson's own legacy is a good example of what he means. We can be content knowing that what we have accomplished in life outlives us: "When life has been well spent, age is a loss of what it can well spare, muscular strength, organic instincts, gross bulk, and works that belong to these. But the central wisdom, which was old in infancy, is young in fourscore years, and, dropping off obstructions, leaves in happy subjects the mind purified and wise. I have heard, that, whoever loves, is in no condition old. I have heard, that, whenever the name of man is spoken, the doctrine of immortality is announced; it cleaves to his constitution. The mode of it baffles our wit, and no whisper comes to us from the other side. But the inference from the working of intellect, hiving knowledge, hiving skill,—at the end of life just ready to be born,—affirms the inspirations of affection and of the moral sentiment."[56]

Emerson has sometimes been criticized for a naive sense of optimism. He was determined to view life positively, in spite of his own personal losses. What he says about the pleasures and advantages of age was borne out in his own life. But this was and is not true for everyone. Some come to the end of life consumed with bitterness and remorse. Others suffer from poverty, loneliness, and ill health. However, Emerson reminds us not to focus on such frailties as white hair, unsteady knees, and short memories. These are only illusions. Eye to eye with ourselves in the mirror, we are the same persons we have always been. He wrote in his journal, "Within I do not find wrinkles and used heart, but unspent youth."[57]

12

TAKING IN THE SAIL

E merson's final essay in *Society and Solitude* was telling. "It is time to be old, / To take in sail," he wrote in the poem "Terminus," but there was still a lot of sail to take in during the last period of his life. He ceased his lecture tours to the West in 1868. But as a well-known public intellectual, he continued to be in demand as a speaker closer to home. He accepted invitations to talk, for example, at a reception for the Chinese Embassy in 1868 and the dedication of Concord's new Free Public Library in 1873. During the 1860s he gave lectures that he revised for publication in the *Atlantic Monthly* magazine and in his final book, *Letters and Social Aims*, in 1875. He also published another book of poetry, *Selected Poems*, in 1876 and edited an anthology of his favorite poems, *Parnassus*, in 1880.

Emerson was instrumental in founding the Free Religious Association in 1867, which charted a new course for liberal religion that has lasted to this day. For several decades already, he and other radical Unitarian ministers had broken with historical Christianity, espousing "a naturalized, post-Christian, and universal understanding of human spirituality," as David Robinson has characterized it. In the years following the Civil War, leaders in the Unitarian Association pressed for "a uniform creedal statement that might link Unitarianism to traditional forms of Christian belief."[1] Objecting, the radical ministers formed their own association, affirming the right of individual conscience and rejecting supernaturalism. In many respects the Free Religious Association extended the tradition of Emerson and Theodore Parker, bringing it much closer to the tenets of Unitarian Universalism today.

Emerson spoke at the inaugural meeting of the new association in 1867 and again the following year. Those who attended the first meeting

included Transcendentalists, Quakers, liberal Jews, agnostics, spiritualists, and scientific theists. All were invited to join. "The first to pay
his dollar was R. W. Emerson."[2] In his address at the second meeting,
Emerson summarized his position: "We are all believers in natural religion; we all agree that the health and integrity of man is self-respect,
self-subsistency, a regard to natural conscience. All education is to accus-
tom him to trust himself, discriminate between his higher and lower
thoughts, exert the timid faculties until they are robust, and thus train
him to self-help, until he ceases to be an underling, a tool, and becomes
a benefactor. I think wise men wish their religion to be all of this kind,
teaching the agent to go alone, not to hang on the world as a pensioner,
a permitted person, but an adult, self-searching soul, brave to assist or
resist a world: only humble or docile before the source of the wisdom he
has discovered within him."[3]

In his later years, Emerson restored his relationship with Harvard, his
alma mater, which opened some exciting new opportunities for him. In
1866 the college awarded him an honorary doctorate degree, mending
a breach that had lasted nearly thirty years following his controversial
address at the Divinity School in 1838. In 1867 he was invited to give his
second Phi Beta Kappa address and was appointed to Harvard's Board of
Overseers. As an overseer, he pushed for the introduction of electives in
the college curriculum. He raised funds for the construction of the grand
Memorial Hall on the Harvard campus, honoring college students and
graduates who had died in the Civil War. He was most proud of being
appointed a lecturer in philosophy in 1870. He welcomed the opportunity to develop a series of lectures on the natural history of the intellect,
a summation of his philosophy.

By the end of the 1870s, however, Emerson's memory was failing,
and he began to rely on help from his daughter Ellen with his lecturing
and from his friend James Elliot Cabot with editing his papers for publication. Despite his eventual decline, several of his later lectures and
essays are among his finest—especially "Inspiration," "Greatness," and
"Immortality" in Letters and Social Aims and "Character," published in
the North American Review in 1866. Owing perhaps to Cabot's assistance,
they are also more succinct and polished than were earlier essays.

"CHARACTER"

James T. Fields, Emerson's friend, book publisher, and *Atlantic Monthly* editor, refused to publish his essay "Character." Emerson had always offered the essays he developed from his lectures to Fields, but the editor felt this one was too provocative. "Ordinary readers would not understand [Emerson] and would consider [the essay] blasphemous," according to Fields's wife, Annie. So Emerson offered the essay to another friend, Charles Eliot Norton, editor of the *North American Review*. In a letter to a friend, Norton explained that he wished to publish the essay for the very reason that Fields had rejected it: "He calls it 'Character,' but it is on the moral sentiment in its relation to religion. It is a confession of faith; the *religio Emersonii*. It is the most unflinching assertion of the supreme right of private judgment; of the wrong done to human nature by 'authority' in matters of religion; of the temporariness of all the forms of religion, the everlasting freshness of the religious spirit. It is, if rightly understood, a profoundly religious paper; wrongly read it is freethinking almost to blasphemy. It will hurt some tender & pious souls, whom it pains me to distress, but it will help some bewildered ones & will open the way to wider views of truth."[4]

Emerson, like most Unitarians of the nineteenth century, grounded human happiness in the cultivation of the moral sentiment, or conscience. Morality is innate in human beings. It is a tendency or bias toward goodness, but it must be developed and directed to universal ends. In Emerson's expression, "He is moral,—we say it with Marcus Aurelius and with Kant,—whose aim or motive may become a universal rule, binding on all intelligent beings."[5]

Morality is rooted in an intuitive sense of a universal mind, common to all persons. "It is the mind of the mind," Emerson says. "We belong to it, not it to us." It is alike in everyone, although there is a "perpetual conflict between the dictate of this universal mind and the wishes and interests of the individual." In fact, Emerson denounces the exclusive pursuit of private ends as shameful: "The moral element invites man to great enlargements, to find his satisfaction, not in particulars or events, but in the purpose and tendency; not in bread, but in his right to his bread; not in much corn or wool, but in its communication. No one is accomplished whilst anyone is incomplete. Weal does not exist for one, with the woe of any other."[6]

Religions and philosophers through the ages have used a variety of words and images to describe this force: "the light, the seed, the Spirit, the Holy Ghost, the Comforter, the Daemon, the still, small voice, etc.,—all indicating its power and its latency." Though intangible and inexpressible, "it creates a faith which the contradiction of all mankind cannot shake." It is in the constitution of our consciousness, confirmed by our own experience. "The Divine Mind imparts itself to the single person," Emerson says. Some are especially receptive to the influence of the Divine Mind, demonstrated by their character. "Character denotes habitual self-possession, habitual regard to interior and constitutional motives," he says, unswayed "by outward events and opinion and by implication points to the source of right motive."[7] Those who achieve it are exemplary persons, few and far between. Virtue consists in emulating such models in the cultivation of our own character. It is not enough to envision ideal virtue; we must develop it through the practice of our own self-culture.

The moral sentiment "is the judge and measure of every expression of it." Religious institutions, with their rituals, doctrines, and scriptures, may try to embody the moral sentiment, but it is "the perpetual critic on these forms," voicing its disapproval. It cannot be bottled and sold. "The religion of one age," Emerson says, becomes "the literary entertainment of the next." Christianity should not rest on the miracles of Jesus but on "the miracle of being the broadest and most humane doctrine." The Christian religion, however, has become narrow and corrupt; "the words pale, are rhetoric, and all credence gone."[8]

The spirit is what matters, not the form. Religion rests upon the moral sentiment, not church doctrines or scriptures. "The mind of this age has fallen away from theology to morals," Emerson states. "I conceive it an advance." Rejecting the idolatry of Christian forms and rituals has made the far-reaching wisdom of other philosophies and religious traditions more accessible. "Socrates and Marcus Aurelius are allowed to be saints, a Mahomet is no longer accursed. Voltaire is no longer a scarecrow. Spinoza has come to be revered."[9] Our spiritual life can be enriched by other traditions and prophets, as long as we draw from the same source they did: the moral sentiment.

In his "American Scholar" address, Emerson said we must have our own distinctly American literature. So, too, we must have an American faith "written on ethical principles, so that the entire power of the spiritual world can be enlisted to hold the loyalty of the citizen." Christianity no longer sustains the vitality of the Western world. "Our religion has gone on as far as Unitarianism," he says. "But all the forms grow pale. The walls of the temple are wasted and thin." Fellow Transcendentalist Theodore Parker put it this way: the forms of religion pass away, but the sentiment that gave rise to them is permanent.[10]

In his Divinity School address and his essay on "Worship," Emerson observed that America was in the midst of a profound spiritual transformation. He returns to that theme in this essay. He is not talking about a religious reformation, in which Catholic rituals and idols are replaced by Protestant ones, for example. He wants to do away with such religious trappings altogether. He wants to transcend religious institutions and rely on the universal moral sentiment that every individual has access to. That is why he claims Christianity has reached its end with Unitarianism. The church still clings to the miracles of Jesus as proof of its claims. But "the soul, penetrated with the beatitude which pours into it on all sides," finds the miraculous everywhere. If the church truly built its faith on morals, it would never have tolerated slavery, racism, or the disenfranchisement of women. Yet "there is no vice that has not skulked behind" false religions.[11]

Emerson does not dismiss religion entirely. Instead, he argues that removing the strictures of religious orthodoxy invites us "to lay down the New Testament, [and] to take up the Pagan philosophers." It is not that the teachings of the Upanishads or Marcus Aurelius are necessarily better than those of the Christian church but that they do not invade our freedom. They are inspirational, not doctrinal. Opening ourselves to other spiritual teachings leads to a religious cosmopolitanism "freed from the idolatry of ages."[12]

"But the inspirations are never withdrawn," Emerson says. We need religion. "We must have days and temples and teachers." Worship, in fact, encourages self-culture and virtuous living. The power of religion, once directed toward crusades and colonization, now inspires reform and social good. But, he predicts, no one religion or group will dominate the faith of the future. Individuals must decide for themselves. "How many people are there in Boston? Some two hundred thousand. Well, then so many sects." We are losing our old ties to the church. No religious authority admonishes us or monitors our attendance at worship. Is this dangerous? Is it a sign of decay? No, Emerson says, "'Tis not wrong, but the law of growth." It is no more dangerous than a "mother's withdrawing her hands from the tottering babe" when the child first learns to walk.[13]

Once we are freed from outside institutional pressures to conform, we will find inner guidance. "The progress of opinion is not a loss of moral restraint," Emerson tells us, "but simply a change from coarser to finer checks." Instead of casting praise or blame on external events, we must rely on our own character. "Character is the habit of action from the permanent vision of truth." It compels virtuous behavior and right relations with others. He cites the Confucian parable, mentioned in a previous chapter, of the great emperor Ke Kang (now usually spelled Kangxi), who was distressed by the number of thieves in the state and asked Confucius how to get rid of them. Confucius replied, "If you, sir, were not covetous, although you should reward them to do it, they would not steal."[14] By this he means that when wise leaders show great character, their people will be good as well.

The movement toward reliance on one's own character rather than religious institutions has already had an impact on America, Emerson observes. "Calvinism rushes to be Unitarianism, as Unitarianism rushes to be pure Theism." In his journal he had written that "Unitarianism rushes to be Naturalism."[15] He, not an editor, likely made the change in the published version of "Character." He may have felt "pure Theism" would be less controversial than "Naturalism." But, clearly, in his journals and late lectures, such as "Natural Religion," what he means is religious naturalism.

Jerome A. Stone, author of *Religious Naturalism Today: The Rebirth of a Forgotten Alternative*, writes about Emerson's influence: "Religious naturalism is the type of naturalism which affirms a set of beliefs and attitudes that there are religious aspects of the world that can be appreciated within a naturalistic framework." Referring to Emerson, Stone writes, "In many ways [he] paves the way for religious naturalism. He had a strong sense of the immanence of the divine in the world. However, his idealism, as in his concept of the Oversoul, kept him from being clearly a religious naturalist." On the other hand, Robert Corrington, author of *Deep Pantheism: Toward a New Transcendentalism*, views Emerson as a deep pantheist who embraces an ecstatic form of naturalism: "I believe that the philosophy of ecstatic naturalism has an inner telos toward the religious dimension of the depths of the nature/sacred dialectic. Emerson represents the fullest expression of both ecstatic naturalism and deep pantheism."[16] Stone bases his view of Emerson on a reading of *Nature* and the "The Over-Soul." But Emerson was in the process of moving from objective idealism (the idea that the universe is the creation of God's mind) toward subjective idealism (the idea that the universe is the creation of the human mind). For Emerson, the divine is a force imminent *in* nature, not apart from it. His address "The Method of Nature" is the best example of the ecstatic naturalism that Corrington is talking about.

Emerson early on recognized the spiritual transformation that was occurring in nineteenth-century America. Secular forces were challenging historical Christianity, from both within and outside the church. Historical biblical scholarship exposed the fallibility of the Bible and undermined church teachings. Romanticism found "sermons in stone," basing religion on intuition and transcendent experiences of the natural world. Individualism valorized authenticity and promoted the right of private judgment in religious matters.

Until about 1870 there were few exceptions to the Christian framework of understanding one's own spirituality, notes intellectual historian James Turner. Thinking outside it was not possible. There was no vocabulary for it. One might be more or less religious, but the culture simply did not allow for religious freethought, much less atheism. Evolutionary biologist Thomas Huxley coined the term *agnosticism* to describe the rising tide of unbelief in England, but that trend was slower to reach America.[17]

Emerson was a bridge between Christianity and religious naturalism, Turner says. He helped create a new religious vocabulary. Although he continued to use God language, he also drew on other religious and philosophical traditions for words to describe the ineffable: oversoul, universal mind, the One, *natura naturans*, "vast-flowing vigor," "that around which the hands of man cannot reach." As philosopher Charles Taylor explains, Emerson looked for an alternative to materialism *and* Christian orthodoxy. He was "in some clear sense spiritual, without being Christian or even theistic."[18] He introduced "a third path" to spirituality.

"INSPIRATION"

In 1866, at the age of sixty-three, Emerson wrote the following in his journal: "I find it a great and fatal difference whether I court the Muse, or the Muse courts me: That is the ugly disparity between age and youth." Inspiration was harder to come by as he grew older. He continued to "believe that nothing great and lasting can be done except by inspiration, by leaning on the secret augury."[19] But inspiration is occasional. It cannot be forced or obtained by any mechanical means, such as drugs or alcohol. To some extent, we can find it, or the like of it, in reading accounts of enlightened persons.

"Thoughts let us into realities," Emerson writes. The real world, as opposed to the actual world of mundane existence, is revealed to us in moments of inspiration. Such revelations are few and far between. "But what we want is consecutiveness. 'Tis with us a flash of light, then a long darkness, then a flash again." How quickly inspiration fades in the memory. "Could we but turn these fugitive sparkles into an astronomy of Copernican worlds!" This is the dilemma faced by every mystic and poet—how to summon inspiration through an act of will. "Are these moods in any degree within control? If we knew how to command them!"[20] In the examples of enlightened persons there is agreement as to the conditions of inspiration, but not the means for getting it.

What good are we without enthusiasm? In the legends of other cultures and the accounts of mystics and seers, we can see "this ardor to solve the hints of thought." We learn that ecstasy is normal or "only an example on a higher plane of the same gentle gravitation by which stones fall and rivers run." It seems "as if tea, or wine, or sea air, or mountains, or a genial companion, or a new thought suggested in a book or conversation could fire the train, wake the fancy, and the clear perception." But an engine is useless if there is no coal or ignition to light it. We all experience those rare moments when we feel superior to our usual selves, "when a light, a freedom, a power" comes to us and we glimpse new heights of wisdom and power. "We might say of these memorable moments of life, that we were in them, not they in us," Emerson says. "We found ourselves by happy fortune in an illuminated portion or meteorous zone, and passed out of it again, so aloof was it from any will of ours."[21]

In this essay, Emerson examines conditions most favorable to the reception of inspiration. The first is good health, including the beneficial effects of fresh air, exercise, and walks in nature, as he had recommended in earlier essays. Sleep, too, is beneficial, not only for sound health but also for dreams, "into whose farrago a divine lesson is sometimes slipped." After a deep sleep we awaken refreshed, "with hope, courage, fertile in resources, and keen for daring adventure."[22] Writing letters is another way of finding inspiration. "In writing a letter to a friend we may find that we rise to thought and to a cordial power of expression that costs no effort," Emerson observes, "and it seems to us that this facility may be indefinitely applied and resumed."[23]

Another consideration—more appreciated by older scholars than younger persons—is rest. This is a "daily renovation of sensibility," reviving the faculties "to their fullest force."[24] Next on Emerson's list is the will. The exercise of the will is not sufficient to summon inspiration, but it is necessary for its reception, in the same way that the ground must be tilled for a garden to grow. Another primal rule, Emerson says, is "to defend your morning." More than getting up early, this means to develop and maintain an attitude of expectancy. As his friend Henry Thoreau so memorably wrote, "Only that day dawns to which we are awake."[25]

Solitude is also important, setting aside an hour every day to meet one's own mind "and learn what oracle it has to impart." Solitary walks in nature are likewise advised. In nature our spirits are lifted, and we learn what is never contained in libraries. A change of scenery and routine can also be good for the soul. Habits can stifle the spirit. Then, too, certain localities, such as "mountain-tops, the sea-side, the shores of rivers and rapid brooks, natural parks of oak and pine, where the ground is smooth and unencumbered, are excitants of the muse."[26]

"Conversation, which, when it is best, is a series of intoxications," is one of Emerson's favorite means of finding inspiration: "In enlarged conversation we have suggestions that require new ways of living, new books, new men, new arts and sciences. By sympathy, each opens to the eloquence and begins to see with the eyes of his mind. We are lonely, thoughtless; and now a principle appears to all: we see new relations, many truths; every mind seizes them as they pass; each catches by the mane one of these strong coursers like horses of the prairie, and rides up and down in the world of the intellect." Poetry, too, can be a stimulus to the imagination. He especially recommends "old poetry that is new to the reader." In this context, he recommends Pindar, Milton, and the Persian poet Hafiz, among others. "Words used in a new sense, and figuratively, dart a delightful lustre; and every word admits a new use, and hints ulterior meanings."[27]

We can't know for certain what the precise conditions are for our "happiest frames of mind." But we can always look for new ones. "The day is good in which we have had the most perceptions," Emerson says. "The analysis is the more difficult, because poppy-leaves are strewn when a generalization is made; for I can never remember the circumstances to which I owe it, so as to repeat the experiment or put myself in the conditions."[28] The mind so often feels altered in moments of inspiration.

Emerson quotes his favorite lines from Wordsworth's poem "The Excursion": "'Tis the most difficult of tasks to keep / Heights which the soul is competent to gain." While the "powers of the human soul" may be cultivated, the soul "itself is the dictator," and we are only its receivers. "All our power, all our happiness, consists in our reception of its hints, which ever become clearer and grander as they are obeyed."[29]

"GREATNESS"

Greatness, in Emerson's view, does not mean being superior to others. Rather, "it is the fulfilment of a natural tendency" in each person. Our admiration of people we consider great shouldn't be just to compliment them or feel ourselves next to greatness, but to aspire to their models of excellence. We should focus not so much on what others have done but on what we might do if we followed their examples. Rather than following in their footsteps, he urges his readers to "follow the path your genius traces like the galaxy of heaven, for you to walk in."[30]

Referring to recent scientific experiments with magnetism and the laws of attraction, Emerson says that "every mind has a new compass, a new north, a new direction of its own, differencing its genius and aim from every other mind." Although we share with all others "the gift of reason and the moral sentiment," there is a teaching unique to each of us that leads us to follow our own path. The more we trust our own genius, the more we will be our own person and of value to society. "We call this specialty the bias of each individual," Emerson says. "And none of us will ever accomplish anything excellent or commanding except when he listens to this whisper which is heard by him alone."[31] This bias is like a magnetic needle, which points us in our proper direction. We will never be happy or strong until we find and follow it.

There is perhaps no better example of what Emerson speaks of in this essay than that of Elizabeth Cady Stanton (1815–1902), abolitionist, feminist, religious freethinker, and women's rights activist. A younger contemporary of Emerson's, she struggled to assert her individuality and her rights as a citizen. In January 1892, she delivered a speech to the House Committee on the Judiciary, to the Senate Committee on Woman Suffrage, and to the National American Woman Suffrage Association, of which she was president. The speech was titled "Solitude of Self," and it reads, in part: "The strongest reason for giving women all the opportunities for higher education, for the full development of her faculties, forces of mind and body, for giving her the most enlarged freedom of thought and action; a complete emancipation from all forms of bondage, of custom, dependence, superstition; from all the crippling influences of ear, is the solitude and personal responsibility of her own individual life. . . . To guide our own craft, we must be captain, pilot, engineer; with chart and compass to stand at the wheel; to watch the wind and waves and know when to take in the sail, and to read the signs in the firmament over all. It matters not whether the solitary voyager is man or woman."[32]

"IMMORTALITY"

"Immortality" was Emerson's most popular lecture in later life. He often offered it free as a Sunday sermon in towns where he had given a lecture the previous evening. If the essay "Old Age" describes advancing age, "Immortality" imagines death and what may lie beyond.

Emerson scholars have found two manuscripts of the lecture, from which Emerson's daughter Ellen and friend James Cabot helped him develop a third version that appears as the final essay in *Letters and Social Aims*. Some have suggested that his two assistants may have wanted to show, in the printed version of the essay, that later in life Emerson had "a growing accommodation to conventional [religious] belief."[33] Whether Emerson's own conclusions were closer to his lectures or the essay is not clear.

Emerson and his peers continued to speculate about immortality long after they had abandoned Christianity. For one thing, other religious and philosophical traditions offer differing accounts of what happens after death. Christians believe in heaven and the resurrection of the dead. The Egyptians, Greeks, Hindus, Buddhists, and others have believed in some version of reincarnation and the immortality of the soul. Spiritualists, common in Emerson's day as well as our own, believe in communion with the dead. For another, people had difficulty envisioning death as their final end, even agnostics like Charles Darwin, who wrote: "Believing as I do that man in the distant future will be a far more perfect creature than he now is, it is an intolerable thought that he and all other sentient beings are doomed to complete annihilation after such long continued slow process. To those who fully admit the immortality of the human soul, the destruction of our world will not appear so dreadful."[34]

At the beginning of the essay, Emerson surveys the various cultures' beliefs about the afterlife. Under "the shadow of Calvinism and of the Roman Catholic purgatory," death was dreadful and gloomy. Emerson welcomes the notion that now "death is seen as a natural event." He observes: "I think all sound minds rest on a certain preliminary conviction, namely, that if it be best that conscious personal life shall continue, it will continue; if not best, then it will not; and we, if we saw the whole, should of course see that it was better so."[35]

Our hope for immortality comes out of "the infinity of the world, which infinitely reappears in every particle; the powers of society in every individual, and of all mind in every mind." It lies in the very structure of consciousness. Inherent in all forms of life is the impulse to grow and perpetuate. We witness immense time—in the geological record, in the life of certain trees, and the age of the pyramids. In a similar fashion, the human species has developed in an environment suited to its needs. This fosters the conviction that there are "immense resources and possibilities proper to us" that we have yet to draw from.[36]

"For every seeing soul there are two absorbing facts," Emerson noted in his journal in 1867: "*I and the Abyss.*"[37] When he wrote these words, he sensed his powers beginning to fail. Facing the abyss, he refused to despair. "All the comfort I have found teaches me to confide that I shall not have less in times or places that I do not yet know." Whatever the future holds, it is sure to "be up to the style of our faculties;—of memory, of hope, of imagination, of reason." Like the Buddha, who taught that grasping at life was a hindrance to rebirth, Emerson does not wish to "hold on with both hands to every paltry possession." He continues: "I have a house, a closet which holds my books, a table, a garden, a field: are these, any or all, a reason for refusing the angel who beckons me away? We wish to live for what is great, not for what is mean. I do not wish to live for the sake of my warm house, my orchard, or my pictures. I do not wish to live to wear out my boots."[38]

Emerson leaves us to ponder whether the soul is not only timeless but also eternal, shooting "that gulf we call death." He observes, "The soul does not age with the body." Looking over the edge of the abyss, he concludes that there is no postmortem existence of the self or individual consciousness. At death we lose our individuality as we are dissolved back into the oversoul or consciousness itself. "I confess that everything connected with our personality fails," he writes. "Nature never spares the individual. . . . We have our indemnity only in the sure success of that to which we belong. *That* is immortal and we only through that."[39] For the soul there can be no private good.

Whether immortality exists is hard to say. "That knowledge is hidden very cunningly." It cannot be proven by reason or theology. If anything, immortality is a timeless state of being. "It is not length of life, but depth of life. It is not duration, but a taking of the soul out of time, as all high action of the mind does: when we are living in the sentiments, we ask no questions about time," Emerson states. People are rarely prepared for the immortality they seek: "Will you offer empires to such as cannot set a house or private affairs in order? Here are people who cannot dispose of a day; an hour hangs heavy on their hands; and will you offer them ages without end?" It is not immortality that we seek, but eternity; "not duration, but a state of abandonment to the Highest."[40]

Emerson concludes the essay with a story from the Katha Upanishad, in which Yama, the lord of Death, grants three boons, or wishes, to a young man named Nachiketas. Yama readily grants the first two wishes but is reluctant to grant Nachiketas's third request: to know if the soul exists after death. Yama tells him he would not understand the answer to this question and offers him a kingdom instead. Nachiketas continues to insist. Yama eventually relents, telling him that the actual world in which he thinks he lives is not the real world. The actual world is transient. The real world is eternal. Yama tells him: "The soul is not born; it does not die; it was not produced from any one. Nor was any produced from it. Unborn, eternal, it is not slain, though the body is slain; subtler than what is subtle, greater than what is great, sitting it goes far, sleeping it goes everywhere. Thinking the soul as unbodily among bodies, firm among fleeting things, the wise man casts off all grief. The soul cannot be gained by knowledge, not by understanding, not by manifold science. It can be obtained by the soul by which it is desired. It reveals its own truths."[41]

Emerson's choice of this ending shows his ability—uncommon in his time—to use other religious and philosophical traditions to answer the perennial questions of life and death. He clearly does not subscribe to the Christian concept of the afterlife. There is no reward in Heaven nor punishment in Hell. Nor does he believe the ego survives. Like so many other spiritual teachers and sages of many times and places, he advises us to live in the moment: "Sufficient to to-day are the duties of to-day," he says. "Don't waste life in doubts and fears; spend yourself on the work before you, well assured that the right performance of this hour's duties will be the best preparation for the hours or ages that follow it."[42]

Immortality belongs only to those who live life to the fullest. "It is not length of life, but depth of life" that counts for Emerson. It is achieved only in the here and now—the only time and place in which it can be had. The wisdom of age tells us that this is a time for learning to let go. The desire to cling to all we have actually robs us of the peace of mind we seek. To prepare ourselves for immortality we must transcend selfhood altogether.

Religious historian Karen Armstrong enlarged on Emerson's view of immortality in a 2006 lecture she gave at Harvard Divinity School: "There is . . . a widespread agreement that the quest for immortality should not concentrate on self-indulgent and exclusive fantasies of paradise but should focus on *this* world. Just as we experience the divine in our very selves, we can experience the peace and enhanced vision of eternity, freed from the constraints of space and time, in this world of suffering and death. We cannot understand the doctrine of immortality in a purely notional way. We can only achieve true knowledge of our immortal souls by undergoing a long discipline of self-emptying, a training in inwardness and self-effacement, [together with the exercise of] compassion and benevolence."[43]

What does it mean, as Emerson and Armstrong suggest, that the soul might survive but not the self? These teachings of ancient mystics and sages are corroborated by recent findings of science. Mainstream neuroscience has concluded that consciousness is an epiphenomenon, or by-product, of the brain. Consciousness is produced by the brain and ceases with death. To the extent that contemporary popular thought persists in believing in a personalized afterlife, it would seem that science holds the stronger hand.

In my view, popular thinking about immortality and life after death suffers from what philosopher Alfred North Whitehead called the "fallacy of misplaced concreteness."[44] It envisions a life pretty much like this one, under better conditions and, of course, of infinite duration. Seen in this way, it is hard to dispute the claims of science to the contrary. But if we can let go of the ego as being part of the afterlife, we can make a case for the immortality of the soul.

As Emerson said, each of us is "an individual rivulet before the flowing surges of the sea of life."[45] It is through our existence as unique human beings that the oversoul, or universal consciousness, finds expression and realizes its own infinite existence. Life itself is a process of individuation and dissolution, of coming into existence as a finite being, then merging again with the infinite when the course of life is run. It is not our individual consciousness that survives, but consciousness itself. Consciousness is the thread on which the beads of life are strung.

Knowing that consciousness has incarnated itself uniquely in each one of us as human beings gives life its preciousness and poignancy. On the one hand, it is comforting to know that we are part of a larger, grander whole from which we have come and to which we return. On the other hand, we know that we must make the most of the one life that we ourselves are aware of. Will we sleep through this life thinking that we will be awake in the next? Or will we awaken to the miracles that exist all around us and savor the only life we know for sure that we have?

13
EMERSON'S LEGACY

In 1869, Charles W. Eliot, the new president of Harvard University, invited Ralph Waldo Emerson to deliver a series of eighteen university lectures. The prestigious offer gave Emerson an opportunity to summarize a lifetime of lecturing and writing. His alma mater, which had shunned him at the beginning of his career, was now recognizing his impact at its end. Honored, he readily accepted the invitation. He titled the series Natural History of the Intellect. In his journal he called it New Metaphysics, writing, "When we read true metaphysics, we shall jump out of our skin."[1]

Producing these Harvard lectures proved to be "a doleful ordeal" for Emerson. They exhausted him intellectually and emotionally. His memory was beginning to fail, and he was losing his command of words. "From the outset of 1870 through the appearance of *Letters and Social Aims* more than five years later," Ronald A. Bosco writes, "Emerson was increasingly incapable of executing lectures or essays on a large or even on a minimal scale."[2] Although he continued with his public speaking, his daughter Ellen accompanied him, helping with his dress and travel arrangements and keeping him on track as he delivered his lectures in case he lost his place. In 1871, his family arranged for a train trip to the West Coast, calling on Brigham Young in Salt Lake City and touring the Yosemite Valley with John Muir.

Another ordeal was the 1872 fire at his home, which the family called "Bush." "The shock was severe," Bosco writes, "and given the steady progress of the various infirmities of which he and, especially, Ellen had taken notice and complained in the previous two-and-a-half years, the impact of the fire at Bush, while not fatal to Emerson, was effectively so."[3]

Concord neighbors rushed to save Emerson's library and put out the fire. He may have suffered a stroke in the upset, and his mental health was in steady decline from this point on. He suffered from aphasia, a form of dementia that eventually forced him to withdraw from public life. The citizens of Concord raised funds to restore his house and send him on a trip to Britain, France, and Egypt while the work was being done.

On his voyage home aboard the *Olympus*, Emerson spent a good deal of time with fellow passenger Charles Eliot Norton, a longtime friend who was also the son of Emerson's nemesis at Harvard Divinity School, professor Andrews Norton. Charles, a much younger contemporary of Emerson's, was highly regarded as an art historian and cultural critic. Norton and his family had been living for a number of years in England and Europe. Tragically, Norton's wife had died giving birth to their fifth child in Germany just three months before. Grief-stricken, Norton fell into a deep depression.

Until this time, Norton had considered Emerson something of a father figure and spiritual guide. Now, after spending so many years abroad in the company of Thomas Carlyle and John Stuart Mill, among others, he had become a committed rationalist. And with the death of his wife, life had lost all meaning for him. Where once he found wisdom in Emerson's philosophy, now he considered Emerson's persistent optimism irritating and dangerous. "To him this is the best of all possible worlds, and the best of all possible times," Norton wrote. "He refuses to believe in disorder or evil. Order is the absolute law; disorder is but a phenomenon; good is absolute, evil but good in the making."[4]

Norton baited Emerson with his cynicism, but Emerson refused to take it. "I found it in vain to suggest instances of misery, of crime, in society, of apparent ruthlessness and disorder in nature, to his view," Norton stated. "He would not entertain them. His faith was superior to any exceptions." But Emerson, according to John McAleer, author of *Ralph Waldo Emerson: Days of Encounter*, "was making a strong personal appeal to Norton to shake off life-threatening moods of depression." Here at sea, Norton asked Emerson how Columbus managed to discover the New World. He was moved by Emerson's answer: "'Not so much of a wonder after all,' said Emerson, 'he had his compass and that was enough for such a soul as his.' The miracle of the magnet, the witness of the Divine spirit in nature; type of the eternal control of matter by spirit of fidelity to the unseen and the ideal. 'I always carry,' he added, 'a little compass in my pocket. I like to hold the visible god in my hand.'"[5] This was a practical demonstration of the moral force of Emerson's confidence in the universe and in humanity, and it routed Norton's cold rationalism.

Although weighed down with his own recent illness and loss of memory, Emerson ministered to Norton, whose spirits began to rise as they neared home. The day before their arrival was Emerson's seventieth birthday. "The day is a melancholy anniversary for me," Emerson told his friend. "I reckon my seventieth birthday as the close of youth." Norton commented to a friend that Emerson had made the voyage a pleasant one. "He had a spirit of perennial youthfulness. He is the youngest man I know."[6]

At a celebration in Concord on the centennial of Emerson's birth, Norton, now seventy-five years old, focused on Emerson's role as a force for good. He quoted Emerson: "To every serious mind Providence sends from time to time five or six or seven teachers who are of the first importance to him in the lessons they have to impart. The highest of these not so much give particular knowledge as they elevate by sentiment, and by their habitual grandeur of view." Emerson himself was just such a teacher, Norton said. "In long future time [those] seeking to elevate and liberate their souls will find help in the words and example in the character of Emerson."[7]

By 1877, Emerson had ceased writing in his journal, which he had kept since 1820. Just a few years earlier he made the following comment: "The grief of old age is, that, now, only in rare moments, and by the happiest combinations or consent of the elements can we attain those enlargements and intellectual *elan*, which were once a daily gift."[8] After attending one of Emerson's last lectures in 1878, Bronson Alcott noted the following in his journal: "Yet the spectacle, brilliant and impressive as it was, was but a faint reflection of his earlier appearances. . . . Then he was the rhapsodist inspired and upon the tripod, uttering oracles as unexpected as they were divine to the illuminated."[9] In the summer of 1879 Emerson delivered his lecture "Memory"—an ironic choice given his almost total aphasia—at Alcott's Concord School of Philosophy. He seldom appeared in public after that.

In April 1882, Emerson became ill after being soaked by a cold spring shower on a walk. A little over a week later, on April 27, the bells of

Concord's First Parish Church tolled his death. The Sage of Concord had died at age seventy-eight.

Visitors to Authors' Ridge in Sleepy Hollow Cemetery in Concord cannot miss the massive rose quartz stone marking Emerson's grave. No doubt he would have preferred something more modest, but such was his stature that nothing less would do. For those who knew him and the thousands more who attended his lectures, he was revered. On the stone is a plaque bearing a few lines from one of Emerson's poems, "The Problem." To me, a more appropriate choice would have been his poem "Character":

> The sun set, but not his hope:
> Stars rose; his faith was earlier up:
> Fixed on the enormous galaxy,
> Deeper and older seemed his eye;
> And matched his sufferance sublime
> The taciturnity of time.
> He spoke, and words more soft than rain
> Brought the Age of Gold again:
> His action won such reverence sweet
> As hid all measure of the feat.[10]

CODA

It seems fitting that one of his last addresses was given in the same place that one of his first was delivered, the chapel at Harvard Divinity School. In May 1879, a little more than forty years after his controversial "Divinity School Address," he lectured on "the preacher." If anyone thought Emerson might have grown more conservative with age, they were quickly disabused of the notion. True, he had become more broad-minded, owing to his embrace of religious cosmopolitanism. But he was just as perceptive as ever of the advance of secularity and its impact on religious faith.

The biggest threat to the church was not rational protest but indifference. "The old forms rattle, and the new delay to appear; material and industrial activity have materialized the age, and the mind, haughty with its sciences, disdains the religious forms as childish."[11] We are caught in a religious no-man's-land, "born too late for the old and too early for the new faith." This predicament troubled other cultivated minds as well, including Matthew Arnold, who wrote,

Wandering between two worlds, one dead,
The other powerless to be born,
With nowhere yet to rest my head,
Like these, on earth I wait forlorn.[12]

But, unlike Arnold, Emerson did not succumb to melancholy or skepticism. He acknowledges the fate of the churches. He hears "aspirations" of a "the new order of things," though it has yet to take shape. "A thousand negatives it utters, clear and strong on all sides; but the sacred affirmative it hides in the deepest abyss." No age is destitute of the religious sentiment, but when it does appear the "Understanding will write out its vision in a Confession of Faith."[13] The religious sentiment will become objectified and idolatrous. Heretics will be burned. Eventually people of good sense will abandon the church, ushering in an age of unbelief.

Without God in the world the soul feels abandoned. Nature lacks beauty. Everything seems superficial. The sacred is hidden, but it is not absent, according to Emerson: "We are in transition, from the worship of the fathers which enshrined the law in a private and personal history, to a worship which recognizes the true eternity of the law, its presence to you and me, its equal energy in what is called brute nature as in what is called sacred. The next age will behold God in the ethical laws . . . and will regard natural history, private fortunes and politics, not for themselves, as we have done, but as illustrations of those laws, of that beatitude and love. Nature is too thin a screen; the glory of the One breaks in everywhere."[14] Faith consists in rising above the myriad details of life to a vision of the whole. We seem to be afflicted with a St. Vitus' Dance, acting from many and conflicting motives. It is when we act out of a sense of wholeness that we will find peace and joy in life.

All creeds and rites are perishable. The universe is "an infinite series of planes, each of which is a false bottom; and when we think our feet are planted now at last on adamant, the slide is drawn out from under us." Instead of focusing on the differences between creeds, we should look to find agreements among them. "I agree with their heart and motive," Emerson says, "my discontent is with their limitations and surface and language." When religion becomes fixated on creeds or persons, then it is merely pew-holding. Sadly, "it is the old story again: once we had wooden chalices and golden priests, now we have golden chalices and wooden priests."[15]

The clergy are always in danger of being co-opted by the "producing classes." Although it is impossible to ignore public opinion and the day's events, it is the preacher's duty to examine these in light of moral principles. ("Life passed though the fire of thought," as Emerson had said in his previous address at the Divinity School so many years before.) Emerson's advice to the young preacher is this: "When there is any difference felt between the foot-board of the pulpit and the floor of the parlor, you have not yet said that which you should say." The proper use of the Sabbath is to check our "headlong racing and put us in possession of ourselves once more."[16] The forms of the Sabbath may change, Emerson concludes, though its benefit continues. Likewise, creeds and rituals are transient and pass away, but the religious sentiment is permanent and universal in human experience.

In closing, Emerson relates the counsel given to Osiris, the Egyptian god of the afterlife, by his father: "There are two pairs of eyes in man; and it is requisite that the pair which are beneath should be closed when the pair that are above them perceive; and that when the pair above are closed, those which are beneath are opened." From this advice, Emerson draws the following conclusion: "The lower eyes see only surfaces and effects, the upper eyes behold causes and the connection of things. And when we go alone, or come into the house of thought and worship, we come with purpose to be disabused of appearances, to see realities, the great lines of our destiny, to see that life has no caprice or fortune, is no hopping squib, but a growth after immutable laws under beneficent influences the most immense. . . . We come . . . to open the upper eyes to the deep mystery of cause and effect, to know that though ministers of justice and power fail, Justice and Power fail never. The open secret of the world is the art of subliming a private soul with inspirations from the great and public and divine Soul from which we live."[17]

"His voice was low, generally weak, but occasionally rose to loudness," one of his listeners observed. "He sat down in the middle of the address. His daughter Ellen was present with her usual careful anxiety that all her father's wants should be gratified."[18] The lecture had none of the rhetorical fireworks of his first address at the Divinity School, but it pulled no punches regarding the fate of the church in the post–Civil War period.

As always, Emerson was trying to navigate a passage between the Scylla of credulity and the Charybdis of skepticism. His friend Charles Eliot Norton described this religious situation very well: "In the decline of the power of the churches, and in the rejection of their authority, many . . . see a rejection of the authority of religion itself. But this is far from being the case. On the contrary, the increased sense of personal responsibility, which is the direct effect of individual freedom, leads rather to an increase of the religious sentiment. The formal religion of tradition and habit gives place to the vital religion, which is a new growth in each man's soul, and the expression of his sincere devotion to the object which he acknowledges to have absolute claim over the whole of his life."[19]

By this time Emerson had resumed his churchgoing, although with some misgivings. (Come time for church, he could never seem to find his gloves.)[20] In spite of his continuing attendance at the meetings of the Free Religious Association and lectures such as this one, some people looked for evidence that he had recanted his views and returned to the Christian faith.[21] It was during this time that the Reverend Joseph Cook, a conservative Unitarian minister from the Midwest, began spreading just such a rumor. Citing evidence from "The Preacher," Edward Emerson issued a public denial. "The statement [made by Rev. Mr. Cook] is in every respect, incorrect. . . . He has not joined any church, nor has he retracted any views expressed in his writings after his withdrawal from the ministry."[22]

LEGACY

Emerson's legacy is difficult to assess. His reputation has waxed and waned over the years. He has had effusive admirers as well as harsh critics. Yet his message has captured the imagination of generations of spiritual seekers.

Emerson was an "anti-mentor," Lawrence Buell says in his book *Emerson*.[23] Emerson noted proudly in his journal that after writing and speaking for many years he had "not now one disciple." The reason was not because what he said was untrue or that he lacked an intelligent audience. Rather, his goal as a teacher was "not to bring them to me, but to themselves." His teaching would be a failure "if it did not create independence."[24] Describing what he calls "the shadow" of Emerson's books,

Walt Whitman wrote, "The best part of Emersonianism is, it breeds the giant that destroys itself. Who wants to be any man's mere follower? lurks behind every page. No teacher ever taught, that has so provided for his pupil's setting up independently—no truer evolutionist."[25]

Emerson may not have been a mentor, but he was certainly a model. He was one of those "representative men" he wrote about, individuals who offer an example of persons who heeded their own genius and forged their own path, uncertain at times where it would lead them. "I am only an experimenter," he said, "an endless seeker with no Past at my back."[26] Yet he was aware of his influence. In his delightful introduction to *Mosses from an Old Manse*, Nathaniel Hawthorne wrote of Emerson: "His mind acted upon other minds a certain constitution with wonderful magnetism, and drew many men upon long pilgrimages to speak with him face to face."[27] In "Uses of Great Men," Emerson cautioned against "the excess of influence of the great man. His attractions warp us from our place."[28] He felt a responsibility to push his acolytes away from him.

Emerson never set out to be a sage. No sage ever does. Nor did he ever consider himself one. "The disagreeable word Sage, often applied to him, would never have pleased him," wrote his son Edward. "Seer is certainly better. He strove to report truly and temperately what he saw, and through all the beautiful and shifting forms he traced the Law with reverence and delight."[29]

From a young age he simply adopted and persistently engaged in a variety of spiritual practices intended to cultivate the soul. In his lectures and essays he offered advice to others on how to do the same. And he did this with uncommon grace. "I am here to represent humanity," he wrote in his journal. "It is by no means necessary that I live, but it is by all means necessary that I should act rightly."[30] His sage-hood—whether he accepted the mantle or not—is the result of his integrity, the congruence between the person and the message.

In the first chapter of this book, I cited the two ways that classical scholar Julia Annas said the virtuous or self-reliant person could be developed. One is "the person living according to an ideal which transcends the everyday, rising above it and regarding ordinary life, its concerns and troubles, as petty and fleeting." The other is a "person whose ideal virtue is displayed not in rising above the everyday but precisely in

staying at that level and dealing with it. This is arguably the more challenging notion, since instead of contrasting the ideal and the practical it
tries to bring them into relation, showing how ideal virtue can be found
in actual practical, goal-directed activity."[31]

Emerson is the second type of sage. He viewed everyday life from a
"higher platform," as he would say, from the perspective of divine reason. When we think of ourselves as part of a larger whole, we loosen the
grip of petty concerns. But instead of avoiding life, this type of sage takes
an active part in it. As Annas says, these sages "see the life detached from
everyday practical concerns devoted to a transcendent ideal, as selfish
and self-indulgent."[32] For sages like Emerson virtue means living life
well—mindfully, in accordance with that which promotes *eudaimonia*,
or human flourishing.

Emerson was engaged in the life of his family, his community, and
society as a whole. He celebrated domestic life and civic duties. He felt
obligated to involve himself in larger causes, such as the abolition of
slavery and women's rights. "We are not permitted to stand as spectators
at the pageant which the times exhibit," he wrote; "we are parties also,
and have a responsibility which is not to be declined."[33]

His gospel of self-reliance has sometimes been taken to mean a radical
individualism at odds with the need for community. But careful readers
understand this was not the case. "The heightened sense of the importance of the individual that emerged in the nineteenth century did not
(as one might imagine) produce a diminished sense of community,"
Daniel Walker Howe writes in *Making the American Self*. "Instead, a
heightened sense of national community actually accompanied the rise
of individualism."[34] This was true for Emerson as well.

Emerson found meaning and joy in everyday life. "I embrace the common, I explore and sit at the feet of the familiar, the low," he wrote. "Give
me insight into to-day, and you may have the antique and future worlds."
He valued common *people* too. He often found his lecture tours arduous,
but he loved meeting people along the way. They energized him. "I meet
in the street people full of life," he wrote in his journal. "I see them pass
with envy at this gift which includes all gifts."[35] The feeling was mutual.
Elizabeth Peabody recalled asking a parishioner at the East Lexington
church where Emerson was an interim preacher why the congregation
had not hired a minister he had recommended. "Oh, Miss Peabody," she

said, "we are a very simple people here; we cannot understand anybody but Mr. Emerson."[36]

Although he mingled with Boston's intellectual elite, he was not an elitist himself. For Emerson, there was no social or religious hierarchy. He encouraged all to grow to their fullest potential. "All that Adam had, all that Caesar could, you have and can do," Emerson wrote in *Nature*. "Adam called his house, heaven and earth; Caesar called his house, Rome; you perhaps call yours, a cobler's [sic] trade; a hundred acres of ploughed land; or a scholar's garret. Yet line for line and point for point, your dominion is as great as theirs, though without fine names. Build, therefore, your own world."[37]

Philosopher John Dewey called Emerson "the one citizen of the New World fit to have his name uttered in the same breath with that of Plato." Emerson was a spokesman for what Dewey called "spiritual democracy": "Against creed and system, convention and institution, Emerson stands for restoring to the common man that which in the name of religion, of philosophy, of art, and of morality, has been embezzled from the common store and appropriated to sectarian and class use. . . . For such reasons, the coming century may well make evident what is just now dawning, that Emerson is not only a philosopher, but that he is the Philosopher of Democracy."[38]

In addition to his spiritual egalitarianism, Emerson embraced an expansive, liberal, progressive view of America's destiny. In his address "Fortune of the Republic," first given in December 1863, following Lincoln's Emancipation Proclamation and the Battle of Gettysburg, Emerson declared: "At every moment some one country more than any other represents the sentiment and the future of mankind. At the present time, none will doubt that America occupies this place in the opinion of nations." America, he said, is "passing out of old remainders of barbarism into pure Christianity and humanity,—into freedom of thought, of religion, of speech, of the press, of trade, of suffrage, or political right." He was deeply saddened that it took the sacrifice of a whole generation to see "a new era of equal rights dawn on the universe." He did not take America's "fortune" as a given. It had to be earned. "The great end of all political struggle," he argued, "is, to establish morality as the basis of all legislation. 'Tis not free institutions, 'tis not a republic, 'tis not a democracy, that is the end,—no, but only the means. We want a state of things in which crime will not pay. A state of things which allows every man the largest liberty compatible with the liberty of every other man."[39]

Despite his praise of America in that moment, Emerson was by no means a nationalist. He understood the tendency of his fellow citizens to put financial gain above humane ideals. "I am a little cynical on some topics," he noted in his journal, "and when a whole nation is roaring Patriotism at the top of its voice I am fain to explore the cleanliness of its hands and the purity of its heart." He stood for "the fusion of races and religions," the advancement of women's rights, the abolition of slavery, just rules for labor, abolition of capital punishment, and social services for the poor.[40]

He also called for a religious revolution in America. "Emerson is in fact the theologian of something we may almost term 'the American religion,'" writes Sydney E. Ahlstrom in his *Religious History of the American People*. Emerson's message wasn't "a mere softening of traditional doctrines, but a dramatic and drastic demand for a complete recasting of religious life and thought."[41] He set in motion a rapid transition from Christian dominance to religious cosmopolitanism in America. As Ahlstrom suggests, this was more in the nature of a revolution than an evolution.

"Shooting the gulf"—one of Emerson's favorite phrases, meaning an exhilarating breakthrough—was most certainly what happened in the chapel at Harvard Divinity School on the evening of July 15, 1838, when he gave his address to the aspiring ministers. He did not pull down the walls of historical Christianity, but he did breach them, opening a doorway for a new way of being religious, grounded in nature and human consciousness. "The world," he said, "is not the product of manifold power, but of one will, of one mind; and that one mind is everywhere active, in each ray of the star, in each wavelet of the pool." The "religious sentiment" is aroused by the elements of nature: the mountain air and the scent of flowers. This teaching, he insisted, "dwelled always deepest in the minds of men in the devout and contemplative East; not alone in Palestine, where it reached its purest expression, but in Egypt, in Persia, in India, in China." It is available to all, "guarded by one stern condition; this, namely; It is an intuition. It cannot be received at second hand."[42]

Emerson was part of a group of young religious radicals preaching this new gospel. They were searching for new ways of being religious, freed from orthodoxy and sectarianism. But he was the most prominent proponent of decentered Christianity, creating what Charles Taylor has called a "third form of secularity." *Secularism* commonly refers to religious unbelief and relegates religion to the periphery of civic life. *Secularity*, as Taylor uses the word, retains what Emerson calls the religious sentiment within "the immanent frame."[43] It is a this-worldly form of spirituality.

The Transcendentalist movement arose in a uniquely American context, observes Perry Miller, whose anthology of its writings reawakened interest in the movement in the 1960s. It "is most accurately defined as a religious demonstration," he said. It broke away from a religion that "was notoriously indigenous to eastern Massachusetts": Unitarianism, which itself had broken away from Calvinist orthodoxy. One might think, Miller says, that "a heresy within so localized a sect may well be thought of little interest or significance for the rest of an immense country."[44] Yet, thanks largely to Emerson, the movement became a religious force in America, validating all those who sought spirituality beyond the bounds of orthodox religion.

Every lecture and essay Emerson wrote revolves around his spiritual vision. He addresses every issue—reform, power, wealth, success, society, politics, religion, social justice—from the perspective of a higher platform, gained through an awareness of the unity of being that we and all of nature are a part of. He promotes the flourishing of individuals and society by means of the spiritual practices of self-culture. Heightened visions of an ideal world and social life could not be summoned at will. As poet William Blake wrote, "If the doors of perception were cleansed everything would appear to man as it is, infinite."[45] In other words, we might become more receptive to visionary experiences when we cultivate our souls.

As to the nature of Emerson's continuing influence, I am reminded of a folktale I heard many years ago, though I do not remember the source. One day, a king summoned his three daughters. "I am going away to meditate," he told them. "You will rule in my absence. Take this grain of rice and keep it until I return." The first daughter threw her grain of rice away. "I'll just go down to the kitchen and get another one when he returns." The second daughter carefully wrapped her grain of rice with a golden thread and placed it in a box which she kept in a drawer.

The third daughter thought about hers for a long time before deciding what to do. Years later, the king returned and summoned his daughters to come before him and bring their grain of rice. The first daughter ran to the kitchen to get a grain of rice. "Thank you," her father said. The second daughter carefully unwrapped her grain of rice and brought it to give to her father. And he said, "Thank you." The third daughter said, "Come, father, I have something to show you." She led him outside of the castle and with a wave of her hand, she showed him a vast field of rice, waving in the wind. "There, father," she said, "is your single grain of rice." And her father said, "You shall rule in my place."[46]

Emerson has inspired intellectuals, world leaders, and everyday people with his message. He has found his way, often incognito, into some of the best literature written and has influenced some of the best thinkers since his death: Walt Whitman, Emily Dickinson, John Muir, William James, Robert Frost, Friedrich Nietzsche, Leo Tolstoy, Rabindranath Tagore, D. T. Suzuki, Annie Dillard, Mary Oliver, Barack Obama, and countless others. He has transformed worship and theology in liberal churches. He has done this all without any school or association in his name, only through his enduring spiritual presence. As his friend Oliver Wendell Holmes said of him, "Here was an iconoclast without a hammer, who took down our idols from their pedestals so tenderly that it seemed like an act of worship."[47] The seeds he planted in the spiritual lives of his many readers have yielded a rich harvest—in his own day and in all the days since.

NOTES

ABBREVIATIONS

AS Ralph Waldo Emerson. *Emerson's Antislavery Writings*. Edited by Len Gougeon and Joel Myerson. New Haven, CT: Yale University Press, 1995.

C Ralph Waldo Emerson. *The Complete Works of Ralph Waldo Emerson*. Edited by Edward Waldo Emerson. 12 vols. Boston: Houghton Mifflin, 1903.

CW Ralph Waldo Emerson. *The Collected Works of Ralph Waldo Emerson*. Edited by Alfred Riggs Ferguson, Robert E. Spiller, Joseph Slater, Douglas Emory Wilson, and Ronald A. Bosco. 10 vols. Cambridge, MA: Harvard University Press, 1971–2013.

EL Ralph Waldo Emerson. *The Early Lectures of Ralph Waldo Emerson*. Edited by Stephen E. Whicher, Robert E. Spiller, and Wallace E. Williams. 3 vols. Cambridge, MA: Harvard University Press, 1961–72.

J Ralph Waldo Emerson. *Journals of Ralph Waldo Emerson: 1820–1872*. Edited by Edward Waldo Emerson and Waldo Emerson Forbes. 12 vols. Boston: Houghton Mifflin, 1909.

JMN Ralph Waldo Emerson. *The Journals and Miscellaneous Notebooks*. Edited by William H. Gilman et al. 16 vols. Cambridge, MA: Harvard University Press, 1960–82.

L Ralph Waldo Emerson. *The Letters of Ralph Waldo Emerson*. Edited by Ralph L. Rusk. 6 vols. New York: Columbia University Press, 1939.

LL Ralph Waldo Emerson. *The Later Lectures of Ralph Waldo Emerson*. Edited by Ronald A. Bosco and Joel Myerson. 2 vols. Athens: University of Georgia Press, 2001.

TN Ralph Waldo Emerson. *The Topical Notebooks of Ralph Waldo Emerson*. Edited by Ralph H. Orth, Susan Sutton Smith, and Glen M. Johnson. 3 vols. Columbia: University of Missouri Press, 1990–94.

W Ralph Waldo Emerson. *The Complete Works of Ralph Waldo Emerson*. Centenary ed. Edited by Edward Emerson. 10 vols. Boston: Houghton Mifflin, 1903.

INTRODUCTION

1. Walt Whitman, *Complete Poetry and Collected Prose*, ed. Justin Kaplan (New York: Library of America, 1982), 1270.
2. Leigh Eric Schmidt also makes this argument in *Restless Souls: The Making of American Spirituality* (New York: HarperCollins, 2005), 1–8.
3. Isaiah Berlin, *The Roots of Romanticism* (Princeton, NJ: Princeton University Press, 1999), 1–2.
4. Quoted in James Elliot Cabot, *A Memoir of Ralph Waldo Emerson*, 2 vols. (Boston: Houghton Mifflin, 1887), 2:245.
5. *C*, 10:325–26.
6. *EL*, 3:202–37.
7. Thomas Carlyle, *Sartor Resartus* (Oxford: Oxford University Press, 1987), 147.
8. *EL*, 3:190–91.
9. Charles Taylor, *A Secular Age* (Cambridge, MA: Harvard University Press, 2007), 2–3.
10. *EL*, 3:194.
11. Taylor, 383; Charles Taylor, *Sources of the Self: The Making of the Modern Identity* (Cambridge, MA: Harvard University Press, 1989), 408.
12. Taylor, *Sources*, 497.
13. John Lysaker, "Taking Emerson Personally," in *New Morning: Emerson in the Twenty-first Century*, ed. Arthur S. Lothstein and Michael Brodrick (Albany: State University of New York, 2008), 122; Matthew Arnold, *Matthew Arnold*, ed. Miriam Allott and Robert H. Super (Oxford: Oxford University Press, 1986), 481.

CHAPTER 1: AN AMERICAN SAGE

1. In John McAleer, *Ralph Waldo Emerson: Days of Encounter* (Boston: Little, Brown, 1984), 387.
2. Julia Annas, *The Morality of Happiness* (New York: Oxford University Press, 1993), 3–10.
3. See Pierre Hadot, *What Is Ancient Philosophy?*, trans. Michael Chase (Cambridge, MA: Harvard University Press, 2004), 220–33.
4. Julia Annas, "The Sage in Ancient Philosophy," http://www.u.arizona.edu/~jannas /Published%20Articles/sage.pdf, 14; Epicurus, "Letter to Menoeceus," in *The Stoic and Epicurean Philosophers*, ed. Whitney J. Oates (New York: Random House, 1940), 32–33.
5. Annas, "Sage in Ancient Philosophy," 16.
6. Annas, 18–19.
7. George Santayana, "Emerson," in *Emerson's Prose and Poetry*, ed. Joel Porte and Saundra Morris (New York: W. W. Norton, 2001), 633.
8. Charles E. Mitchell, *Individualism and Its Discontents: Appropriations of Emerson, 1880–1950* (Amherst: University of Massachusetts Press, 1997), 5.
9. See Bliss Perry, *Emerson Today* (Princeton, NJ: Princeton University Press, 1931), 31–57.
10. Annas, "Sage in Ancient Philosophy," 23.
11. David Robinson, *The Unitarians and the Universalists* (Westport, CT: Greenwood

Press, 1985), 17; David Robinson, *Apostle of Culture: Emerson as Preacher and Lecturer* (Philadelphia: University of Pennsylvania Press, 1982), 13.

12. Robinson, *Unitarians and the Universalists*, 13.

13. William Ellery Channing, *Selected Writings*, ed. David Robinson (New York: Paulist Press, 1985), 95.

14. Another brother, Bulkeley, was developmentally disabled. Waldo was one of seven children born to William and Ruth Emerson, only four of whom lived to adulthood.

15. Daniel Walker Howe, *The Unitarian Conscience* (Cambridge, MA: Harvard University Press, 1970), 46, 63.

16. See Conrad Wright, *The Liberal Christians* (Boston: Beacon Press, 1970), 6–15.

17. This is why philosopher Richard Taylor finds inspiration in the writings of the ancient philosophers, including Epicurus, Epictetus, Plato, Aristotle, Seneca, Marcus Aurelius, and others, but nothing uplifting at all in "the arid trivial writing of modern ethical philosophers." Richard Taylor, *Virtue Ethics: An Introduction* (Amherst, NY: Prometheus Books, 2002), 6–7.

18. Robinson, *Apostle of Culture*, 53–54.

19. Christopher W. Gowans, "Self-Cultivation Philosophy as an Interpretive Framework: The Critiques of Desire" (paper presented to the Columbia Society for Comparative Philosophy, Columbia University, New York, NY, February 24, 2017), https://christophergowans.com/what-are-selfcultivation-philosophies.

20. Pierre Hadot, *Philosophy as a Way of Life*, ed. Arnold I. Davidson, trans. Michael Chase (Malden, MA: Blackwell Publishing, 1995), 102.

21. Channing, *Selected Writings*, 226–27.

22. Howe, *Making the American Self*, 108, 111.

23. See Joseph F. Kett, *The Pursuit of Knowledge under Difficulties: From Self-Improvement to Adult Education in America, 1750–1990* (Stanford, CA: Stanford University Press, 1994), 29–37, 81–97. See also Carl Bode, *The American Lyceum: Town Meeting of the Mind* (New York: Oxford University Press, 1956), 19–27, 41–60.

24. Mark G. Vásquez, *Authority and Reform: Religious and Educational Discourses in Nineteenth-Century New England Literature* (Knoxville: University of Tennessee Press, 2003), 30, 58.

25. Channing, *Selected Writings*, 231.

26. Amos Bronson Alcott, "The Doctrine and Discipline of Human Culture," in *The Spirituality of the American Transcendentalists*, ed. Catherine L. Albanese (Macon, GA: Mercer University Press, 1988), 151–64; James Freeman Clarke, *Self-Culture: Physical, Intellectual, Moral, and Spiritual* (Boston: Houghton, Mifflin, 1880).

27. Frederic Henry Hedge, "The Art of Life, the Scholar's Calling," *The Dial: A Magazine for Literature, Philosophy, and Religion*," October 1840, 175.

28. Hadot, *Philosophy as a Way of Life*, 83.

29. *JMN*, 14:258.

30. Joseph Campbell, "The Hero's Journey," *The Sun*, September 1986, 13–14.

31. *JMN*, 14:258.

CHAPTER 2: THE HERO'S JOURNEY

1. Lawrence Buell, *Emerson* (Cambridge, MA: Harvard University Press, 2003), 7–8.

2. Octavius Brooks Frothingham, *Transcendentalism in New England* (Gloucester, MA: Peter Smith, 1965), 221.

3. *JMN*, 3:15.

4. *JMN*, 2:239, 240.

5. See James Elliot Cabot, *A Memoir of Ralph Waldo Emerson*, 2 vols. (Boston: Houghton Mifflin, 1887), 1:118.

6. Quoted in Cabot, *Memoir*, 1:150.

7. William Ellery Channing, *Selected Writings*, ed. David Robinson (New York: Paulist Press, 1985), 72.

8. Ironically, Channing tried to talk him out of going to Germany, perhaps for fear of William losing his faith. Ronald A. Bosco and Joel Myerson, *The Emerson Brothers: A Fraternal Biography in Letters* (New York: Oxford University Press, 2006), 75.

9. Bosco and Myerson, *Emerson Brothers*, 111. This is how Waldo's daughter Ellen later described the encounter.

10. Bosco and Myerson, 112.

11. *JMN*, 3:237.

12. *JMN*, 318–19.

13. *JMN*, 4:27.

14. *JMN*, 27–28.

15. *JMN*, 30; Romans 14:17.

16. See Phyllis Cole, "A Legacy of Revolt, 1803–1821," in *Mr. Emerson's Revolution*, ed. Jean McClure Mudge (Cambridge: Open Book Publishers, 2016), 13.

17. Joseph Campbell, "The Hero's Journey," *The Sun*, September 1986, 7–8.

18. *JMN*, 3:47.

19. Robert D. Richardson Jr., *Emerson: The Mind on Fire* (Berkeley: University of California Press, 1995), 126.

20. *CW*, 5:7.

21. *JMN*, 4:219; *CW*, 5:9.

22. *CW*, 5:12.

23. *JMN*, 2:278.

24. Samuel Taylor Coleridge, *Aids to Reflection* (New York: N. Tibbals and Son, 1872), 161–62. Critics have pointed out that Coleridge simplifies Kant's philosophy on several points. But, as Robert D. Richardson Jr. says, "what matters here is not whether Coleridge exactly follows Kant or whether . . . Emerson fully understood the nuances of either Coleridge or Kant. What matters is the idea of reason itself and what Emerson does with it" (Richardson, *Emerson*, 93).

25. *L*, 1:412–13.

26. Wordsworth, *William Wordsworth*, ed. Stephan Gill (New York: Oxford University Press, 1984), 134.

27. *CW*, 10:112.

28. Wordsworth, *William Wordsworth*, 409.

29. Wordsworth, 301.

30. Wordsworth, *The Poetical Works of William Wordsworth*, 6 vols. (London: Edward Moxon, 1840), 6:120.

31. Thomas Carlyle, "State of German Literature," in *Critical and Miscellaneous Essays*, 3 vols. (London: Chapman and Hall, 1887), 1:69–70.

32. Thomas Carlyle, "Signs of the Times," in *Critical and Miscellaneous Essays*, 1:473–74, 477, 481.

33. Carlyle, *Characteristics* (Boston: James R. Osgood, 1877), 33, 45, 91.

34. In a letter written to Goethe on May 23, 1830, MS: Goethe and Schiller Archive, Weimar, Germany. Pbd: Norton, GC, 184–93.

35. Thomas Carlyle, *Sartor Resartus* (Oxford: Oxford University Press, 1987), 147.

36. Carlyle, *Sartor Resartus*, 195.

37. Wordsworth, *Poetical Works*, 6:xiii.

CHAPTER 3: BECOMING A SAGE

1. *JMN*, 4:236.

2. *J*, 2:442–43, 541–42, 3:240–41, 428.

3. *JMN*, 4:360.

4. *JMN*, 324.

5. *JMN*, 276–77.

6. *JMN*, 6:202.

7. *JMN*, 5:270–72.

8. *JMN*, 272, 273; Alfred North Whitehead, *Science and the Modern World* (Cambridge: Cambridge University Press, 1932), 64.

9. *JMN*, 274.

10. See David Van Leer, *Emerson's Epistemology: The Argument of the Essays* (Cambridge: Cambridge University Press, 1986), 2–8. As Van Leer remarks, "What we want to know is not Emerson's 'familiarity' with Kantian concepts, or even his 'knowledge' of them, but only his 'understanding' of those concepts" (6).

11. In *The School of Athens*, Raphael's fresco in the Vatican Museum, Plato is shown with his finger pointing upward, a gesture indicating his idealism, whereas Aristotle's finger points downward, connoting his empirical philosophy.

12. Iain McGilchrist, *The Master and His Emissary: The Divided Brain and the Making of the Western World* (New Haven, CT: Yale University Press, 2009), 3.

13. See Jill Bolte Taylor, *My Stroke of Insight: A Brain Scientist's Personal Journey* (New York: Plume Books, 2009), chap. 3. Her stroke paralyzed the left side of her brain, confirming what she, as a brain scientist, knew about the bilateral asymmetry of the brain.

14. McGilchrist, *Master and His Emissary*, 5.

15. McGilchrist, 6.

16. *CW*, 1:179.

17. *JMN*, 5:275.

18. *EL*, 2:17.

19. *EL*, 84, 85.

20. *EL*, 87.

21. *EL*, 92–93, 96–97.

22. *EL*, 216, 220.

23. *EL*, 220–22.

24. See Grace H. Turnbull, ed., *The Essence of Plotinus* (New York: Oxford University Press, 1948), 14–15, and John S. Harrison, *The Teachers of Emerson* (New York: Haskell House, 1966), 125–38.

25. *EL*, 2:250.

26. *EL*, 250, 252.

27. *EL*, 256.

28. *EL*, 261.
29. *EL*, 261.
30. *EL*, 275, 273–74.
31. *EL*, 281, 292.
32. *EL*, 304, 356.
33. Pierre Hadot, *The Present Alone Is Our Happiness,* trans. Marc Djaballah (Palo Alto, CA: Stanford University Press, 2009), 87.
34. See Sarah Ann Wider, *The Critical Reception of Emerson: Unsettling All Things* (Rochester, NY: Camden House, 2000), 85–88.
35. John T. Lysaker, *Emerson and Self-Culture* (Bloomington: Indiana University Press, 2008), 5.

CHAPTER 4: AWAKENING THE GIANT

1. *JMN*, 5:162–63.
2. Mary Kupiec Cayton, "The Making of an American Prophet: Emerson, His Audiences, and the Rise of the Culture Industry in Nineteenth-Century America," in *Ralph Waldo Emerson: A Collection of Critical Essays*, ed. Lawrence Buell (Englewood Cliffs, NJ: Prentice-Hall, 1993), 77–100; quotation on 78.
3. *JMN*, 4:200.
4. *CW*, 1:7.
5. *CW*, 7, 9, 10.
6. *CW*, 12–13.
7. *CW*, 18, 19, 23.
8. *CW*, 26, 27.
9. *CW*, 37, 39.
10. *CW*, 43.
11. *CW*, 27–28, 38.
12. See Samantha C. Harvey, *Transatlantic Transcendentalism: Coleridge, Emerson, and Nature* (Edinburgh: Edinburgh University Press, 2013), 63–66. The distinction goes back to Aristotle. Pantheist philosopher Baruch Spinoza (1632–77) also made use of it. Emerson was familiar with Spinoza's philosophy.
13. *CW*, 3:104, 112.
14. *CW*, 1:124, 127, 130.
15. Robert S. Corrington, *Deep Pantheism: Toward a New Transcendentalism* (Lanham, MD: Lexington Books, 2016), xi, 7. Harvey argues that Emerson was a panentheist. See Harvey, *Transatlantic Transcendentalism*, 110–16.
16. *CW*, 1:145.
17. For an account of the event, see Bliss Perry, *The Praise of Folly and Other Papers* (Boston: Houghton Mifflin, 1923), 81–113.
18. *CW*, 1:53.
19. *CW*, 54–55.
20. *CW*, 55–56.
21. *CW*, 57.
22. *CW*, 59, 61.
23. *CW*, 62.
24. *CW*, 67–68.

25. *CW*, 69.

26. Quoted in Perry, *Praise of Folly*, 95.

27. *CW*, 1:55.

28. The room as it is today is different from the way it would have looked then. According to Conrad Wright, the panels, plaques, and pews date from remodeling done around 1900. See Conrad Wright, "Soul Is Good, but Body Is Good Too," *Journal of Unitarian Universalist History* 37 (2013–14): 4. The description of the event is also taken from this article.

29. *CW*, 1:80.

30. Elizabeth Palmer Peabody, "Emerson as Preacher," in *The Genius and Character of Emerson*, ed. Franklin B. Sanborn (1885; repr., Port Washington, NY: Kennikat Press, 1971), 158.

31. David Robinson, "The Sermons of Ralph Waldo Emerson: An Introductory Historical Essay," in *The Complete Sermons of Ralph Waldo Emerson*, ed. Albert J. von Frank, 4 vols. (Columbia: University of Missouri Press, 1989), 1:31.

32. *CW*, 1:76, 79.

33. *CW*, 81–82. The Unitarians drew on the philosophy of John Locke, who argued that knowledge comes to us by way of sense experience, to validate Jesus's divinity by virtue of the miracles he performed. *CW*, 82.

34. *CW*, 87, 85, 90.

35. As noted in a previous chapter, I have taken the term *ecstatic naturalism* from Corrington, *Deep Pantheism*, xi, who writes: "Emerson in particular pushed hard on the edges of his Unitarian tradition and came out of his intense struggle as a post-Christian deep pantheist. His life arc is one of the purest expressions of ecstatic naturalism, in deed and act, that the world has seen. While there have been numerous ecstatic naturalists both before and after Emerson, his expression of this form of naturalism is exemplary and paradigmatic."

36. *CW*, 1:78, 79, 92.

37. David Robinson, "Poetry, Personality, and the Divinity School Address," *Harvard Theological Review* 82, no. 2 (1989): 190, 192.

38. Robinson, "Poetry," 80–82. Emerson was quite explicit about the personhood of God. In an 1837 journal entry he wrote, "Is God a person? No. That is a contradiction: the *personality* of God. A person is a finite personality, is finiteness." *JMN*, 5:282.

39. *EL*, 3:6.

CHAPTER 5: DOUBLE CONSCIOUSNESS

1. *CW*, 10:180.

2. In a letter from Ripley to Emerson, November 9, 1840, in *The American Transcendentalists: Essential Writings*, ed. Lawrence Buell (New York: Modern Library, 2006), 202.

3. *CW*, 1:145.

4. *CW*, 146, 148–49.

5. *CW*, 152–55.

6. *CW*, 156–57.

7. *CW*, 158–59.

8. Len Gougeon, *Virtue's Hero: Emerson, Antislavery, and Reform* (Athens: University of Georgia Press, 1990), 35.

9. *AS*, 103.

10. This is the conclusion reached by Alan M. Levine and David S. Malachuk in the introduction to *A Political Companion to Ralph Waldo Emerson*, ed. Alan M. Levine and Daniel S. Malachuk (Lexington: University Press of Kentucky, 2011), 17. Other useful information on this topic will be found in writings by Len Gougeon, David Robinson, and Jack Turner.

11. Robert N. Bellah, "Individualism and Commitment in American Life" (speech, University of California, Santa Barbara, February 20, 1986), http://www.robertbellah.com/lectures_4.htm.

12. Levine and Malachuk, *Political Companion*, 4.

13. I was told that this was the Reverend John Haynes Holmes (1879–1964), who was for many years minister of what is now known as the Community Church of New York. A noted antiwar activist, he was also cofounder of the NAACP and the ACLU.

14. David Robinson, introduction to *The Political Emerson: Essential Writings on Politics and Ethical Reform*, ed. David M. Robinson (Boston: Beacon Press, 2003), 16.

15. David Robinson, *Emerson and the Conduct of Life: Pragmatism and Ethical Purpose in the Later Work* (New York: Cambridge University Press, 1993), 52.

16. *CW*, 1:172.

17. *CW*, 173–74.

18. *CW*, 176–77.

19. *CW*, 179–81.

20. *CW*, 182–83.

21. *CW*, 189.

22. *CW*, 195–98.

23. *CW*, 199–200.

24. Quoted in Gougeon, *Virtue's Hero*, 8–9.

25. Apparently, the first name that was proposed for their meeting was the Symposium, after Plato's dialogue by that title. The symposium was a gathering of friends for discussion, poetry, and wine drinking.

26. *CW*, 1:201.

27. *CW*, 202–3.

28. *CW*, 203–4.

29. *CW*, 206, 209–10.

30. *CW*, 213. This "youth," no doubt, is a stand-in for Emerson himself.

31. *CW*, 213.

32. *CW*, 213–14.

33. *CW*, 215.

34. Joseph Campbell, *The Power of Myth* (New York: Doubleday, 1988), 123, 129.

35. *CW*, 1:216.

36. For this discussion I have drawn on an essay by David Lyttle, "'The World Is a Divine Dream': Emerson's Subjective Idealism," *Concord Saunterer*, n.s., 5 (Fall 1997): 93–110.

37. Lyttle, "'World Is a Divine Dream,'" 38.

38. *JMN*, 5:337.

39. David J. Chalmers, "Idealism and the Mind-Body Problem," pdf located at http://consc .net/papers/idealism.pdf, 1.

40. Chalmers, "Idealism," 18. He prefers this term to that of Hegel's notion of absolute idealism in order "to avoid the resonant Hegelian overtones" (4).

41. Chalmers, 28.

42. *CW*, 1:43.

CHAPTER 6: SPIRITUAL PRINCIPLES

1. *CW*, 2:xvi.

2. Quoted in *CW*, xxiii.

3. David Robinson, *Emerson and the Conduct of Life: Pragmatism and Ethical Purpose in the Later Work* (New York: Cambridge University Press, 1993), 10.

4. *CW*, 1:80, 28.

5. See, for example, John Updike, "Emersonianism," in *Odd Jobs: Essays and Criticism* (New York: Knopf, 1991).

6. *CW*, 1:3, 37.

7. *CW*, 27.

8. Epictetus, *Discourses and Enchiridion*, trans. Thomas Wentworth Higginson (New York: Walter J. Black, 1944), 42.

9. Steve Jobs, "You've Got to Find What You Love" (commencement address, Stanford University, June 12, 2005), https://news.stanford.edu/2005/06/14/jobs-061505/.

10. *CW*, 2:29–30.

11. *CW*, 30; Kenneth S. Sacks, *Understanding Emerson: "The American Scholar" and His Struggle for Self-Reliance* (Princeton, NJ: Princeton University Press, 2003), 61.

12. Robert D. Richardson Jr., *Emerson: The Mind on Fire* (Berkeley: University of California Press, 1995), 322.

13. Alexis de Tocqueville, *Democracy in America*, trans. Henry Reeve, 2 vols. (New York: D. Appleton, 1899), 1:280–81.

14. *CW*, 2:37.

15. *CW*, 37.

16. Thomas Moore, *Original Self: Living with Paradox and Originality* (New York: Harper-Collins, 2000), v.

17. *CW*, 2:37, 41.

18. *CW*, 40. It is hard to say where Emerson first encountered the phrase "shooting the gulf," but it is mentioned in Daniel Defoe's *Voyage Round the World* (1725) and in Robert Southey's *Lives of the British Admirals*, 5 vols. (London: Longman, 1834). As Southey expressed it, "To sail around the world was in the popular belief an adventure of the most formidable kind, and not to be performed by plain sailing, but by reaching the end of this round flat earth, and there shooting the gulf, which is the only passage from one side of the world to the other" (3:239). The expression suggests breaking out into something new or crossing from one plane of existence to another.

19. *CW*, 2:40.

20. Social philosopher George Kateb takes strong objection to the criticism of communitarians such as Bellah and Brooks. He writes, "To discredit liberal individualism is

necessarily to strengthen those forces in modern life which work to render people docile. . . . Defenders of liberal individualism must hold to the premise that there is something worse than the wrongs and the deficiencies that the communitarian critics point to, and that is docility. A docile people is a people fit for mobilization; and the purposes of mobilization in advanced countries tend to be destructive and irrational. Only a rights-based individualism provides a steady perspective from which to protest this mobilization." See Kateb, *The Inner Ocean: Individualism and Democratic Culture* (Ithaca, NY: Cornell University Press, 1992), 238–39.

21. Wesley T. Mott, "'The Age of the First Person Singular': Emerson and Individualism," in *A Historical Guide to Ralph Waldo Emerson*, ed. Joel Myerson (New York: Oxford University Press, 2000), 91.

22. *CW*, 2:57–58.

23. *CW*, 59.

24. *CW*, 59–60, 65, 71.

25. David Robinson, *The Spiritual Emerson* (Boston: Beacon Press, 2003), 110.

26. *CW*, 2:77–78.

27. Seneca, *Moral Essays*, trans. John W. Basore, 3 vols. (Cambridge, MA: Harvard University Press, 1932), 2:107, 111.

28. *CW*, 2:79–80.

29. *CW*, 81.

30. *CW*, 94.

31. Alan Watts, *Become What You Are* (Boulder: Shambala Publications, 1995), 21.

32. *CW*, 2:179.

33. *CW*, 181.

34. *CW*, 188.

35. *CW*, 189–90.

36. Anne Morrow Lindbergh, *Gift from the Sea* (New York: Pantheon, 1955), 108; *CW*, 2:189.

37. Stephen E. Whicher, *Freedom and Fate: An Inner Life of Ralph Waldo Emerson* (Philadelphia: University of Pennsylvania Press, 1953), 97–101. Whicher views this essay as a bridge between the idealism of his *Essays: First Series* and the skepticism of the *Essays: Second Series,* as shown, in particular, in the essay "Experience."

38. Whicher, *Freedom and Fate*, 189.

39. *JMN*, 8:228.

40. *EL*, 3:5–6.

41. *EL*, 14, 20, 22.

42. *CW*, 2:159.

43. *CW*, 160.

44. *CW*, 161.

45. *CW*, 161; William James, *The Varieties of Religious Experience* (New York: Longmans, Green, 1925), 388.

46. James, *Varieties of Religious Experience*, 380–81.

47. *CW*, 2:162–66.

48. *CW*, 166–67.

49. *CW*, 168, 171.

50. *CW*, 175.

51. *L*, 1:116–17.

52. *CW*, 2:173–74.

53. Plotinus, *The Essence of Plotinus*, ed. Grace H. Turnbull (New York: Oxford University Press, 1948), 135.

54. Plotinus writes, "Let a quiet soul behold that other mighty soul, externally as it were, on all sides flowing and infused into, penetrating and illuminating the quiescent mass." In John S. Harrison, *The Teachers of Emerson* (repr., New York: Haskell House, 1966), 140.

55. David Lyttle, "Emerson on the Soul: What the Eye Cannot See," *Concord Saunterer*, n.s., 11 (2003): 62.

56. Ken Wilber, *The Essential Ken Wilber: An Introductory Reader* (Boston: Shambhala Publications, 1998), 8.

57. Very little has been written about Emerson's doctrine of the soul. Exceptions include David Lyttle, as noted, and Jonathan Bishop, *Emerson on the Soul* (Cambridge, MA: Harvard University Press, 1964).

58. *CW*, 2:160.

59. *JMN*, 7:435.

CHAPTER 7: LABYRINTH

1. *CW*, 2:xxii.

2. Quoted in *CW*, 3:xxxvii.

3. Quoted in *CW*, 2:xxii–xxxiii.

4. *CW*, xxiv.

5. *JMN*, 8:163–64.

6. *CW*, 10:334.

7. *CW*, 3:27.

8. Dante Alighieri, *The Divine Comedy*, trans. John Ciardi (New York: W. W. Norton, 1970), 3.

9. *CW*, 3:29.

10. *CW*, 30.

11. *CW*, 30–32; Leonard Cohen, *Stranger Music: Selected Poems and Songs* (New York: Pantheon Books, 1993), 373.

12. *CW*, 3:32–35.

13. *CW*, 35–36.

14. *CW*, 39.

15. *CW*, 39–40.

16. *CW*, 41.

17. *CW*, 42–43.

18. *CW*, 44–46.

19. *CW*, 49.

20. *CW*, 2:27.

21. Elizabeth Kübler-Ross, *On Death and Dying* (New York: Simon and Schuster, 1969).

22. *CW*, 3:27–29.

23. *CW*, 1:216.

24. *L*, 1:435.

25. *CW*, 10:110.

26. *CW*, 1:90.

27. Robert D. Richardson Jr., *Emerson: The Mind on Fire* (Berkeley: University of California Press, 1995), 67.

28. *CW*, 9:427.

29. *CW*, 3:3–4.

30. *CW*, 4–6.

31. *CW*, 6–8.

32. *CW*, 9, 15–16.

33. *CW*, 16–17.

34. *CW*, 17–19.

35. *CW*, 20.

36. Walt Whitman, *Complete Poetry and Collected Prose*, ed. Justin Kaplan (New York: Library of America, 1982), 1326.

37. Whitman, *Complete Poetry*, 14–15.

38. *CW*, 3:23–24.

39. Whitman, *Complete Poetry*, 57.

40. *CW*, 3:149–50.

41. *CW*, 151.

42. *CW*, 154.

43. *CW*, 156–57.

44. *CW*, 158–59.

45. *CW*, 161, 163, 167.

46. See Stephen E. Whicher, *Freedom and Fate: An Inner Life of Ralph Waldo Emerson* (Philadelphia: University of Pennsylvania Press, 1953), 170–72.

47. See, in addition to Whicher, Sarah Ann Wider, *The Critical Reception of Emerson: Unsettling All Things* (Rochester, NY: Camden House, 2000), 34–35; David Robinson, *Emerson and the Conduct of Life: Pragmatism and Ethical Purpose in the Later Work* (New York: Cambridge University Press, 1993), 69–70; and Robert C. Gordon, *Emerson and the Light of India: An Intellectual History* (New Delhi: National Book Trust, 2007), xv–xx.

48. *EL*, 1:358

49. Marcus Aurelius, *The Emperor's Handbook*, trans. C. Scott Hicks and David V. Hicks (New York: Scribner, 2002), 29, 31.

50. Frederic Hedge, "Writings of R. W. Emerson," in *Christian Examiner and Religious Miscellany*, vol. 38, January 1845, 1.

51. *JMN*, 3:45.

CHAPTER 8: AN EASTERN EDUCATION

1. *CW*, 1:80.

2. Quoted in Arthur Christy, *The Orient in American Transcendentalism: A Study of Emerson, Thoreau, and Alcott* (New York: Octagon Books, 1969), 61.

3. The literature on Emerson's "Eastern education" is considerable. Best sources are Frederic Ives Carpenter, *Emerson and Asia* (Cambridge, MA: Harvard University Press, 1930); Carl T. Jackson, *The Oriental Religions and American Thought: Nineteenth-Century Explorations* (Westport, CT: Greenwood Press, 1981); Arthur Versluis, *American Transcendentalism and Asian Religions* (New York: Oxford University Press, 1993); Robert C. Gordon, *Emerson and the Light of India: An Intellectual*

History (New Delhi: National Book Trust of India, 2007); Alan Hodder, "Asia," in *Ralph Waldo Emerson in Context*, ed. Wesley T. Mott (New York: Cambridge University Press, 2014); Shoji Goto, *Emerson's Eastern Education* (New York: Nova Publishers, 2016); Yoshio Takanashi, *Emerson and Neo-Confucianism: Crossing Paths over the Pacific* (New York: Palgrave Macmillan, 2014); and Christy, *Orient in American Transcendentalism*.

4. Emerson, "The Present State of Ethical Philosophy," in *Ralph Waldo Emerson, together with Two Early Essays of Emerson*, ed. Edward Everett Hale (Boston: Brown and Company, 1899), 109.

5. *JMN*, 6:392–97. The verse can be paraphrased as follows: "He who recognizes in his individual soul (Self, Atman), the universal Soul that exists in all beings, attains peace of mind and enters into the highest state, Brahman."

6. See Carpenter, *Emerson and Asia*, 77. See page 131.

7. *The Upanishads: A New Translation*, trans. Swami Nikhilananda, 4 vols. (New York: Ramakrishna-Vivekananda Center, 2003), 1:206.

8. Quoted in Swami Paramananda, *Emerson and Vedanta* (Cohasset, MA: Vedanta Centre Publications, 1985), 69.

9. *CW*, 9:365. For an insightful analysis of the poem, see Carpenter, *Emerson and Asia*, 113–19.

10. *CW*, 4:23, 27.

11. *CW*, 28–29.

12. *CW*, 30–31.

13. *CW*, 31.

14. *CW*, 43.

15. *JMN*, 16:36.

16. *CW*, 6:114.

17. *JMN*, 11:417.

18. Carpenter, *Emerson and Asia*, 232.

19. *CW*, 10:491.

20. Daniel K. Gardner, *The Four Books: Basic Teachings of the Later Confucian Tradition* (Indianapolis, IN: Hackett Publishing, 2007), xxii.

21. Chu Hsi, *Learning to Be a Sage*, trans. Daniel K. Gardner (Berkeley: University of California Press, 1990), x–xi.

22. *CW*, 10:463.

23. *CW*, 464.

24. See, for example, the discussion of moral cultivation in Philip J. Ivanhoe, *Confucian Moral Self-Cultivation* (Indianapolis, IN: Hackett Publishing, 2000), ix–xiv.

25. See the commentary to this passage by Gardner in *Four Books*, 37.

26. In Henry D. Thoreau, *Early Essays and Miscellanies*, ed. Joseph J. Moldenhauer (Princeton, NJ: Princeton University Press, 1975), 147. The Ethnical Scriptures column was a collaboration between Emerson and Thoreau.

27. *CW*, 3:42.

28. In a commentary on this passage from Mencius, Gardner states that "since heaven and man are one, and no distinction is to be made between them, the vast, flowing psychophysical stuff of the universe is one with our vast, flowing psychophysical stuff; this being the case, if we nurture ours and let no harm come to it, it will merge naturally with the universal vital psychophysical stuff. Thus successfully nurturing

our vast, flowing vital stuff brings about a perfect balance and harmony with the cosmos. The implications of this passage are moral, to be sure, but extend beyond, into the realm of the spiritual." See Gardner, *Four Books*, 65.

29. Quoted in Robert D. Richardson Jr., *Emerson: The Mind on Fire* (Berkeley: University of California Press, 1995), 406.

30. Robert D. Richardson, *Nearer the Heart's Desire: Poets of the Rubaiyat a Dual Biography of Omar Khayyam and Edward FitzGerald* (New York: Bloomsbury USA, 2016), 49.

31. *CW*, 8:149.

32. Richardson, *Nearer the Heart's Desire*, 51–52.

33. *CW*, 8:127, 129.

34. Emerson, *Collected Poems and Translations*, ed. Harold Bloom and Paul Kane (New York: Library of America, 1994), 480.

35. *CW*, 10:442.

36. Quoted in David Lee Maulsby, *Emerson: His Contribution to Literature* (Tufts College, MA: Tufts College Press, 1911), 122–23.

37. Thomas A. Tweed, *The American Encounter with Buddhism, 1844–1912: Victorian Culture and the Limits of Dissent* (Chapel Hill: University of North Carolina Press, 1992), 3.

38. Yoshio Takanashi, *Emerson and Neo-Confucianism: Crossing Paths over the Pacific* (New York: Palgrave Macmillan, 2014), 106–7.

CHAPTER 9: A HIGHER LAW

1. *CW*, 3:154.

2. *JMN*, 3:117.

3. *JMN*, 4:357.

4. For a description of the event, see Sandra Harbert Petrulionis, *To Set This World Right: The Antislavery Movement in Thoreau's Concord* (Ithaca, NY: Cornell University Press, 2006), 43–47.

5. *AS*, 17.

6. *AS*, 20, 24.

7. *AS*, 30–32.

8. *AS*, 54–56.

9. *AS*, 57–64.

10. *AS*, 65–68.

11. *AS*, 68–72.

12. *AS*, 84. This providential viewpoint was shared by others in the Transcendentalist circle, including Theodore Parker (1810–60), who wrote, "I do not pretend to understand the moral universe; the arc is a long one, my eye reaches but little ways; I cannot calculate the curve and complete the figure by the experience of sight; I can divine it by conscience. And from what I see I am sure it bends toward justice." Theodore Parker, *Sermons of Religion*, ed. Samuel A. Eliot (Boston: American Unitarian Association, 1908), 64. This formulation was adopted by Martin Luther King Jr. and, later, Barack Obama.

13. *AS*, 84–89.

14. *AS*, 91–93.

15. *AS*, 103.

16. *L*, 5:179–80.

17. James Elliot Cabot, *A Memoir of Ralph Waldo Emerson*, 2 vols. (Boston: Houghton Mifflin, 1887), 2:597. The passage was not included in the printed version of the lecture. Thoreau made a similar comment in "Plea for Captain John Brown," given on October 30, 1859: "Some eighteen hundred years ago Christ was crucified; this morning, perchance, Captain Brown was hung. These are the two ends of a chain which is not without its links. He is not Old Brown any longer; he is an Angel of Light." Henry D. Thoreau, *Reform Papers*, ed. Wendell Glick (Princeton, NJ: Princeton University Press, 1973), 137.

18. *AS*, 118–19.

19. *AS*, 123.

20. Four of the members of the "Secret Six," Brown's closest advisers, were members of the Transcendentalist circle. The fullest account of Transcendentalists' support of John Brown is David S. Reynolds, *John Brown, Abolitionist* (New York: Knopf, 2005). See also Edward J. Renehan Jr., *The Secret Six: The True Tale of the Men Who Conspired with John Brown* (New York: Crown Publishers, 1995).

21. Reynolds, *John Brown*, 163–65.

22. Reynolds, 425.

23. In his poem "Boston Hymn," Emerson wrote:

> Pay ransom to the owner
> And fill the bag to the brim.
> Who is the owner? The slave is owner,
> And ever was. Pay *him*.

CW, 9:383.

24. *J*, 7:396.

25. *AS*, xl; *L*, 5:206.

26. Len Gougeon, "Emerson, Self-Reliance, and the Politics of Democracy," in *A Political Companion to Ralph Waldo Emerson*, ed. Alan M. Levine and Daniel S. Malachuk (Lexington: University Press of Kentucky, 2011), 189.

27. Jack Turner elaborates on this point in *Awakening to Race: Individualism and Social Consciousness in America* (Chicago: University of Chicago Press, 2002), chap. 2.

28. See Len Gougeon, *Virtue's Hero: Emerson, Antislavery, and Reform* (Athens: University of Georgia Press, 1990), for a thorough debunking of the claim that Emerson had little interest or involvement in the antislavery cause.

29. Margaret Fuller, *Woman in the Nineteenth Century* (New York: W. W. Norton, 1998), 10, 20.

30. Fuller, *Memoirs of Margaret Fuller Ossoli*, ed. R. W. Emerson, W. H. Channing, and J. F. Clarke, 2 vols. (Boston: Phillips, Sampson, 1852), 2:132.

31. See Phyllis Cole, "Women's Rights and Feminism," in *The Oxford Handbook of Transcendentalism*, ed. Joel Myerson, Sandra Harbert Petrulionis, and Laura Dassow Walls (New York: Oxford University Press, 2010), 226–27.

32. *L*, 4:230.

33. *LL*, 2:18–19.

34. *LL*, 25, 26.

35. *LL*, 28–29.

36. *L*, 9:326–27.

37. Phyllis Cole, "The New Movement's Tide," in *Emerson Bicentennial Essays*, ed. Ronald A.

Bosco and Joel Myerson (Boston: Massachusetts Historical Society, 2006), 138; Caroline Healey Dall, *Daughter of Boston: The Extraordinary Diary of a Nineteenth-Century Woman*, ed. Helen R. Deese (Boston: Beacon Press, 2005), 235.

38. Cole, "New Movement's Tide," 138.

39. Tiffany K. Wayne, *Woman Thinking: Feminism and Transcendentalism in Nineteenth-Century America* (Lanham, MD: Lexington Books, 2005), 42–43.

40. Armida Gilbert, "Emerson and the Woman's Rights Movement," in *A Historical Guide to Ralph Waldo Emerson*, ed. Joel Myerson (New York: Oxford University Press, 2000), 234.

41. Quoted in Wayne, *Woman Thinking*, 77.

CHAPTER 10: THE ART OF LIFE

1. *JMN*, 2:294.

2. *CW*, 3:40.

3. Carl Bode, *The American Lyceum: Town Meeting of the Mind* (New York: Oxford University Press, 1956), 221.

4. Wallace E. Williams, "Historical Introduction," in *CW*, 4:xlix–l.

5. Fuller, *Memoirs of Margaret Fuller Ossoli*, ed. R. W. Emerson, W. H. Channing, and J. F. Clarke, 2 vols. (Boston: Phillips, Sampson, 1852), 1:202–3. In *The Lives of Margaret Fuller* (New York: W. W. Norton, 2012), 117, author John Matteson writes the following: "Lidian Emerson, married only ten months and pregnant with her husband's first child, looked on as an unmarried woman, almost eight years her junior, settled under her roof, beguiled her husband with glittering repartee, and was in no rush to leave."

6. *JMN*, 11:258.

7. Stephen E. Whicher, *Freedom and Fate: An Inner Life of Ralph Waldo Emerson* (Philadelphia: University of Pennsylvania Press, 1953), 124–25.

8. Gertrude Reif Hughes, *Emerson's Demanding Optimism* (Baton Rouge: Louisiana State University Press, 1984), x.

9. David Robinson, *Emerson and the Conduct of Life: Pragmatism and Ethical Purpose in the Later Work* (New York: Cambridge University Press, 1993), 134.

10. Robert D. Richardson Jr., *Emerson: The Mind on Fire* (Berkeley: University of California Press, 1995), 500.

11. *CW*, 6:1.

12. *CW*, 2.

13. *CW*, 2–3.

14. *CW*, 3–4.

15. *CW*, 4.

16. *CW*, 8.

17. *CW*, 10.

18. *CW*, 12.

19. *CW*, 12–13.

20. *CW*, 13.

21. *CW*, 14.

22. *CW*, 15.

23. *CW*, 15–16.

24. *CW*, 16.
25. *CW*, 17.
26. *CW*, 20–21.
27. *CW*, 22–23.
28. *CW*, 25–26.
29. *CW*, 26.
30. *CW*, 26–27.
31. *JMN*, 7:167; emphasis in original.
32. Campbell, quoted in Jack Kornfield, *The Art of Forgiveness, Lovingkindness, and Peace* (New York: Bantam Books, 2002), 145.
33. Hughes, *Emerson's Demanding Optimism*, xi.
34. *L*, 1:430–31.
35. *CW*, 8:107–8.
36. *CW*, 108–9.
37. *CW*, 110–11.
38. *CW*, 113–14.
39. *CW*, 114–15.
40. *CW*, 115.
41. *CW*, 117–18.
42. *CW*, 118, 122.
43. *CW*, 123.
44. *CW*, 127–28.
45. *CW*, 128.
46. James Turner, *Without God, without Creed: The Origins of Unbelief in America* (Baltimore: Johns Hopkins University Press, 1985), xii, 163.
47. *CW*, 6:131, 134–35, 139.
48. *CW*, 139, 142.
49. *CW*, 143–44.
50. *CW*, 145.
51. *CW*, 147–48.
52. *CW*, 166.
53. *CW*, 166.
54. *CW*, 167.
55. *CW*, 168–70.
56. *CW*, 171–72.
57. *CW*, 172.
58. *CW*, 172–73.
59. *CW*, 173.
60. *CW*, 174.
61. Robinson, *Emerson and the Conduct of Life*, 152.

CHAPTER 11: THE SOUND OF TRUMPETS

1. *L*, 5:4, 304.
2. *JMN*, 14:308–9.
3. *CW*, 9:383
4. *JMN*, 14:353.

5. *CW,* 10:431.

6. *JMN,* 14:355.

7. *LL,* 2:84; quoted in John J. Chapman, *Emerson and Other Essays* (New York: Moffat, Yard, 1909), 34.

8. *JMN,* XVI: 175.

9. Quoted in Ronald Bosco, "Historical Introduction," in *CW,* 7:xlvi.

10. Quoted in Bosco, "Historical Introduction," *CW,* 7:xlvii.

11. *EL,* 2:261.

12. *W,* 7:345–46.

13. *CW,* 7:3–5.

14. *CW,* 5–7.

15. *CW,* 7–8.

16. Anne Morrow Lindbergh, *Gift from the Sea* (New York: Pantheon, 1955), 49–50.

17. Alfred North Whitehead, *Religion in the Making* (New York: Meridian Books, 1960), 16.

18. *W,* 7:155.

19. *CW,* 7:80, 82.

20. *CW,* 83.

21. *CW,* 85.

22. *CW,* 85–86.

23. *CW,* 87.

24. *CW,* 87–89.

25. *CW,* 89.

26. *CW,* 90.

27. *CW,* 91.

28. *CW,* 91–92.

29. *CW,* 93.

30. *CW,* 94.

31. Joseph Campbell, *The Power of Myth* (New York: Doubleday, 1988), 67; Jameson quoted in Jack Kornfield, *The Art of Forgiveness, Lovingkindness, and Peace* (New York: Bantam Books, 2002), 193.

32. Bronson Alcott, *Tablets* (Boston: Roberts Brothers, 1868), 76.

33. *W,* 9:408.

34. Alfred G. Litton, "Clubs," in *Ralph Waldo Emerson in Context,* ed. Wesley T. Mott (New York: Cambridge University Press, 2014), 180–87. There is some controversy regarding the membership of women in the Town and Country Club. When the club was formed in 1849, Caroline Healey Dall alleged that Emerson opposed the admission of women. "In point of fact," writes Helen R. Deese, editor of Dall's diary, "Dall proves to be an unreliable witness in this matter. Her contemporary journals of the Town and Country Club period reflect no such incident." Helen R. Deese, "Transcendentalism from the Margins: Caroline Healey Dall," in *Transient and Permanent: The Transcendentalist Movement and Its Contexts,* ed. Charles Capper and Conrad Edick Wright (Boston: Massachusetts Historical Society, 1999), 538.

35. *CW,* 7:114.

36. *CW,* 115–18.

37. *CW,* 123.

38. A "marplot" is a meddlesome person whose activity interferes with the plans of others.
39. *LL*, 2:364.
40. *CW*, 7:126.
41. Sherry Turkle, *Reclaiming Conversation: The Power of Talk in a Digital Age* (New York: Penguin Press, 2015), 22–23.
42. *CW*, 6:52–53, 68.
43. *CW,* 7:147.
44. *CW*, 148.
45. *CW*, 151.
46. *CW*, 153.
47. *CW*, 156.
48. *CW*, 158.
49. *CW*, 9:469–70.
50. Edward Waldo Emerson, *Emerson in Concord: A Memoir* (Boston: Houghton Mifflin, 1919), 183.
51. *CW*, 7:159–61.
52. *CW*, 161–62.
53. *CW*, 162–63.
54. *CW*, 163–65.
55. *CW*, 165–66.
56. *CW*, 170.
57. *JMN*, 15:416.

CHAPTER 12: TAKING IN THE SAIL

1. David Robinson, "The Free Religious Movement," in *The Oxford Handbook of Transcendentalism*, ed. Joel Myerson, Sandra Harbert Petrulionis, and Laura Dassow Walls (New York: Oxford University Press, 2010), 617–19.
2. Stow Persons, *Free Religion: An American Faith* (New Haven, CT: Yale University Press, 1947), 50.
3. *W*, 11;487.
4. Quoted in Ronald A. Bosco, "Notes," in *CW*, 10:813, 814.
5. *CW*, 10:448.
6. *CW*, 448–49.
7. *CW*, 450–53.
8. *CW*, 454–55.
9. *CW*, 456–57.
10. *CW*, 459. See Parker's sermon, "The Transient and Permanent in Christianity," in Theodore Parker, *The Transient and Permanent in Christianity*, ed. George Willis Cooke (Boston: American Unitarian Association, 1903), 1–39.
11. *CW*, 459–60.
12. *CW*, 460–61.
13. *CW*, 461.
14. *CW*, 463.
15. *JMN*, 15:228.
16. Jerome A. Stone, *Religious Naturalism Today: The Rebirth of a Forgotten Alternative*

(Albany: State University of New York Press, 2008), 1, 18; Robert S. Corrington, *Deep Pantheism: Toward a New Transcendentalism* (Lanham, MD: Lexington Books, 2016), 7.

17. James Turner, *Without God, without Creed: The Origins of Unbelief in America* (Baltimore: Johns Hopkins University Press, 1985), xii, 171.

18. Charles Taylor, *A Secular Age* (Cambridge, MA: Harvard University Press, 2007), 351.

19. *JMN*, 15:25; *CW*, 8:151.

20. *CW*, 152.

21. *CW*, 153–54, 156.

22. *CW*, 156.

23. *CW*, 157.

24. *CW*, 156–57.

25. *CW*, 158, 160; Thoreau, *Walden* (Boston: Houghton Mifflin, 1995), 324.

26. *CW*, 8:160–62.

27. *CW*, 164–65

28. *CW*, 166.

29. *CW*, 166.

30. *CW*, 167–68.

31. *CW*, 170.

32. Elizabeth Cady Stanton, *Solitude of Self* (Ashfield, MA: Paris Press, 2001), 4–5.

33. *CW*, 8:cclxxiv.

34. Quoted in John Haynes Holmes, *The Affirmation of Immortality* (New York: Macmillan, 1947), 50.

35. *CW*, 8:181.

36. *CW*, 183, 186.

37. *TN*, 3:314.

38. *CW*, 8:186.

39. *CW*, 186–87, 189.

40. *CW*, 190–92.

41. *CW*, 192–94.

42. *CW*, 181.

43. Karen Armstrong, "Is Immortality Important?," Harvard Divinity Bulletin, Winter 2006, https://bulletin-archive.hds.harvard.edu/articles/winter2006/immortality important.

44. Whitehead, *Science and the Modern World* (Cambridge: Cambridge University Press, 1932), 64.

45. *CW*, 1:166.

CHAPTER 13: EMERSON'S LEGACY

1. *TN*,1:134.

2. *TN*, xxix; Ronald A. Bosco, "Historical Introduction," in *CW*, 8:xxviii.

3. Bosco, "Historical introduction," *CW*, 8:clx.

4. John McAleer, *Ralph Waldo Emerson: Days of Encounter* (Boston: Little, Brown, 1984), 620.

5. McAleer, *Ralph Waldo Emerson*, 621–22.

6. McAleer, 623.

7. Social Circle of Concord, *The Centenary of the Birth of Ralph Waldo Emerson* (Concord, MA: privately printed, 1903), 46, 58.

8. *JMN*, 15:416, 422.

9. Amos Bronson Alcott, *The Journals of Bronson Alcott*, ed. Odell Shepard (Boston: Little, Brown, 1938), 485–86.

10. *CW*, 9:490.

11. *W*, 10:217.

12. Arnold, *Matthew Arnold*, ed. Miriam Allott and Robert H. Super (Oxford: Oxford University Press, 1986), 161.

13. *W*, 10:218–20.

14. *W*, 222–23.

15. *W*, 226–29.

16. *W*, 230, 233.

17. *W*, 237–38.

18. *LL*, 2:377.

19. In James Turner, *Without God, without Creed: The Origins of Unbelief in America* (Baltimore, MD: Johns Hopkins University Press, 1985), 261.

20. Henry Thoreau built a drawer under his chair in the hallway so that he would always know where his gloves were.

21. Emerson was vice president of the Free Religious Association for six years.

22. In George Willis Cooke, *Ralph Waldo Emerson: His Life, Writings, and Philosophy* (Boston: James R. Osgood, 1882), 363–64.

23. Lawrence Buell, *Emerson* (Cambridge, MA: Harvard University Press, 2003), 7–8.

24. *JMN*, 11:258.

25. Walt Whitman, *Complete Poetry and Collected Prose*, ed. Justin Kaplan (New York: Library of America, 1982), 1055.

26. *JMN*, 2:188.

27. Nathaniel Hawthorne, *Mosses from an Old Manse* (Philadelphia: Henry Altemus, 1896), 35.

28. *CW*, 4:16.

29. Edward Waldo Emerson, *Essays, Addresses, and Poems* (privately printed by Riverside Press, 1930), 221.

30. *JMN*, 13:327.

31. Julia Annas, "The Sage in Ancient Philosophy," http://www.u.arizona.edu/~jannas /Published%20Articles/sage.pdf, 14, 17.

32. Annas, "Sage in Ancient Philosophy," 18–19.

33. *CW*, 1:171.

34. Daniel Walker Howe, *Making the American Self* (Cambridge, MA: Harvard University Press, 1997), 109.

35. *CW*, 1:67–68; *JMN*, 11:86.

36. Peabody quoted in *Emerson in His Own Time*, ed. Ronald A. Bosco and Joel Myerson (Iowa City: University of Iowa Press, 2003), 153.

37. *CW*, 1:45.

38. John Dewey, "Ralph Waldo Emerson," in *Emerson: A Collection of Critical Essays*, ed. Milton Konvitz and Stephen Whicher (Englewood Cliffs, NJ: Prentice-Hall, 1964), 28–29.

39. *AS*, 140, 153.

40. *JMN*, 2:302; *CW*, 8:108–9.

41. Sydney E. Ahlstrom, *A Religious History of the American People* (New Haven: Yale University Press, 1972), 605.

42. *CW*, 1:80–81.

43. See Taylor, *Secular Age*, 542–57.

44. Perry Miller, *The Transcendentalists: An Anthology* (Cambridge, MA: Harvard University Press, 1960), 8.

45. William Blake, *Complete Writings* (London: Oxford University Press, 1972), 154.

46. This is a story I heard many years ago, but I do not know the source. It may be a Jain parable from the Sixth Anga.

47. *W*, 11:640.

INDEX

BARRY M. ANDREWS was born in Seattle, Washington. A graduate of Gonzaga University, he also earned a doctor of ministry degree from Meadville Lombard Theological School. He has been a scholar in residence at the Thoreau Institute and a Merrill Fellow at Harvard Divinity School. He has written and edited several books on Transcendentalist authors, including Ralph Waldo Emerson, Henry David Thoreau, and Margaret Fuller. His most recent books are *Transcendentalism and the Cultivation of the Soul,* published by the University of Massachusetts Press, and *Transcendentalism Yesterday and Today: Addresses and Sermons on Transcendentalist Themes,* published by Xlibris Books. As a minister he has served Unitarian Universalist congregations in Spokane, Manhattan, San Diego, and Manhasset, New York. He is currently an independent scholar living on Bainbridge Island, Washington, with his wife, Linda.